Western Canada

An Altitude SuperGuide

by
Jennifer Groundwater

Altitude Publishing
Canadian Rockies/Vancouver

Altitude Publishing Canada Ltd.

The Canadian Rockies/Vancouver
Head Office:
1500 Railway Avenue
Canmore, Alberta T1W 1P6
1-800-957-6888
www.altitudepublishing.com

Canadian Cataloguing in Publication Data

Groundwater, Jennifer, 1970-
Western Canada/Jennifer Groundwater

(Altitude superguide)
Includes index
ISBN 1-55153-637-4

1.British Columbia--Guidebooks.
2. Alberta-- Guidebooks. I Title. II. Series
FC3807.G76 2003   917.1104'4
C2003-910268-8   F1087.7.G76 2003

Altitude GreenTree Program

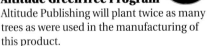

Altitude Publishing will plant twice as many trees as were used in the manufacturing of this product.

Front cover: Lake O'Hara, Yoho National Park in the Canadian Rockies
Frontispiece: Dinosaur Provincial Park, Alberta
Back cover left: The Fairmont Empress Hotel and the Inner Harbour, Victoria
Back cover left: Grain elevators and canola field at Hussar, Alberta

Project Development

Layout	Scott Manktelow
Maps	Mark Higenbottam
	Hermien Schuttenbeld
	Scott Manktelow
Editor	Andrea Murphy

Made in Western Canada
Printed and bound in Canada by Friesen Printers

We acknowledge the financial support of the Government of Canada through the Book Publishing Industry Development Program (BPIDP) for our publishing activities.

A Note from the Publisher

The world described in Altitude SuperGuides is a unique and fascinating place. It is a world filled with surprise and discovery, beauty and enjoyment, questions and answers. It is a world of people, cities, landscapes, animals and wilderness as seen through the eyes of those who live in, work with, and care for this world. The process of describing this world is also a means of defining ourselves.

It is also a world of relationship, where people derive their meaning from a deep and abiding contact with the land—as well as from each other. And it is this sense of relationship that guides all of us at Altitude to ensure that these places continue to survive and evolve in the decades ahead.

Altitude SuperGuides are books intended to be used, as much as read. Like the world they describe, Altitude SuperGuides are evolving, adapting and growing. Please write to us with your comments and observations, and we will do our best to incorporate your ideas into future editions of these books.

Stephen Hutchings
Publisher

Table of Contents

Maps

Vancouver Island, pg.157

Vancouver, pg.137

British Columbia, pg.113

Canadia

ERRITORIES   NUNAVUT   HUDSON BAY

Churchill

Lake Athabasca

N
W   E
S

Wollaston Lake

Reindeer Lake

Churchill River

Nelson River

MANITOBA

Lynn Lake

ort urray

La Loche

Thompson

SASKATCHEWAN

La Range   Lac la Range

Flin Flon

Pierceland

Saskatchewan River

The Pas

Cedar Lake

Grand Rapids

Lake Winnipeg

ONTARIO

Meadow Lake

Saskatchewan River

Lloydminster

Prince Albert

North Battleford

SASKATOON

Swan River

Yorkton

Gimli

Lake Manitoba

Selkirk   Elma

Kenora

South Saskatchewan River

Assiniboine River

WINNIPEG

Swift Current

Moose Jaw   REGINA

Brandon

Portage la Prairie

Fort Frances

Medicine Hat   Maple Creek

Weyburn

Winkler

Lake of the Woods

Estevan

Emerson

MINNESOTA

UNITED STATES OF AMERICA   NORTH DAKOTA   Grand

Introduction

Crowsnest Pass, Alberta

W estern Canada is an immense area that stretches across many varied landscapes. If these four provinces — Manitoba, Saskatchewan, Alberta and British Columbia — were a country, they would be the world's eighth largest. Together, their combined

area of 2,913,037 square kilometres is greater than that of most of the world's countries, yet their population is only just over 9 million, most of whom live within 100 kilometres of the U.S. border. This means that vast portions of the north in each province are essentially uninhabited, save for small villages, mainly home to Native peoples. The northern regions of each province have a lot in common, covered in a long swath of boreal forest that eventually gives way to tundra, dotted throughout with innumerable lakes.

In the south, the prairies of Manitoba and Saskatchewan, the Rocky Mountains of Alberta, and the coastal waters off British Columbia appear to share few observable traits. However, an exploration of these four diverse provinces shows that they have more in common than not. Their economies are based primarily on resource extraction and agriculture — all have plenty of fresh water, timber and other natural resources. Their people are a hardy mix of many different ethnic backgrounds. Their landscapes are immense, varied, and in many cases very beautiful. And each has a wealth of attractions for the visitor, with discoveries to be made in the cities, smaller towns, national and provincial parks, and areas off the beaten track. These attractions and discoveries are the primary focus of this book.

A Very Brief History

The history of each of these provinces has been shaped immeasurably by the fur trade, the railway, and the North West Mounted Police. The names of the same explorers crop up across the west: men of vision and determination who had lofty goals in mind and put up with immense hardship to make

Opposite: Downtown Vancouver rises behind Granville Island and False Creek.

their dreams come true. The same can be said of the settlers who followed in the footsteps of the explorers: whether prospectors, fishermen, or farmers, they worked hard to establish themselves in their chosen provinces.

And through all of this history run the threads of Native life, which was often difficult before the white men came, but was irrevocably changed as a result of contact. The tribes of the western part of the continent, once essentially free to live as they pleased, ended up decimated by disease and pushed into reserves as the new settlers made themselves a home.

Native History

Before the arrival of the European explorers, many different Native groups made their home in the western part of what is now Canada. With such a varied landscape, their lifestyles were vastly different, but they all shared a reverence for the land and the resources it provided.

On the Plains, the culture developed around the buffalo, which were plentiful. For many thousands of years the buffalo hunt took place on foot, with the entire band participating in the same way. The most efficient means of killing buffalo was to stampede the herd over a cliff. Once the animals fell to their death, the band proceeded to process and preserve the meat and every other part of the animal. Head-Smashed-In Buffalo Jump, in what is now southern Alberta, is a site known to have been used for

The Buffalo

The buffalo or bison, the largest land mammal in North America, was the sustenance for many Prairie Native groups, who hunted it on foot, and later on horseback. The story of the disappearance of this massive, shaggy beast from the plains of North America is alarming. From numbers estimated to be about 60 million at the beginning of the 19th century, the buffalo declined in number to only about 1,500 animals by 1900.

The Natives hunted the buffalo en masse, stampeding them over cliffs and killing many animals at one time. However, they used every part of the animal for some purpose, from the skins that were used as clothing and blankets, to the bones that were fashioned into tools, to the meat, which could sustain a group for months on end.

With the introduction of the horse in the 1700s, hunting became more efficient. The Métis were superb buffalo hunters, and their society was structured around the hunt

Buffalo

for many years.

It took a wave of settlers and hunters to begin the rapid decline of the buffalo. In the United States, people would shoot them from trains for sport — influenced perhaps by ignorance, for there seemed such an infinite number of the animals.

Today the buffalo is still occasionally seen on the plains, generally being ranched or within a national park. Their numbers have rebounded somewhat from their historic low, to about 350,000 continent-wide, but the landscape they once roamed is gone forever, and never again will they seem to cover the earth as far as the eye can see.

at least 5,000 years, and complicated rules were developed to regulate its use. Because they depended greatly on the buffalo for all of their needs, the Plains people suffered hardship if they could not hunt enough. Once horses were introduced on the plains, hunting the buffalo became much easier.

The Cree who lived in the woods had perhaps the most challenges of any of the Native groups, as their diet consisted of fish and game that could be hunted. These people were constantly on the move in search of food.

In coastal British Columbia, the Native groups enjoyed abundant food from the sea, and had perhaps the most sedentary lifestyle of all the Native peoples in Canada as a result. Some groups hunted whales, while others relied on the salmon and other seafood. Groups in the eastern B.C. interior were nomadic hunters, much like the Plains groups across the Rockies, while along the rivers of the interior the people depended on the salmon's bounty as well.

In the north, the Inuit ranged across the northern part of Manitoba along Hudson Bay. The Dene were the people of the northern parts of Saskatchewan, Alberta, and B.C. The Cree were the most numerous group, and adapted to many different living environments, reflected in their names: Swampy Cree, Woodland Cree, Plains Cree.

Today the descendants of all of these groups are still living in more or less the same areas as they did historically; however, many are on reserves that were created through treaty in the late 19th century.

The Fur Trade

European explorers arrived in the western part of Canada primarily due to the fur trade. First the French and then the English began to trade furs with the Native peoples in the early part of the 16th century, as the craze for beaver hats in Europe coincided with the extinction of beavers on that continent. It was the English, however, who pushed beyond New France to gain control of new lands to acquire the pelts so prized in Europe. The ketch *Nonsuch*, which arrived in James Bay in 1668, returned to England with a fine load of furs. King Charles II granted a monopoly on future trade to the company formed by his cousin, Prince Rupert, which is how all the lands that drained into Hudson Bay became known as Rupert's Land. The company, formed in 1670, was known as "The Company of Adventurers of England trading into Hudson's Bay", or the Hudson's Bay Company.

Britain and France were at war off and on for close to a century after this. For a time the British lost control of all their trading posts and forts, but by 1763, when the Seven Years' War concluded with the Treaty of Paris, Britain had won French Canada as her own. The fur trade had continued during this time, but the HBC had confined itself to known territory around

Sir Alexander Mackenzie

Mackenzie was born in Scotland in 1764 and came to Canada with his father as a child. He became a partner in the North West Company at the age of 20, and five years later was charged with finding a route over the Rocky Mountains to the Pacific Ocean. He set out from Fort Chipewyan along the river he named "Disappointment", for it led to the Arctic Ocean. That river, one of the longest in the world, now bears his name.

He was determined to make it to the Pacific, however, and acquired more gear and knowledge before his second attempt in 1793. This time he went west along the Peace River, eventually arriving at the Fraser River where, at the urging of the local Natives, he decided to take the overland route. This entailed going back up the Fraser to the Bella Coola River, which does empty into the Pacific. Arriving on July 22, 1793, he became the first white man to cross the continent overland. This was a dozen years before Lewis and Clark made their journey.

After returning east, Mackenzie continued in the fur trade, and became wealthy. He wrote a book about his journey, and eventually entered politics for a brief time, but not surprisingly, after his life of adventure, was "bored to tears" by it. He returned to Scotland, was knighted by the King of England, married and had children later in life, and died in 1820.

His importance as an explorer is honoured by the eleven different places in B.C. and the Northwest Territories named after him.

9

Hudson Bay.

Late in the 18th century, the North West Company was formed by a group of Montreal businessmen who wanted to get in on the fur trade. They saw the benefit in pushing farther into the heart of the continent to trade with the Natives who had previously traded with the French along the network that de la Vérendrye had set up several decades earlier.

The North West Company was very successful at first, though they were dismissed as "pedlars" by the HBC brass, far away in England. Their explorers and partners pushed deep into the continent, often forming attachments with Native women, and bringing in significant amounts of furs. Many of their explorers were responsible for charting the vast new lands and discovering new routes.

A fierce war broke out between the HBC and the North West Company, which kept the two companies fighting for territory and profits from the fur trade, often in the most underhand and sometimes violent ways, until 1821. The Hudson's Bay Company absorbed the North West Company and continued to rule western Canada for all intents and purposes until 1870. The decline of the fur trade and the near extinction of the beaver were among the reasons the company sold Rupert's Land to the Canadian government.

The Canadian Pacific Railway

The story of the building of the CPR is a fascinating one, filled with big personalities and huge crises, as well as scandal. It's worth a book on its own, but a short version of the story follows.

In 1867, the Dominion of Canada came into being. At first, the new country consisted only of four provinces in the east. While the new prime minister, John A. Macdonald, was uninterested in the lands to the west, he nevertheless did want to keep them from becoming part of the United States, a real threat at the time. So, in 1870, he amalgamated much of the west into what was then called the North-West Territories. In 1871 he promised British Columbia a transcontinental railway to link the Pacific Ocean province with the rest of the country. This move would also help to guard the revenue

Beaver

Canada's economy was based on the beaver for several hundred years

The large rodent whose existence sparked the exploration of a continent, the North American beaver today flourishes along the lakes and rivers of Canada. During the 18th century, however, it came near to extinction because of the European fashion for beaver felt hats.

Unlike today's fashions, this one was long-lasting — from the 1600s through to the mid-18th century, when silk hats became the thing to have. The beaver pelt was so important in Canada that it became the unit of trade against which all other things were measured in the trading posts of the Hudson's Bay Company.

The beavers were trapped in the winter, when the fur was long and luxuriant. The pelts were then prepared, mostly by Native women, who scraped the fur clean, tanned the inside, and plucked out the long guard hairs. Once it was this far prepared, it was known as a "made beaver", the unit of trade. The trappers would come into the trading posts with their pelts and trade them for other necessities of life such as blankets and gunpowder. The made beaver theoretically represented the value of a prime pelt on the London market, but the value actually changed very little in Canada once the Natives became used to it as a measure of trade.

Canadian Pacific Railway "Pacific Empress" at Mount Stephen House in Field, B.C., 1898

William Cornelius Van Horne

The man responsible for overseeing the railway through to completion was the American William Cornelius Van Horne, who in 1882 was hired at a huge salary to come to Winnipeg as general manager of the CPR. He was a man of indomitable confidence, who made fantastic promises and somehow managed to keep them. He knew everything about railroads — from the way the locomotives worked to the best way to schedule trains — and ran the railway always with an eye to maximum efficiency.

William Cornelius Van Horne

Van Horne was given ten years to complete the railway. The sooner it could be finished, the better for the government, because it would then begin creating revenue. Van Horne intended to complete it in half that time. He was committed to creating the shortest possible route across the country — a commitment that often had unforeseen consequences and ended up costing more in the long run. The route he chose through the Rockies was a good example of this. Though

it saved some 70-odd miles of track, he was forced to build sheds to protect the trains in Rogers Pass and eventually to build the Spiral Tunnels to make the grade safe at Kicking Horse Pass.

Van Horne also saw the possibility of tourism through the mountains and established lodges along the tracks in the most spectacular locations. Glacier House in Rogers Pass, Mt. Stephen House in Field, and the Banff Springs Hotel were among these luxurious hotels.

Despite all the financial insecurities and undeniable difficulties associated with building the railway, Van Horne succeeded in his mission when the last spike was driven on November 7, 1885, at Craigellachie, B.C.

from the extensive mineral deposits that were still being discovered in B.C.

To build such a railway was clearly a massive undertaking, and what's more, Macdonald promised it would be complete within ten years. The government sought funds from private investors to help build the railway without placing too high an extra tax burden on eastern Canadians.

Unfortunately for Macdonald, it became known that he had accepted substantial campaign funds from Sir Hugh Allen in return for a promise to award Allen the contract to build the railway. The "Pacific Scandal", as it became known, forced the fall of the government. It fell to the next prime minister, Liberal Alexander Mackenzie, to get the railway going, and he was less interested in the whole process than Macdonald. In 1875 the official start of the Canadian Pacific Railway occurred near present-day Thunder Bay, Ontario.

In 1880, once Macdonald's Conservatives were back in power, the government contracted Andrew Onderdonk to begin building the line west from Yale and the Fraser Valley. This was intended to reassure B.C. that the promise would be kept, even though the ten-year completion was looking unlikely at that point.

Andrew Onderdonk built the rails along the Fraser River — a most dangerous undertaking — and well into British Columbia's interior, using Chinese labourers as the majority of his workforce. At the same time, the rails were being pushed quickly westward through Manitoba and the prairies of southern Saskatchewan and Alberta, while surveyors searched frantically for a southern route through the Rockies. The most reasonable way to get through would have been to the north, at Yellowhead Pass, but that idea had been rejected for various reasons in 1881.

Eventually, and just in the nick of time, Major A.B. Rogers found a suitable pass through the Rockies and the Selkirks and the railway could proceed. The grade was very steep and the rails led through major avalanche paths, but construction continued in appallingly difficult conditions.

During this most expensive time of building, the railway was just about broke. In 1885, it was unable to pay its creditors or even meet its payroll. With completion so near, the CPR very nearly went under. The North-West Rebellion, which broke out in spring of 1885, helped to secure the railway when the militia was sent out from eastern Canada along the railway lines and arrived in a matter of weeks. This was an important point for national security and renewed the federal government's commitment to the railway.

Perhaps more importantly, a new investor was found — Barings Bank of London, which bailed out the CPR at the critical time. (The B.C. town of Revelstoke is named for Lord Baring of Revelstoke, the man behind the bailout, without whom the town would probably have faded into obscurity.)

On November 7, 1885, the ceremonial "Last Spike" was driven by Donald A. Smith, Lord Strathcona, at Craigellachie, which is where Onderdonk's team coming from the west had run out of supplies. The country was united as the first transcontinental train took the leaders of the CPR on their historic ride across the country.

The North West Mounted Police

A final element in the history of western Canada is the North West Mounted Police, whose presence in the western provinces was intended first to establish and then to maintain order in these formerly wild places. Their history is interwoven with that of the Native peoples and the railway.

In 1873, near the Cypress Hills in southern

A Note to Readers

This book focuses primarily on summer activities and attractions. It is always a good idea to call before visiting any attractions since many are open only limited hours in winter months. Generally the high season is between the end of May and the middle of October, and visitors can expect most attractions to be open daily during these months.

As well, please note that the book focuses on the southern part of Western Canada. There are many exceptional attractions in the northern parts of the four provinces which are not covered here, as they would be a suitable subject for another volume.

North West Mounted Police inspection in Calgary

Saskatchewan, a group of inebriated wolf hunters and whisky traders killed a number of Natives in what became known as the Cypress Hills Massacre. This terrible incident sparked the formation of the North West Mounted Police, who were given the task of suppressing the whisky trade, bringing law and order to the North-West Territories, and encouraging the Native people to give up their traditional lands and move into reserves.

Just over a year after the massacre, the new police force left Manitoba on horseback, destined for the Belly River area of Alberta, 800 miles away, where the most notorious whisky trading post, Fort Whoop-Up, was located.

Some of the force remained at various places along the way in Saskatchewan, setting up forts there. Along the journey, the Mounties suffered a good deal of hardship, so it was fortunate that they found the trading post abandoned when they arrived in Fort Whoop-Up, and could move right in. Most of them were in no shape for battle by this time.

The NWMP did establish order in the formerly troubled areas and managed to control the whisky trade. As the representatives of the government charged with making treaties with the Natives they were also successful, though from a historical perspective many would question whether this achievement was either moral or fair to the Native people.

The treaties were signed between 1871 and 1877, while the federal government was building the railway through lands belonging to Native peoples. Before the railway could pass, the Natives had to cede their land, so the government was highly motivated to complete these treaties. The first of these post-Confederation treaties was signed in Manitoba in 1871, and Treaty 7 with the Natives in what is now Alberta was signed in 1877. Thus the railway could proceed.

With the building of the railway, the NWMP faced new challenges, as gangs of rough men arrived in the west to work. The NWMP dealt with normal issues of disorder, usually related to liquor, and also found itself involved in labour unrest when workers had not been paid. The superintendent of the NWMP, Sam Steele, managed to calm the justifiably angry workers in 1885 when they went on strike and threatened to riot at Beaver Crossing, taking advantage of the general confusion around the time of the North West Rebellion. He read them the Riot Act and threatened to shoot anyone who got out of line. With only eight men to back him up against several hundred workers, he quelled the violence. The men were eventually paid and work resumed.

Over time, the NWMP eventually evolved to become the Royal Canadian Mounted Police, whose red uniforms are a symbol of Canada worldwide.

Every visitor who passes through Western Canada will be travelling through the pages of the vibrant history of this nation. The many historic sites will enable you to see the way things were in the old days and will illuminate the key events in the story of Canada. Take some time to explore these places. They will bring to life the fur trade, the railway, the North West Mounted Police, and the stories of the First People.

NUNAVUT

MANITOBA

ONTARIO

Birdtail Bench, Riding Mountain
National Park

Churchill

Seal River

Wapusk
National
Park

Sand Lakes
Provincial Park

Numaykoos Lake
Provincial Park

Churchill River

Nelson River

Hayes River

Vollaston
Lake

Reindeer
Lake

Lynn
Lake

Thompson

HBR

Pelican
Narrows

Snow
Lake

Wabowden

Cross
Lake

Cross
Lake

Island
Lake

Flin
Flon

Grass River
Provincial Park

Ronge
al Park

Norway
House

AN

The Pas

Saskatchewan River

Cedar
Lake

Grand
Rapids

Lake
Winnipeg

Hudson
Bay

Lake
Winnipegosis

Atikaki
Provincial
Park

Woodland
Caribou
Provincial
Park

Swan
River

Duck Mountain
Provincial Park

Arborg

Grand
Beach

Nopiming
Provincial
Park

yard

16

Yorkton

Roblin

Dauphin

Gimli

Lake
Manitoba

Whiteshell
Provincial
Park

CNR

Melville

Riding Mountain
National Park

Russell

Stonewall

Selkirk

Beausejour

Elma

Kenora

CPR

1

Fort
'Appelle

Assiniboine River

Neepawa

Portage
la Prairie

WINNIPEG

Minnedosa

CNR

Rivers

REGINA

CPR

Moosomin

Virden

Brandon

Spruce Woods
Provincial Park

Carman

Red River

Steinbach

Lake of
the Woods

Weyburn

Redvers

Winkler

Fort Frances

Estevan

Carnduff

Melita

Boissevain

Morden

Altona

Emerson

NORTH DAKOTA

MINNESOTA

Manitoba

Clear prairie skies over Winnipeg

M anitoba is one of Canada's undiscovered tourism destinations. Most Canadians — except for those who live there — tend to think of the province as one massive prairie, without much in the way of scenic distractions. This impression is actually quite erroneous. Much of

the landscape is rolling, with plenty of lakes and boreal forest, and tundra in the far north that provides some of the best polar bear habitat in the world. The south is rather flat, but the rich agricultural lands and the wide-open skies are beautifully compelling in their own way.

By far the biggest city in Manitoba is Winnipeg. Smaller towns include Dauphin, Portage la Prairie, Brandon, The Pas, Churchill, Selkirk, and Steinbach. As with all of Canada, most of the population is clustered along the U.S. border, leaving vast tracts of more northerly land just about empty, save

for fly-in fishing lodges and other wilderness retreats.

Manitoba's human history is believed to have begun some 15,000 years ago, when nomadic groups began to arrive from the southwest. Natives of the Cree and Sioux nations who settled in the area began to farm as early as 1100 AD, but subsequent climate change forced their return to hunting, trapping and fishing for sustenance.

The first Europeans known to have visited Manitoba arrived in 1612, and by 1670 the explorers of the Hudson's Bay Company were ranging widely throughout the territory in search of fur. The

SuperGuide Recommendations: Manitoba

1) The Forks, Winnipeg
2) The Exchange District, Winnipeg
3) Oak Hammock Marsh
4) Suntanning in Grand Beach
5) Mennonite Historic Village, Steinbach
6) Spirit Sands, Spruce Woods Provincial Park
7) Hiking in Riding Mountain National Park
8) Polar bear tours, Churchill
9) Historic sites, Churchill
10) Attend a performance of the Royal Winnipeg Ballet

The Forks is Winnipeg's most popular destination, summer or winter.

government of Canada purchased Rupert's Land —

Manitoba Festivals

Around Manitoba, there are many festivals celebrating the culture and heritage of the various smaller communities. Here is a selection:

1) The Pas Manitoba Trappers' Festival, February
2) Altona Sunflower Festival, July
3) Neepawa Lily Festival, July
4) Flin Flon Trout Festival, July
5) Killarney Prairie Pioneer Days, July
6) St. Pierre Frog Follies, August
7) Gimli Icelandic Festival, August
8) Morden Corn and Apple Festival, August
9) Dauphin National Ukrainian Festival, August

8 million square kilometres of land stretching from northern Quebec to present-day Nunavut — from the HBC for $1.5 million in 1869. Sir John A. Macdonald's main goal in doing so was to prevent the Americans from buying the land, as the HBC was perfectly willing to sell to the highest bidder.

Manitoba joined Confederation in 1870 with the passing of the Manitoba Act, but not before a series of upheavals involving the original inhabitants of the province, who understandably were not delighted with the change in the status quo.

Winnipeg

Winnipeg is just about bang in the middle of Canada. While some might uncharitably say that this means Winnipeg is far from any of the more interesting Canadian

tourist destinations, in reality there is a good deal for the visitor to enjoy, including a lively arts scene complete with ballet, symphony, opera, and numerous festivals throughout the year. Outdoor activities are numerous, and the people are friendly and welcoming.

For over 6,000 years, Natives used the area near present-day Winnipeg as a fishing and hunting camp and trading post. Fish and game were plentiful, so this was an excellent place to stock up before travelling further along the Red River. There does not appear to have been any permanent settlement by Native groups, however, and occasional battles were fought between the various nomadic groups who used the area.

Winnipeg was founded as Fort Rouge in 1738 by the French Canadian explorer La

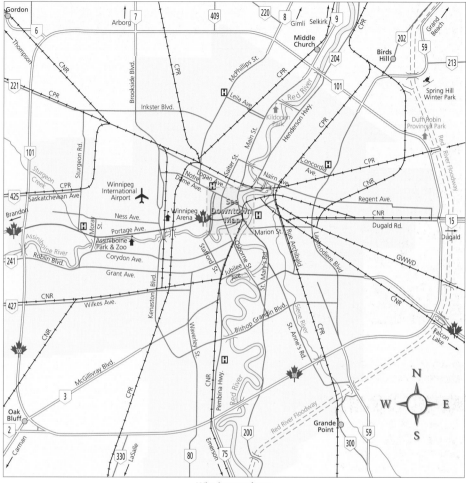

Winnipeg and area

Vérendrye, who established it as part of a network of fur trading posts that were in direct competition with the Hudson's Bay Company. It quickly became an important settlement due to its convenient location at the confluence of the Red and Assiniboine Rivers. The fur trade and the railway were at the base of Winnipeg's development, and grain production was the third element in its rapid growth as Western Canada's most important city.

Attractions in Winnipeg

The Forks
www.theforks.com
201 One Forks Market,
204.942.6302
The Forks is one of the major draws in Winnipeg for both tourists and locals alike. Located right where the Red and Assiniboine rivers meet, the area is also a meeting place for the community — a place to shop, dine, stroll along the river paths, or take in a show or a boat ride. In summer, it hosts outdoor performances

and an open-air market. The river is alive with boats of all descriptions. Canoe rentals are available for those who wish to paddle, and there is a water taxi as well as riverboat tours. Winter sees skating and cross-country skiing on the rivers.

The Forks Market offers a wide range of shops and restaurants that beckon in every season. This is an excellent place to purchase local crafts, as well as items imported from all over the world, and to enjoy a gourmet lunch in the food court atrium.

Manitoba Children's Museum
www.childrensmuseum.com
45 Forks Market Road,
204.924.4000
This is a big draw for families: an interactive museum where kids can get busy in seven galleries with themes ranging from trees to a real TV news studio. Each gallery is totally hands-on and allows children to use their imagination to discover the world around them.

The Forks National Historic Site of Canada
204.983.6757
Commemorating the area's historic significance for over 6,000 years, this part of The Forks features plaques and sculptures explaining the evolution of The Forks from Native meeting place through the fur trade era to its present status. In summer, interpretive guided walks are available, as well as a rotating schedule of theatrical presentations. The gardens are pleasant to stroll through in any season.

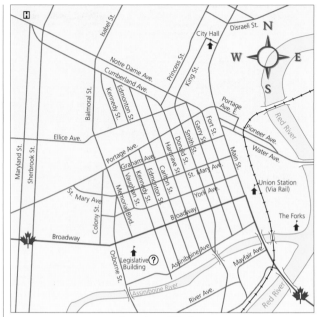

Downtown Winnipeg

Special events often take place at this part of The Forks, including the Winnipeg International Children's Festival and National Aboriginal Day in June. It is also the hub of

Canada Day festivities on July 1.

The Manitoba Museum
www.manitobamuseum.ca
190 Rupert Ave., 204-956-2830

Winnipeg's Elm Trees

Any visitor to Winnipeg will notice the abundance of stately trees that line the streets of downtown and the older residential neighbourhoods. Many of these trees are close to one hundred years old, dating from the boom years at the turn of the 20th century. This remarkable urban forest is made up of over 200,000 elm trees. Native to the area, these trees are extremely hardy and able to withstand Winnipeg's harsh winter conditions where many other trees cannot.

Canadians may recognize these trees with fond remembrance, as elms have all but

died out in many other Canadian cities due to Dutch elm disease. This fungus, carried by bark beetles, was first identified in the Netherlands, and, when it first came to Canada, moved remarkably quickly through the eastern provinces, killing off millions of trees. The trees of Winnipeg have withstood the assault very well so far — the trees are hardy and the winters too cold for the beetles to move in en masse.

Residents and visitors alike enjoy the cool shade and aesthetics of these lovely trees. They are one of Winnipeg's best natural attractions.

Downtown Winnipeg's office towers rise behind The Forks National Historic Site.

This museum brings to life the natural history of Manitoba and the relationship between people and their environment. Seven galleries offer insight into aspects of Manitoba's natural and social history, focusing on the human element within the landscape and some of the issues associated with human impact on the land. One of the highlights of the museum is the full-scale replica of the *Nonsuch*, a ketch whose 1668 arrival in Hudson Bay launched the fur trade in Canada.

Travel further into the history of the HBC in the Hudson's Bay Company Gallery. Over 10,000 artifacts were deeded to the museum in 1994 and the new gallery was created in 1998 to showcase them. The exhibit brings to life the amazing story of this company and its enormous impact on early Canadian history through the fur trade and beyond.

Manitoba Legislative Building
Broadway and Osborne Street,
204.945.5813
This imposing edifice was completed in 1920. In spring and summer, the gardens and fountains are a refreshing sight, and the building, with its neoclassical style, is a tourist attraction in itself. Tours are offered daily throughout the summer.

Winnipeg Art Gallery
www.wag.mb.ca
300 Memorial Blvd.,
204-786-6641
This is the place to see the world's largest collection of modern Inuit art: over 10,000 carvings, prints, drawings and textiles, at least some of which are always on display. The gallery also features contemporary art by Canadians and others, on a rotating schedule.

Métis and Francophones

Manitoba has a large population of French speakers whose presence in the province dates back to the time of La Vérendrye's exploration in the 1730s. His trading posts were subsequently visited by the French voyageurs. Over time, many of the French men intermarried with the Indian women, which led to the formation of the "half-breed" or Métis society. The Métis were active in the fur trade, using their Red River carts as well as boats to transport goods around the prairies and along the rivers.

In the latter part of the 19th century, the majority of the population of Manitoba was Métis, and to this day the culture continues to flourish and thrive. Places to learn more about their customs and colourful history include the St. Boniface Museum, the Grey Nuns' Convent National Historic Site, Riel House and St. Boniface Cathedral in Winnipeg, and the Riel Monument in St. Norbert.

Louis Riel

Perhaps the most controversial figure in Canadian history, Louis Riel (1844-85) had an immense impact on the history of Manitoba and of Canada. He was responsible for bringing Manitoba into Confederation as the fifth province, but was ultimately hanged as a traitor for his role in the North-West Rebellion.

Métis by birth, Riel grew up in St. Boniface and was sent at a young age to Montreal to train for the priesthood. He stayed on in Montreal working as a law clerk after leaving the priesthood, returning to Winnipeg in the summer of 1868.

When Rupert's Land was sold to Canada in 1869, surveyors were sent to Manitoba to begin organizing settlement along new lines. Riel and 18 other Métis halted the surveying process as the first act in what would become known as the Red River Rebellion. He gained much support from the Métis population as a result of this action, and in November 1869 he rode with a group of supporters to Fort Garry and seized control of the fort, setting up a provisional government a few weeks later. He drew up a List of Rights that outlined the Métis demands of the federal government — mainly, that they wished to keep their property rights, and freedom of worship and language. At this time, the Métis were the majority of the population in the territory.

In May 1870, the Manitoba Act was passed, creating a new province and granting most of Riel's conditions, but Riel himself had to leave the country, due to a court martial having ordered the execution of an Ontarian, Thomas Scott, during Riel's occupation of Fort Garry. He went to the States and returned a few times before the fateful events of 1885.

In 1884, the "half-breeds" (the Métis of French as well as those of Scottish and English descent) of the prairies were unhappy with the government's land policy. They turned first to Gabriel Dumont, a beloved leader who was known far and wide for his good character. Dumont, however, spoke no English and knew he was not the right man to be negotiating with the federal government. He turned to Riel, then living in Montana but still filled with a sense of purpose and willing to take up the cause of his people once again.

Riel returned to Canada and began to meet with the Native groups as well as the "half-breeds", organizing to act in concert and peacefully to have their demands met. However, events escalated and Riel declared a provisional Métis government in Batoche, Saskatchewan. His followers began to run riot in the area. A battle broke out between the

Louis Riel

Métis and the police, which the police lost. This marked the beginning of the North-West Rebellion. The militia was sent from eastern Canada to quell the rebellion and by mid-May the last battle had been fought. The Native and Métis began to surrender to the inevitable. Riel was tried in Regina for treason and sentenced to death — a controversial decision that split the country along linguistic lines. Most English speakers felt he was a traitor, while most francophones believed he was a patriot. Riel was hanged on November 16, 1885.

Dalnavert Museum
www.mhs.mb.ca
61 Carlton Street, 204.943.2835
A restored Queen Anne-style house that was built for Sir Hugh John Macdonald, son of Sir John A. Macdonald, Canada's first prime minister. The house was built in 1895 for Sir Hugh, a lawyer (and briefly Premier of Manitoba, in 1900). After undergoing many transformations, it was eventually refurbished and is now a museum highlighting the lifestyles of the wealthy in the boom days of Winnipeg — the early part of the 20th century — when the city was known as the Chicago of the North.

Riel House
www.parkscanada.gc.ca/riel
330 River Road, St. Vital, 204.257.1783
The home of the Riel family until 1969, this site explores the life of Louis Riel, the Métis leader who founded Manitoba as a province, yet who was considered a traitor by some for starting the North-West Rebellion of 1885. Riel House also highlights the lifestyle of the Métis in the late 19th century. The house has been refurbished and shows the living room in a state of mourning, for it was here that Riel's body lay in state for two days after his execution, before his burial in St. Boniface Cemetery. Costumed interpreters offer a guided tour, and special events happen throughout the year.

Assiniboine Park
2355 Corydon Ave.
One of Winnipeg's nicest natural attractions, Assiniboine Park was officially opened in 1909. The park was designed in the English landscape style, which emphasizes large open meadows, wilder-looking gardens, and free-form bodies of water. Several gardens adorn the park, including the English Garden, the Formal Garden and the Leo Mol Sculpture Garden.

Assiniboine Park Zoo
www.zoosociety.com
54 Zoo Drive, 204.986.2327
Located within Assiniboine Park, the zoo features over 300 species of animals, and wisely specializes in animals from cold-weather zones of the world. It is a leader in breeding animals in captivity, so most of the species on display were not captured in the wild. Lovers of more southern animals can see them in various indoor pavilions.

Indoors, the Assiniboine Park Conservatory features a palm house and floral displays, as well as a restaurant and gallery featuring the work of local artists. Visit the Pavilion Garden Museum, in the restored 1929 Pavilion Building, to discover the work of three artists or to enjoy a meal in the Tavern in the Park.

Fort Whyte Centre
www.fortwhyte.org
1961 McCreary Road, 204.989.8355
Just south of Assiniboine Park, Fort Whyte is a place to learn about and experience the natural world. Four hundred acres feature walking trails, boardwalks, birdwatching

Take a Tour

Get a different viewpoint of Winnipeg and learn a little more about the city.

On a boat:
MS *Paddlewheel Queen*
www.paddlewheelcruises.com
204.942.4500
Paddlewheelers have been used on the Red River for almost 150 years. Tour the river today on the MS *Paddlewheel Queen*. Public cruises depart daily in summer months

On your feet:
Marche Donc
866.808.8338
This highly entertaining guided tour, led by a longtime local resident, starts at St. Boniface City Hall. It highlights some of St. Boniface's most important landmarks, and includes many interesting anecdotes about the area's history.

With a horse:
Bar 32 Horse Drawn Ventures
204.736.2836
Custom bookings for tours through St. Boniface and many other areas of Winnipeg. One of their popular tours travels through the streets of Old St. Boniface past many of the area's important historical landmarks.

On a train:
Prairie Dog Central,
www.vintagelocomotive
society.mb.ca
204.832.5259
You don't have to be a train buff to enjoy this tour on a vintage train that travels from Winnipeg to Warren, a small prairie town northwest of the city, stopping at a country market or two along the way. This tour runs weekends only, May through September.

sites, and even a bison prairie and deer enclosure. The 10,000-square-foot Interpretive Centre features an aquarium and a glassed-in honeybee hive. You can canoe or fish in designated spots in summer, and toboggan or skate in winter, or take a guided snowshoe tour.

Living Prairie Museum
2795 Ness Ave., 204.832.0167
Prior to the arrival of white settlers, tall-grass prairie covered one million square kilometres of land in central North America. Today, thanks to agricultural and residential pressure, it is almost all gone. Manitoba, for example, has less than 1% of its original grasslands left. The Living Prairie Museum is a place to discover the beauty of the grassland ecosystem, on 30 acres of land within Winnipeg. It's home to wildlife, songbirds, and amazingly tall grasses native to the area. An interpretive centre is open all summer, and guided or self-guided tours are available.

Manitoba Crafts Museum and Library
161 Ash St., 204.487.6117
This independent museum is devoted to the understanding, preservation and study of handcrafts, mainly of Manitoban origin, but some from around the world. The collection features a wide variety of handmade objects, including embroidery, beadwork, quillwork, basketry, crochet, knitting, quilting, weaving, spinning, dying, tatting, sewing, Inuit and Aboriginal stone sculpture, woodwork and pottery.

Winnipeg Railway Museum
Via Rail Station, 123 Main St., 204.942.4632
The railway was essential to the development of Winnipeg as a boom town. By 1911, 24 rail lines met in Winnipeg, making it the most important transportation hub in western Canada. The museum features many vintage railway cars as well as displays on the history of the railway.

Royal Canadian Mint
520 Lagimodière Blvd., 204.257.3359
The first Canadian Mint is in Ottawa, but Winnipeg has a modern money-making facility, opened in 1975, that creates money for over 40 countries as well as Canada. Over 4 billion coins are produced annually. Take a tour to watch the process.

A Prairies Bodice Ripper

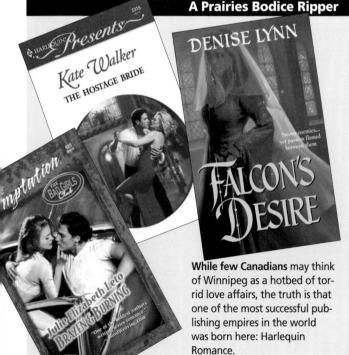

While few Canadians may think of Winnipeg as a hotbed of torrid love affairs, the truth is that one of the most successful publishing empires in the world was born here: Harlequin Romance.

Richard Bonnycastle was the man behind the company. He had previously had an adventurous life working for the Hudson's Bay Company in the Canadian Arctic. In 1949 he founded Harlequin Enterprises, which began by publishing a range of books. In 1957 the company began to buy the rights for love stories put out by British romance company Mills and Boon.

Mary Bonnycastle, Richard's wife, noticed the popularity of the "nice little books with happy endings", and by 1964 the company was publishing Harlequin Romances exclusively. Today the company sells over 160 million romance novels every year and has branched out into online romances with its eHarlequin.com website.

Manitoba Sports Hall of Fame and Museum
www.halloffame.mb.ca
450 Portage Ave. (5th Floor of The Bay), 204. 774.0002
This unusually-located museum celebrates the history of sport in Manitoba, and honours outstanding athletes from the province. The galleries include bowling and curling exhibits as well as a space for various rotating exhibits.

Western Canada Aviation Museum
www.wcam.mb.ca
Ferry Road at Ellice Ave., 204.786.5503
One of Winnipeg's largest museums, the WCAM holds over 20 vintage aircraft and has many displays that illuminate the history of aviation in Canada. Children will appreciate the large interactive section and the chance to watch aircraft landing and taking off.

Air Force Heritage Park and Museum
Air Force Way, 204.833.2500 ext.5993

A must for aviation and military buffs, this museum features 15 military aircraft on display.

Fire Fighters Museum of Winnipeg
www.winnipegfire museum.ca
56 Maple St., 204.942.4817
This unusual museum, housed in a restored 1904 firehall, is dedicated to Winnipeg's firefighters from 1882 to the present, and features displays and artifacts from various eras of firefighting.

Grant's Old Mill
2777 Portage Ave., 204.986.5613 or 204.837.1775
A picturesque working replica of the first gristmill built in the western prairies.

Culture
The long, cold prairie winters (it's not nicknamed "Winterpeg" for nothing!) have inspired Winnipeg to become a haven for the arts. When it's 40 below outside, there is still plenty of fun to be had indoors, whether at the ballet, the opera, the theatre, or other music venues around the city. Check out these venues to see what's happening culturally in Winnipeg.

Centennial Concert Hall
555 Main St., 204.957.4311
In the heart of the Exchange District, this is Manitoba's premier performing arts facility. It is home to the Royal Winnipeg Ballet, the Winnipeg Symphony Orchestra, and the Manitoba Opera.

The Royal Winnipeg Ballet
www.rwb.org
204.956.2792
A Canadian cultural tradition, the company was founded in 1939 and received its royal title in 1953 (the first one granted by Queen Elizabeth II). The company has been touring since 1945 and is now internationally recognized as a world-class ballet. They are on the road more than 20 weeks per year and offer up four programs per year.

The Winnipeg Symphony Orchestra
www.wso.mb.ca
204.949.3999
Winnipeg's symphony season runs from September to May and features classics, contemporary composers, concerts for schoolchildren and families, and the innovative New Music Festival, held in February every year.

Emily Grizzell and Dmitri Dovgoselets perform in the Royal Winnipeg Ballet's Sleeping Beauty. **23**

Winnipeg Festivals and Special Events

Winnipeg is host to many special events and festivals over the course of the year.

February: Festival du Voyageur
www.festivalvoyageur.mb.ca
A celebration of French-Canadian heritage and the fur trade era. This is Western Canada's largest winter festival, featuring international dog sled races, traditional voyageur cuisine, ice sculptures, and fiddling and jigging contests.

June: Winnipeg International Children's Festival
www.kidsfest.ca
This celebration of and for children features performers from around the world, in tents and outdoor stages at The Forks Market.

June: Scottish Heritage Festival
This traditional Highland festival takes place at Red River Exhibition Park, and features music, dancing, drumming, and heavy sports.

June: Red River Exhibition
www.redriverex.com
The official kickoff to summer, the Red River Ex features an agricultural exhibition and midway, craft and baking competitions, musical performances and plenty of old-fashioned fun for the whole family.

June: Jazz Winnipeg Festival
www.jazzwinnipeg.com
A ten-day event that takes place every year at the end of June, when a wide range of acts take to the stage at various venues around the city. As with most jazz festivals, not all performers stick strictly to jazz, so you don't have to be a jazz lover to enjoy the festival — just a music lover.

July: Winnipeg Fringe Theatre Festival
www.winnipegfringe.com
Over 120 theatre companies arrive in Winnipeg for ten days of adventurous theatre.

July: Winnipeg Folk Festival
www.winnipegfolkfestival.ca
The Winnipeg Folk Festival takes place every summer in Birds Hill Provincial Park. This musical feast features over 60 acts representing an incredible range of genres and nations.

August: Folklorama
www.folklorama.ca
This event, unique to Winnipeg, celebrates the more than 40 cultures from around the world that make up Winnipeg's population. This two-week festival is a chance to experience food, music and culture from all over the planet. The festival itself is spread out in different venues around the city and each pavilion has a 45-minute show three times a night. It is possible, if ambitious, to see three shows a night, though with venues all over the city it requires careful planning to drive from one to the other yourself. A bus service simplifies the travel time between events.

August: Manitoba Dragon Boat Festival
Three days of dragon boat racing and other activities at The Forks.

September: Winnipeg International Writers Festival
www.winnipegwords.com
A week of readings, workshops, seminars and other literary events, this event celebrating writers and readers takes place at venues around the city.

October: Oktoberfest
www.winnipegoktoberfest.com
A ten-day Bavarian celebration at the Winnipeg Convention Centre, featuring oom-pah bands, polkas, and plenty of beer and bratwurst.

On the Fringe

Winnipeg's Fringe Theatre Festival is the second-largest event of its kind in North America (after Edmonton) and features hundreds of performances, from noon until midnight, throughout ten days in late July every year. The idea is to present live theatre in an informal, accessible and inexpensive environment, with a mix of work from seasoned actors and well-known pieces to total unknowns. All the action takes place within a five-minute walk of old Market Square in The Exchange District, some indoors and some outdoors. There's something to delight everyone and while it's a bit of a gamble to select a play — some work will inspire a joyful feeling of discovery while some may leave you feeling confused — that's the point of a fringe festival. Tel. 94-FRINGE or visit www.winnipegfringe.com

Winnipeg's Folklorama celebrates more than 40 cultures from around the world.

St. Boniface

Just across the Red River from The Forks is St. Boniface, the French Quarter of Winnipeg. There is a different feel to this side of town, with its sheltering trees and historic buildings along the river, and its streets named in French. Over 25% of the population of this area speaks French as a first language. This is a wonderful place for a stroll along the riverside path known as Promenade Taché, which is easily reached by crossing a bridge from The Forks. Be sure to visit the following sites in St. Boniface:

St. Boniface Cathedral
190 ave. de la Cathédrale, 204.233.7304

The cathedral has been rebuilt five times since the original building went up in 1818. A fire swept through in 1968, destroying most of the structure that had been built in 1908. Only the facade and part of the walls remained and

have now been incorporated into a new building. A provincial historic site, this imposing building attests to the strong Catholic presence in the area. Louis Riel is buried in its cemetery.

Musée de St. Boniface
494 ave. Taché, 204.237.4500

Originally a convent for the Grey Nuns, this log building was constructed between 1846 and 1851. Today it is home to a museum exploring the fascinating history and lives of the Métis and Franco-Manitobans. It is the oldest building in Winnipeg and also the oldest oak log structure in North America.

Gabrielle Roy House
375 rue Deschambault

This was the home of well-known Canadian author Gabrielle Roy. Several of her novels and stories are set right in this neighbourhood.

Sports Action in Winnipeg

Winnipeg has several professional sports teams. Check out a game or two while you are in the city.

The **Winnipeg Blue Bombers** (www.blue-bombers.com) are the city's Canadian Football League team, playing out of Canad Inns Stadium. Their regular season runs from June through November.

The **Manitoba Moose** (www.manitobamoose.com) hockey team is the farm team for the Vancouver Canucks, playing out of the Winnipeg Arena. Their season runs from October through April.

The **Winnipeg Goldeyes** (www.goldeyes.com) are part of the Northern League of independent baseball teams, playing out of CanWest Global Park. Their regular season is from May through August.

Manitoba Opera
www.manitobaopera.mb.ca
204.780.3333
Accompanied by the WSO, the Manitoba Opera stages two classic pieces every year as well as smaller operatic events from time to time.

The Manitoba Theatre Centre
www.mtc.mb.ca
174 Market Ave., 204.942.6537
The MTC was founded in 1943 and continues to offer up a strong calendar of performances featuring local talent. Every year, the company produces ten professional productions (six on its Mainstage and four on the Warehouse). In addition, the Manitoba Theatre Centre is the founder and epicentre of the yearly Winnipeg Fringe Theatre Festival, one of the more popular fringe festivals in the world.

Pantages Playhouse
www.pantagesplayhouse.com
180 Market St., 204.989.2889
For over 80 years this playhouse has hosted any number of performances, from vaudeville to musical performances and live theatre.

Théâtre de la Chapelle
825 rue St-Joseph, 204.233.8053
This is the venue of Le Cercle Molière, the oldest active theatre company in Canada. Every year it produces four innovative and entertaining theatrical pieces in French.

Lyric Theatre
Assiniboine Park, 204.888.5466
This classical Tudor-style stage hosts outdoor summer performances by the Royal Winnipeg Ballet and the Winnipeg Symphony Orchestra, as well as jazz, folk, and drama festivals. Just bring along a lawn chair or blanket (and insect repellent!) and enjoy the performance.

Rainbow Stage
www.rainbowstage.net
Kildonan Park, 204.780.7328
Outdoor musicals take place here every summer, while the company produces winter musicals out of Pantages Playhouse.

Shopping and Dining

Winnipeg has many malls, both downtown and in the neighbouring areas, offering plenty of choice from well-known chains. As well, the city boasts over 900 restaurants, with a wide range of cultural choices. For unique shopping and dining, visit the following areas.

Corydon Avenue
Winnipeg's "Little Italy" is the largest outdoor shopping area in Winnipeg and features pretty flower planters, unique shops and a wide choice of restaurants.

Osborne Village
Just across the Assiniboine River is Osborne Village, a charming, densely populated neighbourhood with more than 25 restaurants and lots of trendy little shops to discover.

Academy Road
One of Winnipeg's more upscale neighbourhoods is found along Academy Road on the south side of the Assiniboine River, with designer fashions, gift shops, and plenty of gourmet food stores and restaurants.

Exchange District
Visit this area for the beautiful buildings as much as for the varied shopping and dining opportunities.

The Exchange District of Winnipeg — Heart of a City

This national historic site is centred around the Winnipeg Grain and Produce Exchange, which was established in 1887 in the basement of Winnipeg's City Hall. The Exchange was the basis for the generation of many a fortune in Winnipeg's boom era, which lasted until the start of the First World War. The historic Exchange building was built in 1906 and kick-started the development of the area, with over 20 banks setting up their western headquarters along "Bankers' Row". At one time Winnipeg had as many millionaires as Chicago, and much of the wealth in Winnipeg flowed through the Exchange.

The area has been remarkably well-preserved and restored. Many graceful old buildings here attest to Winnipeg's former position of pre-eminence in North America, and the area was designated a National Historic Site in 1997. Today, thirty blocks of handsome terra cotta and cut-stone architecture house a thriving arts and business community.

Guided walking tours run May through September (204.942.6716).

Step back in time with costumed interpreters at Lower Fort Garry.

St. James

A neighbourhood in the process of rejuvenation, St. James is located along Portage Avenue West. Cafés, fine dining, and antique shops are just some of the businesses found here. A unique feature of this neighbourhood is the galvanized steel trees.

Selkirk Avenue

This smaller neighbourhood offers many tempting Ukrainian restaurants and shops.

Boulevard Provencher

The main artery for shopping and dining in St. Boniface, this is the ideal place to come for innovative and delicious French cuisine.

Around Winnipeg

It's worth staying in Winnipeg a few extra days to see some of the surrounding areas, which offer plenty of attractions and things to do. These three trips can be divided into attractions north and west of Winnipeg, and a day in Mennonite Country.

North of Winnipeg

Well worth a day trip, the area just north of Winnipeg offers several historic attractions in Selkirk, as well as Oak Hammock Marsh, a popular outdoor destination. Drive out to Selkirk along the east side of the Red River and return along PTH 67 to get to Oak Hammock. Visit Selkirk in July, when the annual Manitoba Highland Gathering takes place, with all the events associated with a Highland Games, from sheep dog trials to heavy sports.

Lower Fort Garry National Historic Site

Highway 9, 1.877.534.3678
This site offers an opportunity to step back in time and explore the workings of a stone fort, circa 1850. Costumed interpreters stroll through the area, and a conversation with each one illuminates another aspect of life in a Hudson's

Treaty One — The Stone Fort Treaty

In August 1871, the first post-Confederation treaty between the Canadian government and the Native people was signed at Lower Fort Garry. The treaty promised the Natives reserves of land, for each band a reserve large enough to provide 160 acres per family of five. The Natives were also promised farm implements, stock, and seed if they wished to begin farming. Schools were to be set up on every reserve, and each man, woman and child received an annuity of three dollars. In return, the Natives were required to give up all of their ancestral lands and keep the peace with the new white settlers.

To a reader of today, the best that can be said about these terms is that they were paternalistic, coming from a school of thought that held that the best thing for the Natives was to settle down and become farmers. At worst, they could be seen as a massively racist and unfair land grab.

The reserves were meant to assimilate the Natives peacefully into the new Canada, and these treaties were used as the blueprint for treaties with Native bands throughout the west. While there was initially a good deal of confusion over the implementation of the treaties — Natives did not receive some of the things they were promised — in the end the administrative system was worked out by which most of the Saulteaux and Swampy Cree were able to live peacefully, if restrictedly, within the new Dominion.

Bay Company fur trading post, from the governor to the Natives bringing in the pelts for trade. Learn about the history of the fur trade and the Red River settlement itself — the fort was where Treaty One was negotiated in 1871, which granted the Saulteaux (Ojibwa), Swampy Cree, and others in southern Manitoba future land, in the form of reserves, within the province.

Weekly interpretive events are held throughout the summer, as well as the Red River RendezVous in August — a lively re-creation of the fur trade days. Lower Fort Garry is open in summer only.

St Andrew's Rectory and Church National Historic Site
5609 Hwy. 9, 204.344.6405
These buildings offer a delightful example of the "Hudson's Bay" style of Red River architecture. The simple stone church is still in use today for worship. Visitors are also welcome to look around the main floor of the rectory, which is now a museum, to learn about the role of the Anglican church in helping to settle the prairies. Enjoy a stroll or picnic in the gardens.

Marine Museum of Manitoba
www.marinemuseum.ca
Eveline St. and Queen Ave., Selkirk, 204.482.7761
Learn about the history of freshwater navigation on Lake Winnipeg and the Red River, so crucial to the development of Winnipeg. Several vessels are permanently berthed on the grass, including an icebreaker, a tug, and a steamship, all of which served for decades on the waterways of Manitoba.

Oak Hammock Marsh is home to more than 295 species of bird.

Oak Hammock Marsh Interpretive Centre
www.ducks.ca/ohmic
North of PTH 67 on PR 220, 204.467.3300
This wildlife management area is an important migratory stop for dozens of species of birds — over 400,000 birds stop here during the fall migration — and features boardwalks and observation decks along the 32 km of interpretive trails. The area includes places to canoe and a lovely tall-grass prairie exhibit with a stunning array of wildflowers throughout summer. The interpretive centre itself is a beautiful building, its rounded contours echoing the curves of the landscape. A visit to the centre will convince you of the importance of wetlands, for animals and people alike. More than 295 bird species make their home here, as well as 25 mammal species and countless reptiles and amphibians.

Return to Winnipeg for the night, or continue to Lake Winnipeg's beach towns for a few more days of exploring.

North of Selkirk, the landscape is dominated by the

La Vérendrye

Pierre Gaultier de Varennes, who became the Sieur de La Vérendrye, was born in Trois-Rivières, Quebec, in 1685. At the age of 40 he embarked on a journey that was the fulfillment of a long-held dream: to explore Canada and reach the Pacific Ocean. He had to raise the funds for this expedition himself, but the French government granted him a monopoly on any furs traded along the way.

Along with several of his sons, he explored the prairies extensively, setting up a network of fur-trading posts along the way in the hopes of financing his travels. He never reached the "western sea" he had heard about from his Native contacts, but his travels as far as the Saskatchewan River opened up the prairies and established the French presence there that continues to this day.

Grand Beach is a favourite summer retreat.

Lake Winnipeg is Canada's fourth largest lake.

massive Lake Winnipeg, which, at 425 km long and 40 km wide, is the fourth largest lake in Canada and the eleventh largest in the world. Winnipeg Beach and Grand Beach are where Winnipeg residents go to beat the summer heat on the famous sandy beaches — the feeling is like being at the seaside.

Gimli
Further up the lake, about 60 minutes from Winnipeg, is the town of Gimli, founded by Icelandic settlers in the late 19th century. It is still the largest settlement of Icelanders outside of Iceland, and today thrives on fishing and summer tourism.

Islendingadagurinn, the Festival of the Icelander, with a parade, fireworks, and festive activities for the whole family, takes place here every August, attracting over 30,000 visitors to this tiny beach community of about 2,000 permanent residents.

On regular days, visit the beach, the New Iceland Heritage Museum, or the H.P. Tergesen Store, which is the oldest operating store in Manitoba (built in 1898) and is now a provincial heritage site.

Further up the lake still is Hecla Provincial Park, a great place to explore the landscape of Manitoba. The park surrounds the shoreline and islands of Lake Winnipeg, with Hecla Island the centre of activity. Learn more about the Icelandic heritage of the area at Hecla Village, the fish station, and the Heritage Home Museum, or take in the views from the wildlife viewing tower or the trails of the Grassy Narrows Marsh. Outdoor activities of all kinds make this a magnet for nature lovers in both summer and winter.

West of Winnipeg
Start out along Hwy. 2, past some small-town sights such as the World's Largest Fire Hydrant in Elm Creek and the World's Largest Smoking Pipe in St. Claude. This area is primarily agricultural and can be quite colourful, with bright yellow canola and sunflower fields along the way.

Spruce Woods Provincial Park
Continue to Glenboro and follow the signs north on Hwy. 5 to Spruce Woods Provincial Park, home of Spirit Sands. This 4-km-square site is the remains of what was once a much larger sandblow. This near-desert area is 30 metres (83 feet) higher than the surrounding prairie, and is home to wildflowers, snakes, spiders, and cactus, as well as several animal species that are unique to Manitoba, such as the Northern prairie skink.

The park also features plenty of forest — hence the name — and a scenic blue-green lake called the Devil's Punch Bowl. Visitors can hike, mountain bike, swim, or take a guided tour of Spirit Sands in a covered wagon. This is a great place to spend the better portion of a day.

Manitoba Agricultural Museum
After you've had your fill of the park, continue north to

Canola fields are vibrant under the brilliant prairie sky.

Carberry, and then head east on Hwy. 1. Stop in Austin, which features the Manitoba Agricultural Museum, a large heritage complex featuring over 500 farm implements and more than 20 heritage buildings in a pioneer village. Visit in late July for the Threshermen's Reunion and Stampede, and the Central Canada Fiddle Festival

Fort La Reine Museum and Pioneer Village

Next is Portage la Prairie, named by La Vérendrye, who stopped here while portaging from the Assiniboine River to Lake Manitoba in the 1730s. Portage is the third-largest city in Manitoba. Visitors here may want to explore the downtown on a self-guided heritage tour or visit the Fort La Reine Museum and Pioneer Village, which features a recreated version of the

Who are the Mennonites?

The Mennonite faith grew out of the Protestant Reformation in the 1500s as a grassroots movement. The earliest adherents, called Anabaptists, believed that the church should be separate from the state, and that people should come to the church by their own free will, through adult baptism.

The name Mennonite evolved from Menno Simons, a priest who became one of the early leaders of the Anabaptist movement in 1536, when he renounced Catholicism.

The core beliefs of the Mennonite church are pacifism (loyalty to God rather than a state), adult baptism, and following the actions of Jesus through service to others and a virtuous life based on plenty of New Testament study.

The Mennonite people settled in Manitoba between 1874 and 1879 at the invitation of the Canadian government, which was anxious to settle the lands closest to the U.S. border in order to safeguard Canadian sovereignty. The pacifist Mennonites were being persecuted in Russia, so the offer of free land as well as "an entire exemption from any military service" brought in entire villages to rebuild in Canada.

The Mennonites of Manitoba, while sharing religious traditions with the Amish, are not generally as separatist and insular as that sect, and are more involved in their surrounding communities.

original fort built in 1738 by La Vérendrye. The village shows what life was like in the area during the mid-to-late 19th century, and also features William Van Horne's personal railway car.

Mennonite Country

This picturesque tour includes a visit to a fascinating attraction, and some scenic driving around southern Manitoba.

Steinbach's Mennonite Heritage Village

Begin an exploration of Mennonite country by driving east on Hwy. 1, then south on Hwy. 12, to Steinbach's Mennonite Heritage Village (Tel. 204.326.9661). This exceptional 40-acre site, laid out like a traditional Mennonite village, tells the story of the Mennonite people from 1525 to the present day. The Village Centre has interpretive displays, but the history really comes alive in the village buildings, where the daily activities of this industrious people are carried out. There are special events year-round at the village.

From Steinbach, head west across several country roads to Hwy. 75, then continue south to Hwy. 201, which will lead into the heart of Mennonite country.

Altona

Altona is known as the Sunflower Capital of Canada and is one of the larger communities of Mennonite origin. A midsummer visit will reveal the fields of flowers in all their glory. Turn south on Hwy. 30, then west at Gretna, then north on Hwy. 32 for a brief drive through the Mennonite country. From Winkler, return to Winnipeg on Hwy. 14 and 75.

Brandon

Less than a two-hour drive west of Winnipeg, Brandon is the next largest community in Manitoba (at 42,000 residents) and the service centre for a large surrounding area. Known as the Wheat City for its location in the some of the richest agricultural land in the world, Brandon has some interesting historical and outdoor attractions. It's also home to the Wheat Kings, a very successful WHL Major Junior A hockey team, and the Grey Owls professional baseball team.

Brandon is located in the Assiniboine River Valley, and has many scenic walking and biking trails along the Assiniboine Riverbank Trail System. In town, take a self-guided walking tour to discover many of the handsome Victorian buildings that have been designated heritage sites.

Within an hour of Brandon to the south is the International Peace Garden, and a little further to the north is Riding Mountain National Park.

The International Peace Garden, located on the border of Manitoba and North Dakota, is well worth a detour off the Trans-Canada, especially for garden lovers — follow the signs and head south on Hwy. 10. Another short detour to the charming small town of Souris, to see the

Brandon Festivals and Special Events

Brandon is home to several major festivals:

January: First Nations Winter Celebration

At the Keystone Centre, this event features arm-wrestling competitions and many more activities for the whole family.

February: Brandon Film Festival

Canada's answer to Sundance, without the mountains. This is a great chance to view some independent films.

March: Royal Manitoba Winter Fair

This is one of the largest agricultural events in Canada and features a wide range of events and displays, including show jumping, a heavy horse show and competitions, a poultry and rabbit display, Canada's largest shows featuring swine, eggs, and seeds, and lots of entertainment.

June: Manitoba Summer Fair

The Summer Fair has more of an emphasis on the midway and other attractions than on agriculture. It features a demolition derby, a car show, a parade and many other activities.

July: Folk Music and Arts Festival

Performances by plenty of well-known musicians of many genres from all over Canada, as well as artists and craftspeople working and selling their wares under the canvas.

November: Manitoba Livestock Expo, Manitoba Rodeo Championship Finals

suspension bridge and the Hillcrest Museum, adds another element to this trip.

Riding Mountain National Park, about an hour north of Brandon via Hwy. 10, is Manitobans' favourite wilderness retreat, and an excellent place to spend a day or more. The park is made up of over 3,000 square kilometres of land — a mix of aspen parkland, deciduous forest, boreal forest and meadows — making it a wonderful place for hiking, camping, fishing, mountain biking and horseback riding.

Many visitors will spend some time in the town located within the park, Wasagaming, which has accommodation and a large campground as well as a wide choice of recreational activities. Wasagaming was set up in the 1930s to emulate an English resort village.

Brandon is known as the Wheat City, due to its location amidst fertile farmland.

Grey Owl

One of the more well-known residents of Riding Mountain National Park was Grey Owl (1888-1938), who lived in a cabin on Clear Lake for a short time with his common-law wife and their two pet beavers, Rawhide and Jelly Roll. He was the first naturalist hired by Riding Mountain National Park after its establishment in 1931. A passionate conservationist, Grey Owl wrote several books and essays about the natural world.

Due to his name and lifestyle, people assumed he was Native, an impression he used to the fullest, even touring North America and the UK giving talks on Native ways. However, his real name was Archibald Belaney and he was English by birth. While his character was somewhat dubious, he sometimes had more than one wife at a time, and he perpetrated a major fraud about his identity, nobody can doubt his commitment to the environment, which shines through in his written works.

He stayed only six months in Riding Mountain before moving to Prince Albert National Park, where he stayed for several years. However, his

Grey Owl feeding his pet beaver

cabin at Beaver Lake has been maintained and is now a hiking destination within the park.

Take a Hike at Riding Mountain

The Manitoba Escarpment overlooks many Riding Mountain National Park trails.

As with most national parks, the best thing to do is to get out of town and enjoy a walk or hike on the trails. Here are several great choices of short walks and hikes, in order of their proximity to Wasagaming:

Lakeshore (2.6-km loop). A great place to stroll, right in the townsite of Wasagaming, this loop is especially pretty at sunset.

Arrowhead (3.4 km return). Learn about the animals, flowers and trees of the park on this gently rolling self-guided trail.

Brulé (4.2-km loop). Take this trail to learn about wildflowers and the development of the area through fire and other natural processes. A 2.2-km version of this loop is also available.

Loon's Island (2.4 km return). This trail along the shores of

Katherine Lake is an excellent place to watch loons diving and calling.

Bead Lakes (4-km loop). A pleasant stroll through a white birch forest, passing a small chain of lakes along the way.

Boreal Island (1 km). Keep an eye out on this short trail for moose, which are plentiful in the park.

Kippan's Mill (1.2 km return). Enjoy a walk through history at the remains of this 1940s logging camp.

Beach Ridges (3.5 km return). Thousands of years ago, the area around Riding Mountain, as well as much of Manitoba and beyond, was covered by a huge glacial lake known as Lake Agassiz. Learn about the natural history of the area on this walk and be sure to climb the Agassiz Tower to get a good view of the surrounding farmland.

Churchill

A long way from anywhere, 1,600 km north of Winnipeg, Churchill has become famous as the polar bear capital of the world. Originally established as a fort, then as a grain shipping port, this small Arctic community on the shores of Hudson Bay is now famous as a naturalist's paradise. It is accessible only by train or by air.

An entire industry has sprung up in Churchill relating to the presence of the magnificent and terrifying polar bear. It's quipped that in high polar-bear season, mid-October to early November, there are as many bears in town as residents. At this time of year, the bears are waiting for the ice to form on the bay, which is their prime seal-hunting habitat in winter. In June, as the ice is melting, they return to the land, where they spend the summers ranging widely on the tundra.

The bears are usually found at the Cape Churchill Wildlife Management Area in Wapusk National Park south and east of town. If a bear wanders into town, it is usually escorted back out of town on a helicopter. Despite their lovable appearance, these bears can grow to be 10 feet tall, weigh in at about 1,300 pounds, and will attack humans. Moreover, they live off the seals they hunt all winter, and during the five months of the year that they are on land, they fast, which makes them pretty eager to get some food by the time October rolls around.

Clearly it is not safe to wander around on the tundra hoping to run into a polar bear. Guided tours are the

Tundra buggies from Churchill offer close encounters of the polar kind.

Take a Historic Tour near Churchill

Due to the absence of roads in the area, and the boggy nature of the landscape, it can be hard for visitors to get around on their own. Take a tour to get the most out of your trip.

Prince of Wales Fort
This enormous star-shaped fort, across the river mouth from Churchill, is one of Canada's most remote National Historic Sites and now stands as a monument to the long enmity between the British and the French. The fort was begun in 1733 by the Hudson's Bay Company, with the intention of providing a refuge for British fur-trading ships in times of war with France. It took close to forty years to complete the stone fort, but just over a decade later, in 1782, the French took the fort. It was never used again.

Take a boat tour to visit this forlorn site and try to imagine passing a winter here in the early days, when a chief occupation was chopping wood to try to keep the place warm, or summer, when the bugs were fierce and the work

of building the fort seemed endless.

Cape Merry
A short distance from town and right across the river from the fort, Cape Merry is the site of a gun battlement that was intended to protect the river from enemy occupation. In summer it is an excellent place to spot belugas and to gaze from afar at Prince of Wales Fort. There is a monument here to commemorate the ill-fated expedition of Jens Munk, a Danish explorer whose crew was forced to winter here in 1619-1620. Only Munk and two of the crew of over 60 men survived.

Sloop Cove
Just south of Prince of Wales Fort is Sloop Cove, a natural harbour that was used by English ships as early as 1689. Today there is no harbour left, due to land heaves resulting in changes to the area's topography. Its historic interest is in the graffiti left by the Hudson's Bay Company employees throughout the 18th century.

only reasonable way to go — take a Tundra Buggy or other large bus-like vehicle to get out to where the bears are. Several local outfitters offer day trips or longer tours that include accommodation at remote lodges outside of Churchill. These tours should be booked well in advance, as many fill up a year ahead.

Churchill is a treasure trove for other wildlife viewing as well. Beluga whales, caribou, seals, arctic and red foxes, and over 200 bird species can be sighted near town. While winter in Churchill may seem monochromatic — even the bears are white, after all — colour can be found from September through March, when magnificent displays of aurora borealis (the northern lights) flame across the night sky.

In spring and autumn the tundra lights up with plants, mosses and lichens. Take a guided walking tour to learn about the fragile life of the tundra.

The belugas move into the bay after the ice breaks up — over 3,000 of them make their summer home here. A whale-watching tour is one of the highlights of a visit to Churchill, whether it is on a conventional boat, in a kayak, or even on a snorkeling trip. Again, these trips need to be booked well in advance.

Icebergs are also a common and much-photographed sight in the bay during the summer months.

Visit the Eskimo Museum (Tel. 204.675.2030) to see an extensive display of Inuit artifacts, art and carvings, some modern, some dating from as early as 1400 BC.

Opposite: Polar bears are the largest bears in the world.

SASKATCHEWAN

Native traditional dancer

Skate River

Buffalo Park

Lake Claire

Fort Chipewyan

Lake Athabasca

Athabasca Sand Dunes Provincial Wilderness Park

Wollaston Lake

Cree Lake

Reindeer Lake

Lynn Lake

Wabowden

MA

Fort McMurray

Clearwater River Provincial Park

La Loche

Buffalo Narrows

Pinehouse Lake

Lac La Ronge Provincial Park

Pelican Narrows

Snow Lake

Flin Flon

Grass River Provincial Park

La Ronge

Lac La Ronge

Dore Lake

The Pas

Saskatchewan River

Cedar Lake

G R.

Lac La Biche

Cold Lake

Pierceland

Meadow Lake

Prince Albert National Park

Lake Winnipegosis

St. Paul

North Saskatchewan River

k

ville

Lloydminster

Prince Albert

Melfort

Hudson Bay

Swan River

Duck Mountain Provincial Park

North Battleford

Unity

SASKATOON

Humboldt

Roblin

Dauphin

se

Biggar

CNR

Wynyard

Yorkton

Riding Mountain National Park

heller

Kindersley

Rosetown

Watrous

Melville

Minnedosa

CNR

Rivers

ussar

South Saskatchewan River

Lake Diefenbaker

Fort Qu'Appelle

Assiniboine River

Russell

Brooks

CPR

Swift Current

Moose Jaw

CPR

REGINA

Moosomin

Virden

Brando

Medicine Hat

Gull Lake

Weyburn

Redvers

Melita

Boisse

Maple Creek

Cypress Hills Interprovincial Park

Shaunavon

Assiniboia

Estevan

Carnduff

Grasslands National Park

Saskatchewan

Big Muddy Badlands

Historically, the area now known as Saskatchewan was peopled by five First Nations cultures: Assiniboine, Cree (Plains, Woodland and Swampy), Dakota, Dene and Saulteaux, each occupying a particular area. While each had its own region, customs, and traditions,

the tribes sometimes overlapped in territory and did not always get along with each other.

With the advent of the fur trade in the 18th century, French voyageurs arrived in Rupert's Land, and many of them married Cree or Saulteaux women. By the late 19th century, their descendants, the Métis, formed the majority of the population of the province, but pressure from white settlers eventually forced their numbers into decline, especially after the North-West Rebellion in 1885. Today this trend is reversed — Saskatchewan's First Nations and Métis people are the fastest-growing segments of the population.

Today, Saskatchewan is probably the most heavily agricultural of all the Canadian provinces, producing an astounding 54% of Canada's wheat and a high percentage of other grains as well. Barley, flax, canola and mustard fields add vibrant colour to a drive through this prairie province, while in the south a series of rolling hills adds drama to the landscape. Among Canadians, Saskatchewan has a reputation of being flat, but it really has a wide range of terrain with plenty to offer visitors, especially those with an interest in outdoor activities and Canadian history.

SuperGuide Recommendations: Saskatchewan

1) Western Development Museum: Saskatoon, Battleford, Moose Jaw and Yorkton
2) Wanuskewin Heritage Park, Saskatoon
3) Little Manitou Lake
4) Prince Albert National Park
5) RCMP Training Academy and Centennial Museum, Regina
6) Tunnels of Moose Jaw
7) Big Muddy Badlands
8) Cypress Hills
9) Great Sand Hills
10) Grasslands National Park

Saskatchewan rodeo

Saskatoon

Archaeological evidence shows that the Northern Plains Indians, and possibly other groups, as well lived in the area around today's Saskatoon for at least 6,000 years. The Saskatoon that we know today was founded as a temperance colony in 1882 by John Lake, an Ontario Methodist preacher who promised "Homes for all where you will be forever free from the accursed influence of the liquor habit."

The original settlers took the train from Ontario as far as Moose Jaw, then continued by horseback or wagon to build their new colony high above the South Saskatchewan River.

Other settlers not interested in temperance also arrived, and the town remained dry for only a few decades. In 1906 Saskatoon became a city, and in 1908 the CPR tracks came through to secure its future. By 1912 Saskatoon was known as the "Instant City" — its population had expanded to 30,000 due to a boom in settlement, agriculture and transportation.

Today it is Saskatchewan's largest city, with a population of just over 230,000. Known as the City of Bridges, the city is centred around the South Saskatchewan River, with the Meewasin Valley Trail running 22 km along both sides of the river. Look for the American white pelicans, which congregate at the weir near the CPR bridge. A major redevelopment of the weir area is underway to make it more interpretive and visitor-friendly.

Attractions in Saskatoon

Western Development Museum
www.wdm.ca
2610 Lorne Ave. South,
306.931.1910
There are four Western Development Museums around the province, each with a different theme. The Saskatoon outlet of the WDM features a recreated "Boomtown Street" echoing Saskatoon's heyday in 1910, when agricultural expansion and settlement

Saskatoon

swelled the city's population. See daily activities from that era and discover the buggies and wagons of the time, as well as vintage cars and the agricultural machinery that began to make farming easier.

Wanuskewin Heritage Park
www.wanuskewin.com
Off Hwy. 11, 306.931.6767
Built around 19 archaeological sites in the Opamihaw Valley, some more than 6,000 years old, this excellent site features exhibits, nature trails, archaeology digs, and interpretive programs. Dance performances take place every day at 2 p.m. in summer, and crafts demonstrations go on from 11 a.m. to 3 p.m. daily.

Stop in at the interpretive centre, an attractive building built to complement its natural environment, to learn about the Northern Plains culture. It's possible to spend a night in a teepee here or to enjoy a traditional Native meal in the restaurant overlooking the river valley.

Mendel Gallery
www.mendel.ca
950 Spadina Cres. East,
306.975.7610
This gallery features a rich variety of contemporary artists in rotating exhibits, as well as the work of some well-known Canadian painters such as Emily Carr and Lawren Harris in the permanent collection. A conservatory is attached — a pleasant place to while away an hour during the prairie winter.

Meewasin Valley Centre
3rd Ave. South at 19th St. East,
306.665.6888
Learn about the natural and human history of Saskatoon by exploring the photos and displays at this riverside visitor centre.

Saskatoon's evening lights are reflected on the South Saskatchewan River.

Saskatchewan Craft Gallery
813 Broadway Ave.,
306.653.3616
This small gallery features frequently-changing shows of handcrafted artwork, including works in fibre, wood, glass, and metal, with a special focus on pottery.

Diefenbaker Canada Centre
101 Diefenbaker Pl.,
306.966.8384
Located at the University of Saskatchewan, this museum is about Canadian politics as illustrated through the life and times of John Diefenbaker, the 13th prime minister of Canada. He was a member of Parliament for 39 years and PM from 1957-1963, and is buried nearby with his second wife.

Ukrainian Museum of Canada
www.umc.sk.ca
910 Spadina Cres., 306.244.3800
This museum explores the Orthodox Ukrainian tradition in Canada, featuring the history of Ukrainian settlement in the area, with a strong emphasis on daily life: housing, every-day tools, and religion. The textile collection is outstanding.

Saskatoon Zoo
1903 Forest Dr., 306.975.3382
This zoo features mainly species native to North America, with over 350 animals and birds. It also has a children's petting zoo, botanical displays, and a train ride. Plenty of special events and guided tours will help you get the most out of a visit to the zoo.

Shearwater Boat Cruises/Day Tours
www.shearwatertours.com
888.747.7572
View the city from the South Saskatchewan River aboard the *Saskatoon Lady*. Tours depart daily in the summer from the Mendel Gallery.

Horse Drawn Rides
306.373.0754
Fridays or Saturdays, take a horse-drawn carriage ride for a scenic city tour. In the winter, step into a cutter for a spin around Meewasin Park. For a private tour, call anytime to book.

Saskatoon Festivals and Special Events

Saskatoon is host to many special events and festivals over the year. Here is a sampling:

June: Northern Saskatchewan Children's Festival; Cameco Victoria Park Summer Festival; Sasktel Saskatchewan Jazz Festival
July-August: Shakespeare on the Saskatchewan Festival
July: Pion-Era; Great Northern River Roar; A Taste of Saskatchewan
August: Saskatoon International Fringe Festival; Saskatoon Exhibition; Clarica Midsummer Masters Horse Show; Folkfest
October: CCA Finals Rodeo

Bridge over the South Saskatchewan River

Street musicians light up the evening in Saskatoon.

Saskatchewan Railway Museum

www.saskrailmuseum.org
Hwy. 60, 306.382.9855
Numerous railway cars, streetcars, artifacts, and buildings are featured on seven acres of display space just west of Saskatoon.

Culture

Saskatoon's cultural scene offers something for everyone, from dance to community theatre. The lucky visitor might even spot musician Joni Mitchell on one of her periodic visits to her old home town. Check out these venues to see what's happening in the arts around town.

Centennial Auditorium

www.saskcent.com
35 22nd St. East, 306.938.7800
This is the place to see the Saskatoon Symphony Orchestra's Master Series throughout the year. The symphony also performs at smaller venues around town. The Centennial also hosts touring productions of well-known musicals and musical acts, as well as local productions and special events.

Castle Theatre

1904 Clarence Ave. South
This theatre, on the campus of Aden Bowman Collegiate, is home to the Saskatoon Gateway Players from October through April (Tel. 306.653.1200), and the Saskatoon Summer Players in June . For either community theatre or musical productions, this is the place to be.

Persephone Theatre

www.persephonetheatre.com
2802 Rusholme Road, 306.244.5828
This theatre company puts on six productions a year, with a wide range from comedy to big musicals, contemporary plays, and the classics.

Off Broadway Dinner Theatre

www.offbroadway.ca
639 Main St., 306.652.4799
For a lighthearted evening out, try this theatre, which features a full-length comedy production as well as a meal.

Barn Playhouse

Hwy. 12, 306/239.4600
About 25 km north of Saskatoon, this working farm offers horse-drawn wagon rides, food booths, live music, and community theatre throughout the summer evenings.

Shopping and Dining

Downtown

Saskatoon's downtown area is between Kinsmen Park and Idylwyld Drive North, and features plenty of excellent restaurants and shops, including Mid-Town Plaza, a large mall.

Broadway

Just across the bridge at 4th Ave. and 19th St. East, this revitalized area is the funkiest area of Saskatoon, with a high concentration of unique shops and restaurants.

Riversdale District

This is the place to see some great street art in the way of murals and sculptures in a neighbourhood that includes Saskatoon's Chinatown and over 170 shops and restaurants of various ethnic origins.

The Farmers' Market

With the motto "Make it, bake it, grow it and sell it", the weekly Farmers' Market offers a wealth of wares and produce for sale every Saturday from 8 a.m. - 2 p.m., on 23rd Street in front of City Hall.

Valley Road

Drive a few kilometres south of the city for a country shopping experience, with plenty of roadside stands offering produce and crafts, as well as U-Pick farms.

North of Saskatoon

North of Saskatoon, several attractions along the Louis Riel Trail are worth a day trip or a longer detour.

Take a day trip along Hwy. 11, the Louis Riel Trail, and learn about the North-West Rebellion at three historic sites. While in the area, visit the Station Arts Centre in Rosthern (Tel. 306.232.5332). During the day it features an art gallery and a tearoom, and their summer theatre during the evening is not to be missed. Also, make time for a visit to the Seager Wheeler National Historic Site (see below).

Batoche National Historic Site

Route 225, 306.423.6227
On the South Saskatchewan River, 90 kilometres northeast of Saskatoon, this was the site in 1885 of one of the few battles of Canadians against Canadians, as well as the last stand of the Métis provisional government during the North-West Rebellion. At the village of Batoche, where there are several restored buildings and an interpretive centre, visitors can learn about the Métis way of life. Stroll along the now-peaceful paths to the cemetery where several Métis leaders are buried.

Duck Lake Regional Interpretive Centre

Hwy. 11 at Hwy. 312, 306.467.2057
Learn more about the Métis and Cree culture at the regional interpretive centre in Duck Lake.

Fort Carlton Provincial Historic Park

Hwy. 212, 306.467.5205
Fort Carlton was first established by the Hudson's Bay Company in 1795. It was

Gabriel Dumont

One of the most charismatic Métis leaders, Gabriel Dumont was the de facto leader of the North-West Rebellion, providing the military strategy where Louis Riel played the messianic figurehead.

Dumont was born in 1837, and from a young age was adept at marksmanship and horsemanship. Although illiterate, he spoke several Native languages as well as French. He was very highly regarded by all who came into contact with him, and he met many people in his travels through the prairies and through his leadership of the buffalo hunt.

When in 1884 the Métis began to agitate for a share in the Native rights to the land in the North-West Territories, they turned to Dumont to lead them. He in turn went to Riel and brought him back to Canada to lead the fight for Métis rights.

Dumont led the Métis to their last stand at Batoche, and after their defeat there he eventually left the west and joined Buffalo Bill's Wild West Show as a top attraction. In 1893 he returned to Batoche. He died in 1906 and is buried there on a ridge overlooking the South Saskatchewan River, near his fallen comrades and his brother who died in the battle.

Gabriel Dumont

Northern Saskatchewan is dominated by boreal forest.

Wolves

Wolf

Wolves, even more than bears, have been demonized in the popular imagination for centuries. Prince Albert National Park's mixed ecoregions offers the ideal habitat for wolves, and here timber wolves are said to live undisturbed — except for the wolf howl tours. It is not uncommon to hear them howling, unprompted, in many locations in the park.

They tend to den in the wooded areas but will cross open ground readily in search of their prey (elk, deer, beaver and other mammals), especially in winter when more animals forage on the meadows.

Wolf packs are strongly family-oriented and territorial, though a pack may range widely across its home territory. Winter wolf packs average about 10-20 members in size for more efficient hunting. Working together, a pack can easily bring down a moose, deer or elk — something the average pack needs to do every few days.

Wolves are elusive, and it's possible to live many years in wolf habitat without seeing one. If you come across a kill, it's a good idea to leave the area. However, in most other circumstances, an encounter with one of these graceful wild animals is likely to be a truly positive and memorable experience.

moved a few times before settling into its present location in 1810. Its strategic location, on the North Saskatchewan between Fort Garry (Winnipeg) and Fort Edmonton, made it an important provisioning stop as well as a fur depot.

Visitors to the site today will see it as it was circa 1860, with several reconstructed buildings that recreate life in an HBC trading post. Interpretive trails lead past teepees where visitors can learn about the involvement of the Natives in the fur trade. Treaty Six was signed here by the Plains and Woodland Cree in 1876 — a treaty that was almost immediately broken by the government and was at least partly responsible for the North-West Rebellion. It is still being contested today.

Seager Wheeler National Historic Site
www.seagerwheelerfarm.org
Hwy. 312, 306.232.5959
At Maple Grove Farm, Seager Wheeler became known as the "World Wheat King" for his innovative work in dryland farming and agriculture. Learn about his story and the cycle of agricultural production in Saskatchewan at this restored farmhouse and surrounding farm, which is being restored to its 1919 condition. Enjoy a stroll around the English garden, or a home-baked treat on the veranda.

Prince Albert National Park
Further north of Batoche, the landscape sees the end of the prairies and the beginning of the vast boreal forest. Prince Albert National Park, 230 km

Whooping crane on Last Mountain Lake

Future mounties go through their paces at Regina's RCMP Centennial Training Academy and Museum.

north of Saskatoon, established in 1927, protects this environment and affords visitors many recreational opportunities. Over 3,875 km² of wilderness include lovely aspen parkland and boreal forest. The park is home to coyote and wild bison in the prairie section, moose, bear, wolf, caribou, elk and badger in the wooded sections, and more than 230 species of birds.

Most visitors make their first stop at the townsite of Waskesiu, where there is a beach along Waskesiu Lake, a visitor centre, accommodation and shopping. This is a great jumping-off point for activities such as camping, canoeing, wildlife viewing, birding, fishing, golfing, and hiking. It's even possible to take in a guided wolf howl tour. If you hear the wolves howling back, you will remember it for the rest of your life. For more information, call 1.877.255.7267, ext.130.

The Battlefords

Northwest of Saskatoon, along the Yellowhead Highway, are Battleford and North Battleford, which face each other across the North Saskatchewan River. A trip to this area from Saskatoon is an enjoyable half-day journey, and it's well worth a stop if you are continuing along west to Alberta. Visit in July and take in the Saskatchewan Handcraft Festival.

In 1876 the North West Mounted Police set up a fort at Battleford. This was the capital of the North-West Territories from 1876 until 1883, when the decision to run the CPR through the southern part of the province ended the strategic importance of Battleford.

Fort Battleford National Historic Site
Hwy. 4, 306.937.2621, open in summer only
One of the original goals of the NWMP fort was to try to push the Natives into reserves in order to create peaceful conditions for the white settlers. Natives began to starve as the buffalo died out, and after two years of unsuccessful crops. Some Cree tried to fight the NWMP in conjunction with Riel's Métis, but they were unsuccessful. During the uprising, settlers took shelter at the fort, and troops used it as an operational base. On November 27, 1885, eight Native men were hanged in Fort Battleford for their role in the Frog Lake Massacre, a key event in the North-West Rebellion.

Today, five buildings from the original fort still stand, including the Commanding Officer's Residence — an imposing log structure — and the Sick Horse Stable. The fort's displays examine the relations between the Natives and the Mounties, and commemorate the events of 1885.

Colourful gardens adorn the grounds of the Saskatchewan Legislative Building.

Western Development Museum
www.wdm.sk.ca
Hwy. 16 at Hwy. 40,
306.445.8033
This Heritage Farm and Village features 36 restored or rebuilt buildings that show what life was like for settlers around 1925. An exhibit called "The Jolly Life of a Farmer's Wife", as well as displays of tools and appliances, further illustrate the development of agriculture in Saskatchewan.

Allen Sapp Gallery/ The Gonor Collection
www.allensapp.com
1091 100th St., 306.445.1760
Allen Sapp (b. 1929) is a well-known Native artist whose work is inspired by his childhood on the Red Pheasant Reserve in North Central Saskatchewan. This gallery showcases his many paintings and is well worth a visit for an insight into Northern Plains Cree life in the early part of the 20th century.

Regina

Regina owes a great deal to the CPR, whose decision in 1882 to route the railway through the southern part of western Canada ensured its rise from a tent settlement known as Pile O' Bones to the capital of the North-West Territories in a few short years. This decision was influenced in no small part by Edgar Dewdney.

Regina Festivals and Special Events

June: Mosaic Festival of Cultures; Bazaart; Children's Festival
July: Flatland Music Festival
August: Buffalo Days; Folk Festival; Royal Red Arabian Horse Show
September: Regina Dragon Boat Festival
November: Canadian Western Agribiton
December: SaskPower festival of Lights

Attractions in Regina

RCMP Training Academy and Centennial Museum
Dewdney Ave. West,
306.780.5838
This is where the best-known symbol of Canada, the Mountie, goes through basic training. Watch RCMP recruits taking karate lessons, practicing handcuffing, and marching at the Academy on a daily guided tour that includes the splendid chapel. Other events open to the public are the Sergeant Major's Parade, which takes place every summer Monday, Wednesday and Friday at 12:45 p.m., and the Sunset Retreat, every Tuesday at 6:45 p.m. in July and August.

The Museum details the Long March West and the evolution of the role of the RCMP in Canadian law enforcement, with an extensive array of artifacts.

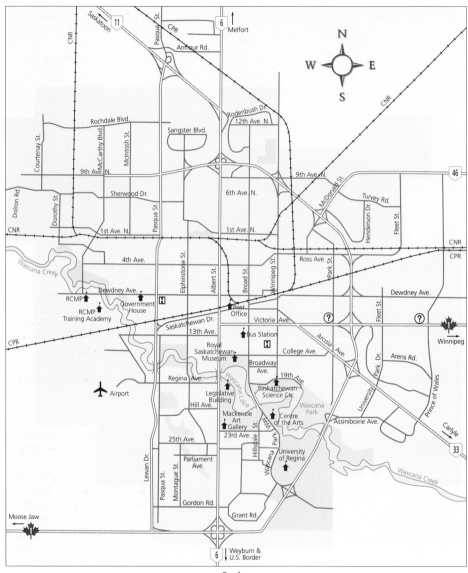

Regina

Regina Plains Museum
www.reginaplainsmuseum.com
1835 Scarth St., 306.780.9435
This museum highlights the growth of Regina, with a focus on the social history of the city through the display of thousands of artifacts. It is also home to a uniquely beautiful piece of art known as The Glass Wheatfield, created by Jacqueline Berting. This piece is composed of 14,000 waist-high stalks of wheat made out of glass and mounted in steel.

Government House Museum and Heritage Property
4607 Dewdney Ave.,
306.787.5773
Residence of the governors of the North-West Territories and Saskatchewan from 1891 to 1945, this splendid building has been restored to how it would have looked around 1900. Try to visit on a day when high tea is served in the ballroom.

Wascana Park, in the heart of Regina, offers 2,300 acres with walking paths, gardens, and a man-made lake with

Modern Regina is a far cry from its origins as a tent settlement.

Pile O' Bones

In 1881 Edgar Dewdney, already the Indian Commissioner for the North-West Territories, also became its lieutenant-governor. He was charged by John A. Macdonald with finding a new capital for the territories, and in 1882 decided on this unprepossessing location along Pile O' Bones Creek — an area where he owned land. The capital was hurriedly moved from Battleford and the new town began to take shape.

The original name ("Wascana", or pile of bones) referred to an enormous heap of buffalo bones that lay on the prairie — remnants of a buffalo pound that had been used for decades by Natives for processing their kills. Clearly the name could not remain, and Dewdney's friend, the Governor General's wife Princess Louise Caroline Alberta, chose the new name of Regina in honour of her mother, Queen Victoria. (Perhaps this is why both Lake Louise and the province of Alberta were subsequently named for her.) In 1883 the new capital was officially named, and when Saskatchewan became a province in 1905, Regina remained the provincial capital, as it does today.

Willow Island in the centre, a popular picnic spot reachable by ferry. The park is also home to many of Regina's major attractions, listed below.

Royal Saskatchewan Museum
www.royalsaskmuseum.ca
2445 Albert St., 306.787.2815
This museum features three distinct galleries. The Earth Sciences Gallery shows how Saskatchewan was once a vast inland sea, and highlights the tropical conditions that prevailed in prehistoric times. See replicas of several dinosaurs that used to live here. The First Nations Gallery brings to life 12,000 years of living history through dioramas, murals and other displays. The new Life Sciences Gallery explores the interdependence of all living creatures, with a strong environmental thrust.

MacKenzie Art Gallery
www.mackenzieartgallery.sk.ca
3475 Albert St., 306.584.4250
This gallery is home to a strong permanent collection of Saskatchewan, Canadian and international work, plus various galleries devoted to visiting exhibits. *The Trial of Louis Riel* is staged here in the Shumiatcher Theatre during the summer months. This re-enactment of the most bitterly debated trial in Canadian history is based on the court transcripts from the trial. In June, the MacKenzie Gallery hosts Bazaart, a one-day outdoor show that features entertainment and food, as well as the work of over 100 artists, artisans and craftspeople.

Saskatchewan Legislative Building

www.legassembly.sk.ca
2405 Legislative Dr.,
306.787.5357
This handsome building was built between 1908 and 1912 in the Beaux-Arts style. Take a free tour to learn about the architecture and history of the building, or stroll the grounds.

Saskatchewan Science Centre

www.sciencecentre.sk.ca
2903 Powerhouse Dr.,
306.522.4629,
toll-free: 800.667.6300
This museum is a popular one with families, as it features over 100 interactive displays and an IMAX theatre.

Casino Regina

www.casinoregina.com
1880 Saskatchewan Drive
306.365.300,
toll-free: 800.555.3189
Featuring 19th-century train station architecture, slots, table games, and a Las Vegas-style show lounge.

Culture

Regina has a small but thriving arts scene. Check out what's happening culturally in Regina at these venues.

Saskatchewan Centre of the Arts

www.centreofthearts.sk.ca
200 Lakeshore Dr.,
306.525.9999, toll-free
800.667.8497
This concert theatre is the home of the Regina Symphony Orchestra, the longest continually-running orchestra in Canada. It's also the place to see major concerts and theatre productions, both local and visiting.

Regina Performing Arts Centre

1077 Angus St., 306.779.2279
Home to Saskatchewan Community Theatre and Regina Little Theatre, as well as several other groups, this centre is a venue for many events throughout the year.

Globe Theatre

www.globetheatrelive.com
1801 Scarth St., 306.525.6400
Located in the old city hall building, the Globe is a theatre-in-the-round that aims to provide an intimate theatre experience that will challenge as well as entertain. The professional company puts on half a dozen productions every year.

Applause Feast and Folly

www.applausedinnertheatre.ca
Broad St. at Victoria Ave.,
306.791.6868
This is a dinner theatre where the servers are also the performers — a lighthearted evening out featuring a meal with a two-act live musical comedy.

Shopping and Dining

Downtown

The downtown area known as Market Square features over 700 stores, restaurants and service providers. It's bordered by Saskatchewan Drive, Osler St., Albert St., and 13th Ave.

Scarth Street

This historic area features a pedestrian mall and unique shops located within refurbished older buildings.

Western wood lily

Warehouse District

Not far from the Scarth Street area, this district was once devoted to storage and transportation of goods. Today it's home to boutiques, restaurants bars, and a slew of new loft condominiums.

Cathedral Village

Centred around 13th Ave., this is one of the most interesting areas in Regina, with clothing, gift and lifestyle boutiques, coffee shops, and great restaurants.

Antique Mall

1175 Rose St., 306.352.7450
Some may call it "junque", but there are definitely treasures to be found here among the 28 shops that make up the Antique Mall.

Around Regina

The area around Regina yields a number of interesting attractions and activities. Take a day or two to explore Little Manitou Lake and the Qu'Appelle Valley.

Farmland in the Qu'Appelle Valley

Little Manitou Lake

Enjoy some of Saskatchewan's natural attractions on this delightful day trip, or en route to Saskatoon from Regina. Depart Regina along Hwy. 20 north, and within a short time you will be at Last Mountain Lake National Wildlife Area (Tel. 306.484.4483). This is North America's oldest aviary preserve, established in 1887, and still a very important nature preserve due to its central location. Up to 250 species of birds have been sighted here during the migration periods, and an astounding 50,000 cranes, 450,000 geese and several hundred thousand ducks may be observed when migration peaks in the fall. There are two walking trails that lead to good viewing sites, as well as a self-guided driving tour through part of the preserve. Stop at the information kiosk for further details.

After enjoying some time at the preserve, head further north along Hwy. 20 until Nokomis, then turn west onto 15, then north onto 2. Your destination is Little Manitou Lake, three times saltier than the ocean, which means that everyone can float here. The water, with its extremely high mineral content, has been thought for centuries to have healing properties. The town that has built up around the lake and beach is rather touristy, but offers plenty of amenities and activities.

Check in to the Manitou Springs Resort and Mineral Spa for a few days of pampering and treatments, or just for the afternoon. There's big band music every Saturday night at Danceland, a 1920s dance hall with a massive dance floor.

Once you are thoroughly refreshed, you can return to Regina or continue along to Saskatoon.

The Qu'Appelle Valley

Another interesting day trip from Regina involves heading east to discover some of the small towns in the area. Leave town on Hwy. 1 east and head to Wolseley, a picturesque village noted for its Opera House, which was built in the late 19th century. It originally housed the town office, council chambers, a jail cell, library, fire hall and the opera house, and was completely restored in 1994. There are also several other Victorian buildings of note here.

From Wolseley, head north on 617 and then west on 22 to

Yorkton Short Film & Video Festival

Every year in late May, dozens of Canadian filmmakers descend on Yorkton for this cinematic event, the longest-running of its kind in Canada. The first festival was held in 1950, and the prestigious Golden Sheaf Award for the most outstanding production of the festival was first handed out in 1958.

Awards are given in close to 30 categories ranging from commercials to documentaries. For filmmakers and producers, this four-day event is a chance to network, take in a workshop or two, and see what competitors are up to. Each is hoping to take home a Golden Sheaf — Saskatchewan's answer to the Oscar!

For the general public, the festival is a wonderful opportunity to see some innovative and creative films made right here in Canada.

For more information, visit www.yorktonshortfilm.org

reach the Motherwell Homestead National Historic Site (Tel. 306.333.2116). This rather incongruous though lovely Italianate fieldstone house with extensive ornamental gardens was built in 1897 for pioneer farmer and politician W.R. Motherwell, who had moved here from Perth, Ontario and recreated an Ontario farm on the prairie. The farm has been restored to its appearance circa 1910-14.

From Motherwell, head towards Fort Qu'Appelle, which must be the most scenically located town in southern Saskatchewan. Recognizing a natural meeting place, the Hudson's Bay Company established a trading post here in 1864. The HBC store here is the oldest in Canada, dating from 1897.

Visit the Fort Qu'Appelle Museum on Bay Ave. at 3rd St. (Tel. 306.332.6443). This museum is built on the site of the old fort, and has a collection of fur trade and NWMP artifacts, as well as other more eclectic items collected over the last century and items relating to the sanatorium that flourished here after World War I.

Those interested in Native history will do well to visit the Treaty Four Governance Centre, which at 21 metres (70 feet) in diameter and 33 metres (111 feet) tall is the largest inhabited teepee in the world. The Visitors' Centre features replicas of the treaty documents and information on the first nations (Cree, Saulteaux and Dakota) who signed the documents.

Further northeast is the fourth branch of the Western

Temple Gardens Mineral Spa Hotel and Resort

Tunnels of Moose Jaw

Under the city is a network of tunnels. Nobody knows why they were built, or by whom, but the story of how they have been used over the years is a fascinating one. Take an interactive guided tour to learn more. Two tours are available:

The Passage to Fortune
In the early 1900s, the Canadian government wanted the Chinese workers who had built the Canadian Pacific Railway to go back home. An exorbitant $500 head tax was set up to penalize those who stayed. The tunnels were used by some Chinese workers to evade the taxmen. This tour brings the Chinese immigrant experience to life.

The Chicago Connection
Gangsters used the tunnels during prohibition to hide out and do liquor deals. This tour explains Moose Jaw's history as a bootlegging town, involving the visitor in an exciting story of booze, gangsters and crooked cops.

Log on to:
www.tunnelsofmoosejaw.com
306.693.5261

Grasslands National Park

Development Museum, located in Yorkton. The focus of this museum is "The Story of People" — the various waves of settlers who arrived in Saskatchewan over the years and what their life was like. Call 306.783.8361 for more information and consider adding Yorkton to your day trip from Regina.

Return to Regina along Hwy. 10 through the broad and picturesque Qu'Appelle River valley. Along the way are eight lakes known as the Fishing Lakes, with provincial parks in between.

Moose Jaw

The fourth largest city in Saskatchewan (Prince Albert is the third), Moose Jaw was established by the CPR in 1882, although it had been a Native settlement as early as 1703, when it first appeared on a French map as "Moozemlek".

Moose Jaw's boom years were the first two decades of the 20th century, when the railway made it an important distribution centre for agricultural products. Improbably, it became a bootlegging centre in the 1920s, as the source for booze smuggled along the Soo Line to Chicago. Al Capone even spent some time here. Today it has several interesting attractions for the visitor, including 36 large murals adorning the downtown streets, showing scenes from Moose Jaw's history.

Attractions in Moose Jaw

Western Development Museum
50 Diefenbaker Dr.,
306.693.5989
The theme of the WDM branch in Moose Jaw is "History of Transportation". The museum features a fine collection of planes, trains and automobiles, as well as a tribute to the Snowbirds, Canada's aerobatics team.

Saskatchewan Burrowing Owl Interpretive Centre
At the Moose Jaw Exhibition,
306.692.8710 or 306.692.1765

Learn about these endangered owls by exploring the displays, visiting with the permanent residents and watching the rehabilitation of those that will be released back into the wild. These tiny owls are among the cutest birds you will ever see.

Temple Gardens Mineral Spa Resort Hotel
24 Fairford St. East,
306.694.5055, toll-free
800.718.7727
This oasis in the prairie features a naturally heated mineral pool connected to an outdoor hot pool, all atop the Temple Gardens Resort Hotel. Come here for a treatment or to while away the afternoon in the soothing atmosphere.

Yvette Moore Fine Art Gallery
www.yvettemoore.com
76 Fairford St. West,
306.693.7600
This attractive gallery is located in the historic Land Titles building and showcases the work of Yvette Moore, well-known artist and illustrator of *A Prairie Alphabet*. Her work, depicting rural domestic scenes, is somewhat reminiscent of Norman Rockwell. The gift shop features work by other prairie artists and artisans, and the café offers a wide selection of lunches and treats.

Wild Places of Southern Saskatchewan

There are several outstanding wild areas in the southern part of the province that are well worth visiting, though they are not that close to any major towns or cities.

Big Muddy Badlands

South of Regina near the U.S. border, this area features colourful eroded sandstone buttes and caves where Butch Cassidy and his gang the Wild Bunch, as well as rum-runners and other outlaws, cached supplies and hung out while on the run.

Visit St. Victor's Petroglyphs Provincial Historic Park to see carvings of turtles, bison, and human hands and feet. Even more intriguing are the stone circles and effigies created by early First Nations, which are found all through the valley, but concentrated near Minton and Big Beaver.

The best way to see the highlights of the Big Muddy is to hire a guide from Coronach, as many of the sites are

Fort Walsh National Historic Site in the Cypress Hills

on private land. Contact Coronach & District Tours at 306.267.3312 or 306.267.2150.

Grasslands National Park

This is one of Canada's youngest national parks,

Chief Sitting Bull and Major James Walsh

Chief Sitting Bull

After defeating General Custer at Little Big Horn in 1876, Chief Sitting Bull came to Saskatchewan with 5,000 followers who were as determined as he not to be placed on reservations against their will. In 1877 Major James Walsh

visited the famous Sioux chief at his camp, where he was surrounded by 1,000 warriors. His message to Sitting Bull was that he was welcome in Canada as long as he obeyed the law of the land — a somewhat ludicrous request, since there were only a handful of NWMP in the area.

Nevertheless, Sitting Bull agreed and lived peacefully for the four years he stayed in Saskatchewan, during which time he and his people hunted buffalo and roamed the prairies. The buffalo began to die out during this time, and eventually Sitting Bull and the approximately 500 other Sioux who hadn't already left returned to the States, where they ended their days on a reservation in Minnesota.

Sitting Bull and Walsh had great respect for each other.

Major James Walsh

Both were men of integrity, and their relationship allowed the Sioux to spend a few years more living their traditional way of life.

Great Sand Hills, north of Maple Creek

officially established in 2001. At present it consists of two blocks of land, the Killdeer Badlands and the Frenchman River Valley (more poetically known as "The Valley of Hidden Secrets"). The federal government intends to purchase the land in between to complete the park.

The park features some of the last untouched prairie left in North America, where western wheat grass, snowberry, and silver sage grow. It's home to many kinds of animals, including pronghorn antelope, golden eagles, black-tailed prairie dogs, burrowing owls, sage grouse, mule deer, white-tailed deer, rattlesnakes, bobcats, and porcupines. The Killdeer Badlands are fantastically eroded and very rugged.

When visiting Grasslands, stop in at Wood Mountain Post Provincial Historic Site, a partly restored NWMP post dating from 1874. You can learn about the NWMP and the Sioux, including Sitting Bull, who frequented the area.

Cypress Hills

The Cypress Hills area is an area of remarkable beauty and surprising elevation, rising up from the nearby prairie. It is the highest point of land between Labrador and the Rocky Mountains. It's home to the Cypress Hills Interprovincial Park, which features Fort Walsh National Historic Site (Tel. 306.662.3590). The site has displays on the Plains Indians, the history of the fort, and the evolution of the RCMP. Built in 1875, the fort was moved to Maple Creek only seven years later. The fort and village have been restored to their original appearance and tours are available from guides in period costume.

Take the bus trip over the hills to Farwell's Whisky Trading Post at Battle Creek on a guided tour of the site of the 1873 Cypress Hills Massacre, which was the catalyst for the establishment of the NWMP.

East of Cypress Hills, the nearly complete remains of a Tyrannosaurus Rex are on display at the T-Rex Interpretive Centre in Eastend (Tel. 306.295.4009). Take a Dinocountry tour to learn more, or join a day dig at the archaeological site near Eastend.

Maple Creek

Near Cypress Hills is Maple Creek, a pretty little town in the heart of the ranching country.

Visit in September, when the Cowboy Poetry Gathering takes place.

SW Saskatchewan Old Timers' Museum
218 Jasper St., 306.662.2474
This is one of the oldest museums in the province, with an extensive collection of photos and artifacts of Native people, settlers and RCMP.

Jasper Cultural and Historical Centre
Jasper St., 306.662.2434
This museum, which includes an art gallery, features numerous displays about life in the "Old Cow Town", and the circa-1900 Maple Creek boardwalk.

Great Sand Hills

North of Maple Creek are the Great Sand Hills: 1900 km^2 of active sand dunes. home to kangaroo rats, sharp-tailed grouse, mule deer and antelope. In this varied landscape, sand dunes are interspersed with grasslands, saline lakes, cottonwood groves and aspen bluffs. Stop in at the Great Sandhills Museum in Sceptre (Tel. 306.623.4345) to learn about the area and to get directions on touring the dunes.

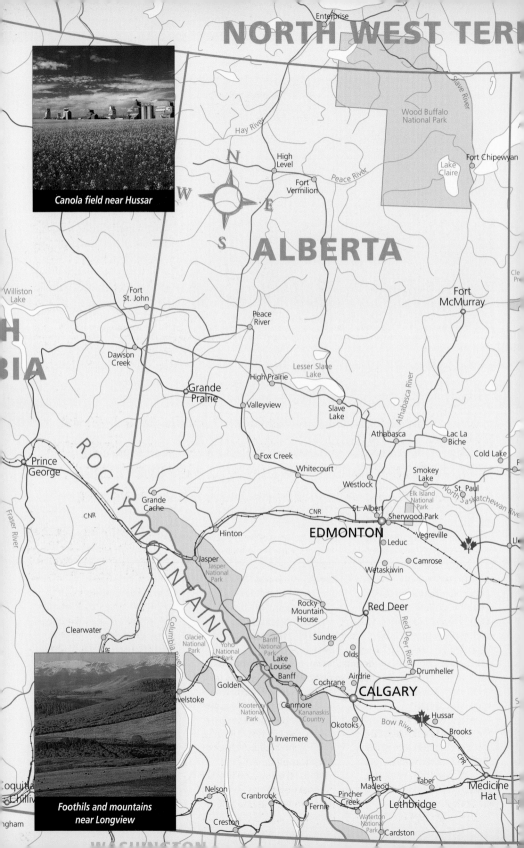

NORTH WEST TER

ALBERTA

Enterprise

Wood Buffalo
National Park

Slave River

Lake
Claire

Fort Chipewyan

Hay River

Peace River

High
Level

Fort
Vermilion

N
W E
S

Fort
McMurray

Williston
Lake

Fort
St. John

Peace
River

Dawson
Creek

Lesser Slave
Lake

High Prairie

Grande
Prairie

Valleyview

Slave
Lake

Athabasca

Lac La
Biche

Cold Lake

Athabasca River

Prince
George

Fox Creek

Whitecourt

Westlock

Smokey
Lake

St. Paul

North Saskatchewan River

CNR

Grande
Cache

Hinton

St. Albert

Sherwood Park

Elk Island
National
Park

CNR

EDMONTON

Leduc

Vegreville

Fraser River

Jasper

Jasper
National
Park

Camrose

Wetaskiwin

Clearwater

Rocky
Mountain
House

Sundre

Red Deer

Red Deer River

Glacier
National
Park

Yoho
National
Park

Banff
National
Park

Olds

Drumheller

Lake
Louise

Banff

Airdrie

Revelstoke

Golden

Cochrane

CALGARY

Canmore

Kananaskis
Country

Okotoks

Hussar

Bow River

Brooks

Invermere

Fort
Macleod

Taber

Medicine
Hat

Nelson

Cranbrook

Pincher
Creek

Lethbridge

CPR

Fernie

Waterton
National
Park

Creston

Cardston

Columbia River

Kootenay
National
Park

Chilliw

oquitl

ROCKY MOUNTAINS

CNR

ELBERTA

Canola field near Hussar

Foothills and mountains
near Longview

WASHINGTON

Alberta

Ranchland near Calgary

Alberta is one of Canada's premier tourist destinations. It is also one of the most geographically varied provinces in Canada, offering grasslands, badlands, ranchlands, farmlands, and the majestic Canadian Rockies, along with the urban centres of Calgary and Edmonton.

During the Mezosoic era, which ended 65 million years ago, dinosaurs roamed the land. Before that, what is now the Rockies was a vast inland sea. Alberta was swampy coastal lowland, subject to floods and hurricanes.

Human habitation in this region began over 11,000 years ago, with Native groups like the Blackfoot, Cree, Sarcee, and Assiniboine. They had quite different ways of life depending on their location, and frequently fought each other.

European explorers in the fur trade, arrived in the mid-18th century. Forts and trading posts were established, but no real settlement got underway until the late 19th century, when the North West Mounted Police arrived to establish order in the formerly lawless territory. Shortly thereafter, the Canadian Pacific Railway began to make its way through Calgary to Vancouver, physically uniting the country in 1885. Settlers arrived in great numbers on the railway and began to farm and ranch on the prairie and in the foothills.

*Please note that the **Canadian Rockies**, being a destination in their own right, are covered in the next chapter.*

SuperGuide Recommendations: Alberta

1) Glenbow Museum, Calgary
2) West Edmonton Mall
3) Waterton Lakes National Park
4) Head-Smashed-In Buffalo Jump
5) Royal Tyrrell Museum, Drumheller
6) David Thompson Highway
7) Crowsnest Pass
8) Fort McMurray Oil Sands
9) Reynolds Alberta Museum, Wetaskiwin
10) Remington Alberta Carriage Museum, Cardston

Alberta became a province in 1905. Both it and Lake Louise were named for Princess Louise Caroline Alberta, the fourth daughter of Queen Victoria.

The discovery of oil at Turner Valley (southwest of Calgary) in 1914 and at Leduc (south of Edmonton) in 1947 launched Alberta's fortunes. Today the energy industry dominates the provincial economy, but tourism is also a very strong element. Most visitors come to experience the Canadian Rockies, the West Edmonton Mall, and the Calgary Stampede. However, there is a wealth of discovery to be made and activities to be experienced in the smaller centres of the province as well.

Calgary

Located on the banks of the Bow River, Calgary is a young and ever-growing city that thrives on its image as the "Heart of the New West". Fort Calgary was established in 1875 by the North West Mounted Police. The city grew up around this site (which is still standing, and operates as Fort Calgary Historic Park) and spread into the current downtown location after the railway came through.

The Calgary of today is a far cry from its early agricultural days. The oil boom years of the 1970s saw a sustained period of construction, and the downtown skyscrapers built during that time still dominate the cityscape today. Historic buildings from the turn of the 20th century are still visible downtown, but the city's suburbs continue to expand at a great rate. Despite

Two of Calgary's most distinctive landmarks are the Calgary Tower and the Pengrowth Saddledome.

this suburban sprawl, downtown is compact with the Bow and Elbow Rivers providing welcome natural beauty amidst the concrete. A network of riverside trails is heavily used by Calgarians for running, rollerblading, and strolling.

Attractions

Glenbow Museum
www.glenbow.ab.ca
130 9th Ave. SE, 403.268.4100
Western Canada's largest museum highlights many aspects of western life through paintings and cultural artifacts collected over many years. The section on Native life and culture is truly outstanding. One of the highlights is the Blackfoot teepee in the *Nitsitapi-isinni: Our Way of Life* gallery. Numerous other exhibits focus on the social and cultural history of the west, displaying a wide-ranging and eclectic collection of items. The section on religious art is a beautiful and unexpected pleasure.

Canada Olympic Park
www.coda.ab.ca/COP
88 Canada Olympic Rd. SW,
403.247.5452
Everyone who leaves Calgary heading west on Highway 1 will pass Canada Olympic Park, with its distinctive ski jump towers. It's well worth a visit. This was the site of several events (ski jumping, bobsleigh, luge, and freestyle) at the 1988 Winter Olympics and is now a year-round training centre, as well as a museum devoted to the winter games.

SuperGuide Recommendations: Calgary

The following attractions and activities represent the best of Calgary. Take in as many of these as possible:

1) Glenbow Museum
2) Calgary Zoo
3) Canada Olympic Park
4) Spruce Meadows
5) Calgary Tower
6) Heritage Park
7) Fort Calgary
8) Eau Claire and Prince's Island Park
9) Kensington
10) The ranch country surrounding Calgary

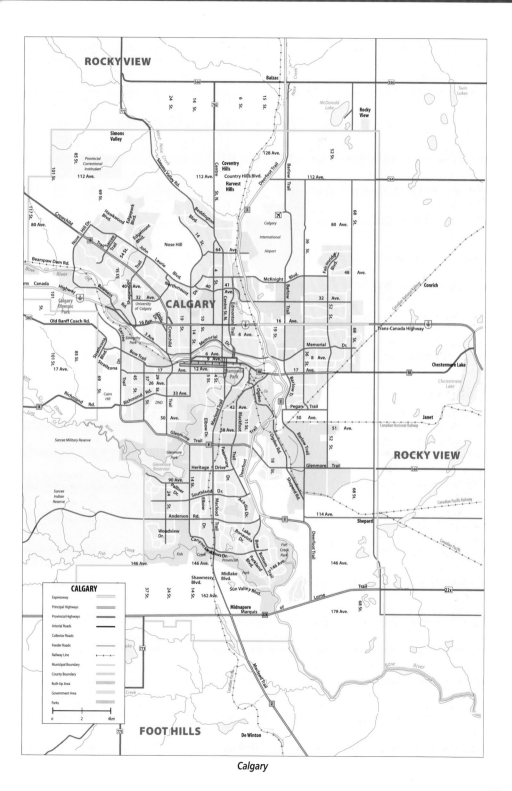

Calgary

A ski jumper takes to the air at Canada Olympic Park.

Heritage Park's steam train is a favourite attraction.

Guided tours include admission to the Olympic Hall of Fame and Museum, the luge track and the 90-metre ski jump tower. You can take a guided tour, or a self-guided tour for a slightly smaller fee.

For an additional charge, thrill-seekers may ride the Road Rocket, a speedy ride down the Olympic bobsleigh track. Bike rentals are also available for exploring the 25 kilometres of mountain bike trails.

The Calgary Zoo, Botanical Gardens and Prehistoric Park

www.calgaryzoo.com
1300 Zoo Rd. NE, 403.232.9300, toll-free 800.588.9993
This is one of North America's premier zoos. It offers a full day's experience in several different areas, each of which aims to recreate the animals' natural habitat as much as possible. There is a prehistoric park with life-sized dinosaur replicas, splendid gardens throughout the park, and the animals themselves, which are the most compelling reason to visit. Australian animals, nocturnal animals, big mammals (check out the baby warthogs), and the new Desti-

nation Africa make for enthralling viewing. As of 2003, the only indoor underwater viewing of hippos in North America will be possible as well. The Canadian Wilds section is the surest place to see a grizzly bear on a visit to Alberta.

The zoo has a year-round calendar of special events, from spring flower festivals to "Boo at the Zoo", a Halloween event.

Calgary Special Events and Festivals

Calgary is host to numerous special events and festivals throughout the year. Here is a sampling:

February: Winter Festival
May: Mother's Day Road Race
June: Carifest; Calgary Jazz Festival
July: Calgary Stampede; Calgary Marathon; Calgary Folk Festival
August: Hispanic Festival; Afrikadey
October: Banff-Calgary International Writers Festival

Heritage Park

www.heritagepark.ca
1900 Heritage Dr. SW, 403.268.8500
This is Canada's largest living historical park (different from Fort Edmonton Park, Canada's largest living history

Bernard Callebaut

One of Calgary's most delicious names is Bernard Callebaut, chocolatier extraordinaire.

He grew up in Belgium, began his Canadian operation in 1983, and moved in 1994 to the distinctive building at 1313 1st St. SE. The chocolates produced are of the highest quality and really do melt in your mouth. M. Callebaut ensures quality control by eating 10-15 chocolates daily to make sure all is up to scratch — a tough job, but somebody has to do it! Stores are popping up all over the Pacific Northwest and even abroad, but this is the source of it all.

Visitors can tour the facility to watch their favourite treats being made — and yes, there are samples at the end. Call 403.265.5777 to book a tour.

museum, in that there are rides as well as exhibits). It recreates a pioneer village with over 150 buildings, most of which are real buildings built before WW I and subsequently moved to the grounds. There is a free pancake breakfast with admission every day between 9 and 10 a.m.

Take a boat ride on the *SS Moyie*, a replica sternwheeler, on the Glenmore Reservoir, or take a steam train ride around the grounds of the park to round out the day.

Spruce Meadows
www.sprucemeadows.com
18011 Spruce Meadows Way SW, 403.974.4200

Spruce Meadows is a unique show-jumping facility with a yearly tournament roster that attracts international competitors. There are three major events every season, beginning with the National in early June. The highlight of the season is the Masters tournament in September, with its rich prize purse of al-

Balloons in Calgary

Balloons floating overhead on a warm summer evening are one of the prettiest sights in Calgary. The city is home to an enthusiastic ballooning community that pursues the sport year-round. The balloons fly at an altitude of about 1,000 feet. Commercial operators offer balloon trips for visitors — an experience not to be missed. The ascent is very gentle, like rising in an elevator, and the views over the city and surrounding countryside are simply spectacular.

most $1.5 million. The North American in early July is also very popular. The facility is open year-round and the entry fee to stroll around the grounds is very reasonable. With more than 20 buildings and all sorts of activity going on, it's well worth a visit any time of year.

The Calgary Tower
www.calgarytower.com
101 9th Ave. SW, 403.266.7171
The Calgary Tower is one of the city's most recognizable structures and among its busiest tourist attractions. Built in 1968 as the Husky Tower, this 190.8-metre-high (625-foot) structure offers sublime views of the city, prairie, foothills and mountains. Visit the observation deck or splurge on fine dining at the Panorama revolving restaurant.

Devonian Gardens
TD Square, 317 7th Ave. SW, 403.268.3888
This wonderful indoor green space takes up the fourth floor of the Toronto Dominion Centre and stretches almost a whole city block. Admission is free. Offering a delightfully refreshing break from shopping or work, the gardens are a popular place for local office workers to have lunch, surrounded by more than 20,000 plants and soothed by the sounds of several waterfalls.

Fort Calgary
www.fortcalgary.com
750 9th Ave. SE, 403.290.1875
The original fort building, erected in haste by fifty members of the North West Mounted Police, is in the process of being rebuilt, but a

visit to Fort Calgary is still an authentic way to learn about Calgary's history. The displays highlight various stages of Calgary's development from 1875 through the 1940s. The setting near the river, with plenty of trails, is a very pleasant place for a stroll or a picnic. You can also drop into Deane House, built in 1906, for a gracious lunch or afternoon tea.

Calgary Chinese Cultural Centre
197 1st St. SW, 403.262.5071
This showpiece of Calgary's Chinatown features art exhibitions, as well as displays about Chinese culture and history. It's worth a visit just to see the building, which is patterned on the Temple of Heaven in Beijing.

Calgary Police Interpretive Centre
316 7th Ave. SW, 403.266.4566
This museum features a recreation of the old pioneer jail, a courtroom, and a flophouse. More contemporary exhibits illustrate the issues and situations faced by modern-day Calgary police.

Calaway Park
www.calawaypark.com
Hwy. 1 and Springbank Rd., 403.240.3822
Open from the May long weekend through mid-October, this amusement park is a delight for children. There are over two dozen rides, including a roller coaster, a Ferris wheel and a log ride.

Science Centre
www.calgaryscience.ca
701 11th St. SW, 403.268.8300
This facility offers hands-on

exhibits and multimedia productions that illuminate science in a fun and informative way. There is a wonderful skateboard park just next door, so the kids can blow off a little steam after their learning experience.

Culture

Calgary has a wealth of cultural activities, special events and festivals to take in over the course of the year. Be sure to check out the variety of performances available at these venues.

Jubilee Auditorium
1415 14th St., 403.297.8000
This is the home of both the Alberta Ballet and the Calgary Opera. It also plays host to a varied calendar of theatrical and musical performances.

Nickle Arts Museum
434 Collegiate Blvd. NW (University of Calgary),
403.220.7234
Rotating exhibits of contemporary and historical works are presented in three galleries.

Loose Moose Theatre Company
403.265.LMTC
This company might best be described as zany. Their performances are high-energy and hilarious, and as often as not, completely improvised. The Loose Moose was the birthplace of TheatreSports — group improv in which two teams compete for points awarded by a panel of judges. If you've ever seen *Whose Line is it Anyway?*, you are familiar with the basic idea. It's an extremely amusing way to spend an evening.

Shopping and Dining

Alberta is one of the best places to shop in all of Canada. American and international visitors can rejoice in the weak Canadian dollar that makes their budgets stretch further, while visitors from the rest of Canada can enjoy a break from provincial sales taxes.

Several large downtown malls are connected by above-ground walkways, but smaller neighbourhoods offer a better chance to experience the flavour of Calgary.

Kensington
Billing itself as the Village in the City, this is a pleasant area to explore, with small boutiques, restaurants and services. At the junction of 10th St. and Kensington Rd. NW, Kensington is easy to get to and makes a welcome change from downtown, which is only a 20-minute walk away.

Inglewood
Located along 9th Ave SE just past Fort Calgary, at the confluence of the Bow and Elbow Rivers, Inglewood is a burgeoning shopping destination. This is an excellent place to shop for home decor items as well as arts and crafts. Inglewood was the first city of Calgary until the CPR established its station further west, near today's Fairmont Palliser Hotel.

Uptown 17th
This trendy area stretches for a dozen or more blocks just

EPCOR Centre

The EPCOR Centre has five theatres: the Max Bell Arena, the Martha Cohen Theatre, the Engineered Air Theatre, the Jack Singer Concert Hall and the Big Secret Theatre. The complex takes up an entire city block and is home to three resident theatre companies. There is almost always a performance of some kind happening at one venue or the other, whether it be a local production or a touring company. Musical series are presented throughout the year in the Jack Singer Concert Hall and the Engineered Air Theatre.

The resident theatre companies in the EPCOR Centre are:

Alberta Theatre Projects
www.atplive.com
403.294.7402

ATP presents contemporary theatre pieces from Canada and around the world. Their goal is to produce work that is entertaining, relevant, and a celebration of Canadian theatrical talent.

Theatre Calgary
www.theatrecalgary.com
403.294.7440
This company produces well-known plays and musicals throughout the year.

One Yellow Rabbit
www.oyr.org
403.264.3224
An innovative company with a 20-year reputation for excellence, One Yellow Rabbit produces at least three new pieces every year.

www.theartscentre.org
205 8th Ave. SE, 403.294.7444

Calgary Stampede

The Midway at Stampede is a colourful and bustling place to be with rides lighting up the evening sky.

A bull rider hangs on for eight seconds in rodeo's flashiest event.

By far the most compelling event in Calgary's calendar is the annual Stampede, billed as the "Greatest Outdoor Show on Earth". A ten-day party in early July celebrating Calgary's western heritage, the Stampede features daily afternoon and evening rodeos, free performances of all sorts, and a grandstand show that includes chuckwagon races. You can also enjoy midway rides and greasy fare, agricultural exhibits, and an Indian village. The three iconic events of the Stampede are the parade, which is the first Friday in July, the pro rodeo, and the nightly chuckwagon races and grandstand show.

Well over a million visitors pass through the Stampede gates every year. It's theoretically possible to pay only the nominal admission fee and enjoy free entertainment for the entire day and evening. How-

This little dancer celebrates his Native heritage in the Indian village.

ever, part of the charm is eating Stampede treats like "those little mini-donuts", winning ugly stuffed animals in games of skill, and going on a ride or two.

During Stampede, downtown Calgary comes alive — though not a lot of business gets done during this period. Free pancake breakfasts take place every morning. Local companies sponsor the breakfasts, cooked by volunteers. While people line up for their free pancakes in Olympic Plaza, they are entertained by performers: marching bands, an Indian parade, a hat-stomping contest, and so on. Along Stephen Avenue Mall, passers-by get pulled into square-dancing lessons while strolling along the streets. It's hard to resist the charm of Calgary at this festive time of year.

south of downtown. A great place to dine, shop, or enjoy a drink on a patio, this area has plenty going on all year round.

The Mission area
This is another older district undergoing a revival. Located near the Elbow River, it's known for its unusual shops and a wide range of restaurants along 4th Street.

Eau Claire Market
www.eauclairemarket.com
Second Ave. at Second St. SW,
403.264.6460
This colourful market offers a selection of boutiques, galleries, food stores, and restaurants. It is a very busy place in summer months for patio aficionados, with several restaurants offering alfresco dining. Eau Claire is home to Calgary's IMAX theatre, as well as a regular cinema, and it's an excellent place to catch buskers of all kinds.

Chinatown
Canada's second-largest

If you have only a day in Calgary:

1) Breakfast at Nellie's or the 1886 Café
2) Dive into the past at the Glenbow Museum
3) Take in the views from atop the Calgary Tower
4) Visit Eau Claire Market and take a stroll along the river paths to Prince's Island
5) Dine along Stephen Avenue Mall — make sure it's Alberta Beef!

If you have two days in Calgary, on day two:

1) Visit the zoo
2) Say hi to the horses at Spruce Meadows
3) Drop in to the Loose Moose to enjoy improv comedy
4) Ride the Rocket at the Calgary Olympic Park
5) Discover Kensington
6) Make a trip to Mountain Equipment Co-op for big savings on outdoor gear

---

Chuckwagons

Fast-paced chuckwagon racing is a highlight of the grandstand show.

Chuckwagon racing is a pastime unique to the Canadian West. Chuckwagons were used for storing food and essential supplies for cowboys working on the range. Nobody is completely sure how the racing event got started. A popular theory is that at the end of the week, cowboys would race their chuckwagons from out on the range into town, and the last one in bought the beer.

The first official chuckwagon race was held at the 1923 Calgary Stampede, and was a great success with the crowds. Today's races are the highlight of the nightly evening rodeo and grandstand show at the Stampede. Four thoroughbreds pull each wagon. The driver is trailed by outriders, who load the wagon, then run to their horses and follow the wagon as fast as they can.

Smaller-scale races, under the auspices of the World Pro Chuckwagon Association Tour, are held throughout the summer and fall in Drumheller, Grande Prairie, Medicine Hat, Lethbridge, High River, Ponoka, Edmonton, Strathmore, and Dawson Creek.

This is a fast-paced and dangerous sport. Each race lasts only a few minutes, including loading time, and represents a link to the living history of the Canadian West.

Eau Claire Market

The Rockies make a majestic backdrop for Calgary's gleaming towers.

Sports Action in Calgary

Calgary is intensely loyal to its sports teams. A great way to experience this feeling is to take in a hockey or football game.

The Calgary Flames are the local National Hockey League team, playing out of the Pengrowth Saddledome, an excellent venue for watching hockey. Hockey is the quintessential Canadian sport, and Flames fans are among the most ardent in Canada. Regular season begins in October and runs through April, though playoff season stretches well into June.

The Calgary Stampeders are the local Canadian Football League team, playing out of McMahon Stadium. The team has been around since 1945 — not with the same players, of course! — but football has a long tradition in the city. The rules are mostly the same as American football, with a larger field and only three downs. Games are played from June through November.

Chinatown, the area between the Bow River and 4th Avenue downtown features plenty of Asian specialty shops and excellent restaurants.

Stephen Avenue
Connecting the Telus Convention Centre and Olympic Plaza with the larger downtown malls, Stephen Avenue is one of the oldest streets in Calgary. A stroll along this pedestrian mall reveals some of the city's best historic buildings, some over 100 years old. The area is gradually becoming more gentrified, with new upscale shops and restaurants. Interesting street art, pageantry, and luxuriant flower baskets add to the appeal.

Chinook Centre
6455 Macleod Tr. SW, 403.255.0613
The destination mall of choice in Calgary, and recently completely renovated and expanded, this is an excellent place to while away a day of bargain hunting.

Natural Distractions in Calgary
In addition to Calgary's trail system along the Bow River Valley, there are a number of outstanding natural areas within the city limits, offering beauty and tranquility.

Nose Hill Park
Now surrounded by new housing developments, Nose Hill is a wonderful grassland oasis in north-central Calgary. There are plenty of walking and hiking trails and some splendid views to the west from the top of the hill.

Fish Creek Provincial Park
Just about surrounded by Calgary's southern suburbs, this park nonetheless offers a wonderful sanctuary from the city along its 46 kilometres of trails for hiking, biking and riding. Sikome Lake offers swimming and skating, depending on the season. Visit the restored 1800s Bow Valley Ranch House or do some birdwatching in the wetlands.

Inglewood Bird Sanctuary
www.gov.calgary.ab.ca
2425 9th Ave. SE, 403.221.4500

Learn about Calgary's wildlife and enjoy the trails in this little gem of a park not far from the heart of downtown. Over 250 species of birds have been sighted here.

Edworthy Park
Along the Bow River between Sarcee and Bow trails, this

Home on the Range

Have a day on the range in the ranchlands outside Calgary. Take a drive northwest of the city to Cochrane, which features a charming small main street with interesting shops and cafés. Be sure to stop at local icon McKay's Ice Cream for one of their decadent flavours, or pick up a homemade treat at the pie shop. Then visit Cochrane Ranche Historic Site, Hwy. 22 at 1A Hwy. (Tel. 403.932.2902). Here, Senator Matthew Cochrane set up the first large-scale cattle ranch in the 1880s. Today visitors can explore the ranch on a variety of interpretive trails.

When you leave Cochrane, follow Hwy. 22 south to Longview (you will have to detour onto Hwy. 8 or the more delightful 762), and visit the Bar U Ranch (Tel. 403.395.2212), where you can learn about the ranching history of the foothills. This was one of the first large commercial ranching operations in Canada, and is now a National Historic Site. Costumed interpreters lead guided walks around the ranch, which is more like a small village. This is a premier place to learn about cowboys, Natives, and ranching life as it was between 1882 and 1950.

Calgary glows in the twilight sky.

Big Rock Brewery

This brewery so dear to the hearts of Albertans was established in 1985 by Ed McNally, a former lawyer and rancher who loved good beer made in the European tradition: no additives, no preservatives, and no pasteurization. Big Rock has grown by leaps and bounds since that time, educating Albertans to the joys of pure beer with big flavour. This beer can be easily recognized by its unusually artistic labels and memorable names. Big Rock's most popular beer is Traditional, known simply as "Trad", but their other beers each have wonderful qualities. Try Grasshopper Wheat Ale, Warthog Cream Ale, McNally's Extra Ale, Pale Ale, Black Amber Ale, and Kold, all of which are readily available throughout the province.

Visitors can tour the state-of-the-art brewing facility at 5555 76th Ave. SE on Mondays, Tuesdays, and Wednesdays, and of course these tours include a tasting at the end. Call 403.720.3239.

Grasshopper Wheat Ale

Downtown Edmonton and the North Saskatchewan River

Bowness Park
48th Ave. and 90th St. NW,
403.268.3888
A great place to canoe (rentals are available) or to ice-skate in the winter. Picnic areas, miniature golf and kids' play areas are part of the family attractions here.

Prince's Island Park
Linked to downtown by a small bridge, this island between the river and a small man-made lagoon is a wonderful pace for a stroll. Many summer festivals are held here.

Edmonton
Edmonton is Alberta's capital city. Its most famous landmark is the West Edmonton Mall, the world's largest shopping and entertainment complex, but Edmonton does have other attractions for the visitor to enjoy.

The Cree and Blackfoot Indians were the first inhabitants of the area around the North Saskatchewan River Valley. Edmonton's settlement by Europeans began in 1795 with the establishment of Fort Edmonton, set up by the Hudson's Bay Company as a fur trading post. For many years after this, Edmonton was a major stopping point for those few folk heading further west or north. Once the Klondike gold rush began, the city grew enormously, swelled by the numbers of prospectors.

When the province of Alberta was formed in 1905, Edmonton was the natural choice for a capital. It had a longer history and greater population than Calgary, which had only been founded some 30 years earlier.

Edmonton Special Events and Festivals

Edmonton bills itself as "Festival City", and it's not hard to see why. Here is a sampling:

January: Comedy Arts Festival
May: Northern Alberta Children's Festival
June: River City Shakespeare Festival; Jazz City International Music Festival
July: Klondike Days; Edmonton International Street Performers Festival
August: Edmonton Folk Music Festival; Edmonton Fringe Festival; Edmonton Heritage Festival; Symphony Under the Sky; Cariwest; Edmonton Blues Festival
November: Canadian Finals Rodeo

park features gardens and the Douglas Fir trail amongst 400-year old trees.

Glenmore Park
Enjoy some beautiful trails and views of the mountains in this park, which surrounds the Glenmore Reservoir.

SuperGuide Recommendations: Edmonton and Area

While the mall is the largest draw, be sure to take in some of the other attractions around the city:

1) West Edmonton Mall
2) Old Strathcona Historic Area
3) Fort Edmonton Park
4) Odyssium
5) Muttart Conservatory
6) Provincial Museum of Alberta
7) Elk Island National Park
8) Ukrainian Cultural Heritage Village

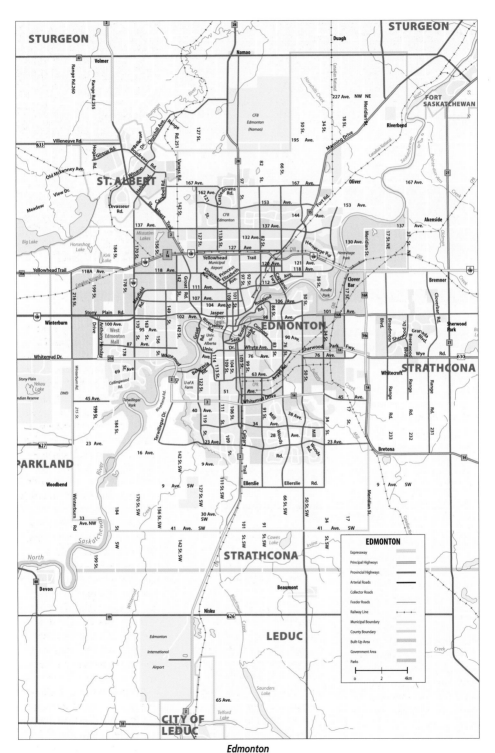

Edmonton

The distinctive pyramids of the Muttart Conservatory

Alberta's Legislature Building

CKUA

One of Alberta's greatest cultural treasures is CKUA radio, a public radio station that has been on the air longer than any other station in North America.

This is not like any other station you've heard — there is a wide and eclectic range of programming, and rarely is the same song played twice in a week. It's perfectly usual to hear a bluegrass tune followed by a song from Cape Verde, followed by a piece of ambient electronica, followed by the daily agricultural report. The variety is amazing.

CKUA broadcasts around the province on AM at 580 or on FM (Edmonton 94.9, Calgary 93.7, Banff 104.3, Red Deer 101.3 and Lethbridge 99.3, plus many other locations) and on the Internet at www.ckua.com, so you can even listen once you get home from your holidays. Tune in and see what you've been missing!

Today, there are many things to see and do in Edmonton. Visitors can enjoy the largest urban parkland system in North America, stretching prettily along the North Saskatchewan and offering trails, golf courses, and winter recreation opportunities. And the "Festival City" of Canada does indeed have many special events going on throughout the summer months.

Attractions in Edmonton

West Edmonton Mall
www.westedmontonmall.com
8882 170 St., 780.444.5200, toll-free 800.661.8890
As mentioned, the West Edmonton Mall is the world's largest shopping and entertainment complex. It's well worth a visit even if you have no interest in shopping. Measuring in at 5.3 million square feet, and spanning 48 city blocks, the sheer size of the place is astounding. Beyond the over 800 shops and 100 eating establishments, there is an astonishing list of extras (all for a fee): the world's largest indoor amusement park, the world's largest wave pool, the world's largest indoor lake, an NHL-sized skating rink, dolphin shows, a life-sized replica of the *Santa Maria*, sea life caverns, an 18-hole mini-golf course, and 27 movie screens. You can even take a submarine ride — it's a joke uncomfortably close to the truth that the West Edmonton Mall has more working submarines than Canada's navy.

The shopping is excellent — Alberta is the only province with no provincial sales tax, and the weakness of the Canadian dollar makes this an incredible bargain for American visitors, many of whom fly in for a weekend of shopping. Where do these savvy shoppers stay? Right at the mall, of course! The Fantasyland Hotel has 355 rooms and is attached to the mall, right next to the World Waterpark. Eleven types of themed rooms are available at the hotel, for guests who want to spend the night in a Polynesian

The Waterpark at West Edmonton Mall is a great way to splash away a day.

The Famous Five

Women in Alberta gained the right to vote in 1916, but they were not allowed to be appointed to the Canadian Senate. In the 1920s, five Alberta women challenged the definition of the word "person" as contained in the British North America Act to include women as well as men.

When the case was first brought before the Supreme Court in 1927, it was unsuccessful. Since it was based on the BNA Act of 1867, it was argued, it should be taken in the spirit of those times, when women were not considered persons. The women refused to give up and took the case to the Judicial Committee of the British Privy Council, the highest court of appeal in Canadian law at the time. This time the courts struck down the archaic law.

Emily Murphy, Henrietta Muir Edwards, Louise McKinney, Nellie McClung, and Irene Parlby were the five women. None of them went on to the Senate, but four months after the ruling, the first Canadian woman, Cairine Reay Wilson, was appointed to the Senate.

Gold Fever!

Crossing Chilkoot Pass in the gold rush

In 1897, word began to spread throughout North America of gold having been found in the far north of Canada. By 1898, thousands of people were on their way north, with little idea of the conditions they would face, but with a healthy desire for gold.

Prospectors had to hike into the area, hauling their provisions with them, over the treacherous Chilkoot Pass, and then take a dangerous boat ride down the Yukon River system to reach Dawson. Needless to say, the ones who made it were euphoric. The Klondike gold rush had begun, and by the summer of 1898 there were over 30,000 people in Dawson City. By the end of it, over 100,000 people had tried their luck, and most had returned home empty-handed. Only a few ever really struck it rich.

The gold rush was a bonanza for Edmonton, which was on one of the routes to the goldfields. Many of the failed miners returned here to settle down after their experiences in the Klondike.

The Edmonton Folk Music Festival is a highlight of the summer calendar.

paradise, an igloo, or the old west, among others. Some rooms even look out onto the waterpark, through one-way glass.

Odyssium
www.odyssium.com
11211 142nd St., 780.451.3344
The Odyssium is one of Edmonton's star attractions. Formerly the Edmonton Space and Science Centre, this striking building houses several galleries devoted to hands-on learning about science. While aimed at children, it offers plenty of things to amuse and interest adults as well.

Enjoy trying to solve a crime on Mystery Avenue, doing a TV weather report in the Greens' House, and imitating the fascinating workings of the human body in The Body Fantastic.

A show about stars and planets runs frequently in the Star Theatre and an observatory is open to the public (times vary). An IMAX theatre shows spectacular films for an extra admission charge.

Fort Edmonton Park
www.fortedmontonpark.com
Fox Dr. and Whitemud Dr.,
780.496.8787
Fort Edmonton Park is the largest living history museum in Canada, and offers portraits of Edmonton life in four different time periods: the Hudson's Bay fur-trading post in 1846, the frontier town of 1885 Street, the bustling young city of 1905 Street (Alberta became a province that year, with Edmonton its capital), and the Roaring Twenties of 1920 Street. Fort Edmonton Park is open seasonally from May to September. The park itself is located along the river, and makes an excellent site for picnics and walking.

Alberta Legislature Building
10800 97th Ave., 780.427.7362
This striking building was completed in 1912, built of imported sandstone and marble. Free tours are offered daily. Explore the grounds with their beautiful gardens in summer, or skate there and enjoy the holiday lights in winter.

Muttart Conservatory
www.edmonton.ca/muttart
9626 96A St., 780-496-8755.
The Muttart Conservatory is a beautiful collection of gardens, each housed in a separate glass pyramid. Each of the four display pyramids has a distinct theme: Arid, Tropical, Temperate, and a Show pyramid with ever-changing displays. The conservatory offers an especially striking contrast to the chilly winter in Edmonton, but is a pleasure all year round.

Provincial Museum of Alberta
www.pma.edmonton.ab.ca
12845 102 Ave., 780-453-9100
Located en route to West Edmonton Mall from downtown, the Provincial Museum offers several appealing galleries, including the Syncrude Gallery of Aboriginal Culture, a live bug exhibit, and displays about the natural and human history of the province. Spend the day; take a walk atop the river valley, and picnic amongst the large sculptures on the grounds of the museum.

Edmonton Queen Riverboat
www.edmontonqueen.com
9734 98 Ave., 780.424.2628
This paddlewheeler offers day and evening trips, featuring dining and dancing, along the North Saskatchewan River below the heart of Edmonton.

Rutherford House
11153 Saskatchewan Dr.,
780.427.3995
This attractive house was built in 1911 for Alberta's first premier, A.C. Rutherford, and was occupied until 1940.

Today you can stroll through the house, enjoy afternoon tea or a light lunch, and feel transported back to an earlier time. There are lots of Sunday special events and the entire atmosphere is one of calm, family-fun activities.

John Walter Museum

www.edmonton.ca/johnwalter
9100 Walterdale Hill,
780.496.8787
Learn about the history of Edmonton, the river valley, and John Walter himself. He was a wealthy entrepreneur who established many diverse businesses in the city around the turn of the 20th century. The museum is located in his three houses.

Edmonton Art Gallery

www.eag.org
2 Sir Winston Churchill Sq.,
780.422.6223
The gallery features visiting exhibits and a permanent collection of western contemporary art. It will also appeal to anyone with an interest in Canadian historical art.

Culture

Edmonton has a vibrant cultural scene with plenty of theatre and music of all kinds to choose from. Check out these venues to see what's going on culturally around the city.

Francis Winspear Centre for Music

www.winspearcentre.com
99th St. at 102nd Ave.,
780.428.1414
This venue is the home of the Edmonton Symphony Orchestra, (www.edmontonsymphony.com; 780.428.1414), and plays host to a number of visiting performers every year. The "World at Winspear" is an ongoing concert series by renowned musicians from around the world.

Jubilee Auditorium

www.jubileeauditorium.com
11455 87th Ave., 780.427.2760
This is Edmonton's performing venue for the Alberta Ballet (www.albertaballet.com;

Klondike Days

Klondike Days is Edmonton's most famous summer event, running for ten days every July. The Klondike Days theme was adopted in 1962 and celebrates Edmonton's role as a gateway to the Yukon during the Klondike gold rush.

The fair offers a ton of free entertainment (the basic admission price for adults is only $5) with agricultural displays, free concerts, and a family-fun zone. Of course there is also a midway, a casino, and chuckwagon races. Downtown Edmonton gets in on the fun too — the streets around Winston Churchill Square feature numerous exhibits and displays, a world beat stage, pancake breakfasts, and free music all day long. Bathtub races between competing office teams careen through the downtown streets every day at noon.

Another highlight that

The Midway at Klondike Days

takes place on the first Sunday of Klondike Days is the annual Sourdough River festival, which sees racers in homemade rafts launch from Terwillegar Park in the southwest part of the city and follow the North Saskatchewan River (even going under the Great Divide Waterfall that runs off the High Level bridge) to land in downtown Edmonton.

For more information, call 780.423.2822 or visit www.klondikedays.com

780.428.6839), and the Edmonton Opera, (www.edmontonopera.com; 780.424.4040), as well as a home for visiting companies. This is another busy place with something happening almost every night.

Citadel Theatre
www.citadeltheatre.com
9828 101A Ave., 780.426.4811, toll-free 888.425.1820
There are five theatres within the Citadel Theatre complex, so there is something going on almost every night.

Walterdale Playhouse
www.walterdaleplayhouse.com
10322 83rd Ave. (Old Strathcona), 780.439.2845
This ambitious amateur group puts on a full slate of productions every year. The theatre itself is an old converted firehall that is now a registered provincial resource.

Shopping and Dining

Edmonton has a number of shopping areas to discover, besides the West Edmonton Mall, which is the king of malls not only in Edmonton but in the entire world. Good choices for dining can be found nearby most of these shopping areas.

Edmonton Area Historical Day Trip

This Ukrainian Church is typical of those in Lamont County.

Spend a day exploring some colourful heritage outside of Edmonton and learn about the area's history. Start by heading to St. Albert and the Father Lacombe Chapel (Tel. 780.459.7663). Then continue east along Hwy. 15 to discover Lamont County and its many historic churches.

Head towards Vegreville to see the Ukrainian Cultural Heritage Village (www.cd.gov.ab.ca/uchv; 780.662.3640). There are over 300,000 Albertans of Ukrainian descent, and this excellent facility celebrates their heritage. As a living history museum, the site recreates daily life from 1892-1930 as it was for Ukrainian settlers in Alberta. The costumed interpreters never come out of character, and the

restored buildings are truly historic (not replicas), making for an authentic experience. Various special events and festivals occur throughout the season.

On the way back to Edmonton, stop in at Elk Island National Park, an ideal place to see herds of bison, elk, moose and deer, as well as trumpeter swans and many other birds. Located in aspen parkland, where the forests of the north meet the grasslands of central Alberta, the park has over 90 kilometres of hiking trails. Some are short and accessible, others are longer and more challenging, so there's something for everyone. Drive out in the late fall or winter on a clear night to spot the northern lights.

Sports Action in Edmonton

Edmonton has several professional sports teams. Check out a game or two while you are in the city.

The **Edmonton Oilers** are the city's National Hockey League team, playing out of Skyreach Centre at Northlands Park. The Oilers were once the team of hockey's greatest-ever player, Wayne Gretzky. While Gretzky has left and it's been a few years since the Oilers won the Stanley Cup, taking in a hockey game is still a typical Edmonton activity that's sure to offer an exciting evening, October through April.

The **Edmonton Eskimos** are the city's Canadian Football League team, playing out of Commonwealth Stadium.

The **Edmonton Trappers** are the city's Triple A baseball team, playing out of Telus Field.

Downtown

Several malls downtown are connected by pedways for shoppers' convenience. There is also a good choice of restaurants in the downtown area. Visit Rice Howard Way, along 100 St. and 101A Ave. It's a pleasant outdoor pedestrian avenue with numerous of patios, and is very popular in summer.

124th Street

This area offers a wide variety of mostly independent shops and restaurants with a relaxed atmosphere. Here is the place to take in a Gallery Walk (www.gallery-walk.com; 780.488.3619) and explore seven art galleries. Formal walks are arranged three times a year, each season except summer, but it's easy to arrange an unguided walk anytime.

Old Strathcona/ Whyte Avenue

This is the place to discover the true heart of Edmonton — the original site of the city that was built up around the railway. Today it has an ambience not found elsewhere in the city, with interesting shops, restaurants, and a thriving farmers' market.

Alberta North

Lloydminster

Anyone driving west along the Yellowhead Highway #16 from Saskatchewan will pass through Lloydminster. This city actually straddles the border between the two provinces.

Visit the Barr Colony Heritage Cultural Centre, 4415

Elk Island National Park, east of Edmonton

Father Lacombe

Father Albert Lacombe

Born in Montreal in 1827, Oblate Father Albert Lacombe came to Alberta in 1852. He travelled extensively, attempting to convince the Cree and Métis to settle down into an agricultural lifestyle. He developed a strong relationship with Native groups, learned the Cree language, and wrote a Cree grammar and dictionary. With help from some Métis, he built what is now the oldest existing building in Alberta, the eponymous Father Lacombe Chapel, in 1861. In the same area a gristmill was built, as well as the first bridge in Alberta.

In his missionary work, Father Lacombe aimed to "show his love for God by showing his love for his People." He travelled tirelessly by horse, dogsled and snowshoes to reach the scattered bands of nomadic Natives to minister to them. He also negotiated with Chief Crowfoot on behalf of the CPR in 1883, when the railway came into conflict with the Blackfoot. Lacombe was well-known by both Cree and Blackfoot, who are traditional enemies. When he died in 1916, his body was buried in Cree territory, while his heart was buried in Blackfoot territory, for both wanted to keep some part of him near their people.

Royal Tyrrell Museum of Paleontology

Fort McMurray

Located about a 4.5-hour drive from Edmonton, this community is booming as a result of oil and gas — over 30% of the world's petroleum reserves are located here, though extracting the oil from the sands is a tricky business. Visitors to the area may wish to learn more on a tour of the oil sands. Others come to see the northern lights, which are visible every clear night between September and April, or to experience some excellent fly-in fishing on remote lakes.

The Oil Sands Discovery Centre explains the story of the development and technology of these vast oil deposits. Tours depart daily at 1 p.m. to see the sites, with their massive machinery, in action.

Alberta Central

Drumheller

Drumheller's prehistory is what attracts visitors today — its weathered and eroded badland scenery and its plentiful dinosaur fossils are the most compelling reasons to visit. The more recent history of the area has much to do with coal mining. Today, it's a town with a dinosaur theme.

There are cute stylized dinos all over town, the world's biggest T-Rex, and the amazing real dinosaur bodies and replicas at the Royal Tyrrell Museum.

Drumheller Attractions

Royal Tyrrell Museum of Paleontology
www.tyrrellmuseum.com
North Dinosaur Trail,
403.823.7707
Plan to spend at least 2-3 hours at this magnificent facility — or more, if you are a real paleophile. The museum welcomes over half a million visitors every year. The building itself appears to rise right out the cliffs that surround it, fitting in perfectly with its environment. Inside are more than 35 complete dinosaurs on display — a real microcosm of Alberta's prehistory. The galleries are put together with wit and imagination, allowing everyone to visualize what life was like in prehistoric times.

If you have an extra day, consider a day-dig program. Limited to 12 people per day, these digs allow you to get a feel for what a day in the field would be like. Participants get to work on excavating real dinosaur bones under the supervision of the Tyrrell staff. There is also a similar program for children. It's essential to book these programs in advance.

Historic Atlas Coal Mine
www.atlascoalmine.ab.ca
Hwy. 10 East (Hoodoo Trail),
403.822.2220
A provincial historic resource, this former coal mine features the only remaining wooden

44th St. (Tel. 306.825.5655), which includes several diverse attractions:

The Imhoff Art Gallery displays over 250 pieces of religious artwork painted in the Renaissance style by a local count, Bertold Von Imhoff (1868-1939).

The OTS Heavy Oil Science Centre explains the local oil industry through hands-on interactive displays (gloves are provided).

The Fuchs Wildlife Display is believed to be the largest taxidermy collection mounted by one man in North America.

The Richard Larsen Museum takes a look at the Barr Colonists, who came from Britain to Lloydminster about 1903 and settled the area. It features restored buildings and various artifacts.

ore-sorting tipple in Canada. Also on site are interpretive trails, historic buildings, mining artifacts, and demonstrations.

World's Largest Dinosaur
403.823.8100
This is one big dinosaur (much taller than an actual T-Rex would have been). Climb the 106 steps to the viewing platform inside the dinosaur's mouth for a view of Drumheller and the surrounding landscape.

Horseshoe Canyon
Coming into Drumheller from Calgary, the first stop is the small and dramatically coloured Horseshoe Canyon. If you have time, meander into the canyon on the trails and immerse yourself in the area. Watch for the cacti, especially lovely when in bloom.

What are the Northern Lights?

Northern lights

The northern lights, also known as the aurora borealis, are a frequent sight in northern Alberta, especially in the winter months. The lights are created by charged particles from the sun colliding with atmospheric particles near the magnetic north pole. The most commonly seen colour is green, but red, pink, purple and orange can also be observed. The lights are not static, but move across the sky in patterns and waves, sometimes making a hissing noise. Most Native cultures have an explanation for the lights that is considerably more poetic than the currently accepted scientific one, and most cultures believe the lights to be benevolent, for they are a truly magical sight.

Odd Alberta

The Vegreville Pysanka stands 32 feet high.

Alberta is home to many objects that bear the moniker "World's Largest". Other oddities include the World's First UFO Landing Pad, the Vulcan Trek Station, and the Torrington Gopher Hole Museum. A tour of these sites will take the intrepid visitor all over the province in search of the following World's…:

1) Largest mallard duck – Andrew. It has a 23-foot wingspan.
2) Largest lamp – Donalda
3) Largest Pysanka (Ukrainian Easter egg) – Vegreville. It's 32 feet high and very beautifully coloured.
4) Largest Piggy Bank - Coleman
5) Largest T-Rex – Drumheller. This dinosaur is four times larger than life.
6) Largest Sundial – Lloydminster
7) Largest Honey Bee – Falher
8) Largest Pyrogy – Glendon. This dumpling is 27 feet tall, speared on a giant fork.
9) Tallest teepee – Medicine Hat
10) Largest Ukrainian Sausage – Mundare. Six tons of this local delicacy are 42 feet tall.
11) Largest Mushrooms – Vilna. These three fun guys are 10 feet, 12 feet and a whopping 20 feet in height.

Canadian Badlands Passion Play
www.canadianpassionplay.com
403.823.2001
This re-enactment of the life of Jesus takes place every July. There are only six performances a year, in the middle two weekends of the month. Set dramatically against the eroded cliffs in a natural amphitheatre, this is a unique theatrical experience.

The Dinosaur Trail
This 48-km trail (road) leads past some of Drumheller's most popular attractions. Look for antelope at Midland Provincial Park and dinosaurs at the Royal Tyrrell Museum. Meditate at the Little Church and admire the views at Horsethief Canyon, Bleriot Ferry (surely one of the world's shortest ferry rides), and Orkney Viewpoint. This is an interesting drive any time, but is especially pretty late in the day.

Rosebud Theatre
www.rosebudtheatre.com
Hwy. 9 at Hwy. 840,
403.677.2001,
toll-free 800.267.7553
Just east of Drumheller, this dinner theatre has three different productions each year, put on by the students of the Rosebud School of the Arts.

The Hoodoo Trail
Enjoy 25 kilometres of scenic driving through small towns that once were bustling with the business of coal extraction. Visit the Historic Atlas Coal Mine (see above) and explore the hoodoos along the way.

Red Deer
Red Deer was named by Scottish fur traders, who mistook the elk common to the area for the red deer native to Scotland. Halfway between Calgary and Edmonton on Highway 2, the town of Red Deer has much more to offer than can be seen from the unattractive "Gasoline Alley" that lines the highway. A good time to visit is in July, when Westerner Days takes place. This five-day old-time country celebration kicks off with a parade, and features a midway, an agricultural show, tons of concerts and performances, and nightly pony chuckwagon races.

Visitors to Red Deer can also take in a performance by the Red Deer Symphony Orchestra, or a Red Deer Rebels WHL hockey game.

Attractions in Red Deer

Alberta Sports Hall of Fame
www.albertasportshalloffame.com
Hwy. 2, 403.341.8614
Located in the large new visitor information centre just off the highway, this museum honours Alberta's athletes and offers plenty of interactive displays. Find out how your pitching compares to pro

Red Deer Area Historical Day Trip

Take a day to explore some of the historic attractions around Red Deer. Drive south on Hwy. 2 to Markerville, home to Historic Markerville Creamery (Tel. 403.728.3006) and Stephansson House (Tel. 403.728.3929). See this restored creamery, built by Icelandic farmers in the 1880s, which now demonstrates how butter was made in the Depression era. Visit the nearby house of Stephan G. Stephansson, "Iceland's Shakespeare", a prolific poet who lived here for several decades. The house tells of his life and that of the Icelanders who settled here in the late 19th century.

If you've a taste for the unusual, continue south on Hwy. 2, then go east on 27 to Torrington, home of the Torrington Gopher Hole Museum (Tel. 403.631.2133). One of the odder offerings in Alberta, this museum is a triumph of taxidermy — stuffed gophers in various human costumes,

engaged in daily human activities.

Continue east to Three Hills and then go north on 21, then east on 11 to Stettler, where you can embark on an Alberta Prairie Railway Excursion (Tel. 403.742.2811). This trip on a vintage steam train is a real pleasure — but watch out for train robbers who haunt the area. Each trip lasts about 5-6 hours and includes a buffet meal in Big Valley, the turnaround point.

If trains aren't your cup of tea, head instead further north to the Reynolds Alberta Museum (Tel. 403.361.1351, toll-free 800.661.4726). This museum is the best reason to visit Wetaskiwin, situated between Red Deer and Edmonton. It features a vast collection of vintage airplanes, cars, and agricultural machinery. Take a ride around the extensive site in a vintage vehicle or splurge on a flight in a biplane with an open cockpit.

baseball players', take a shot or two at the net, and then admire the feats of those who have true athletic talent.

Heritage Ranch
www.heritageranch.ca
Hwy. 2, 403.347.4977
Heritage Range is the gateway to Waskasoo Park, which is a natural wildlife corridor. Enjoy a hayride or trail ride, or in winter take a sleigh ride or go for a cross-country ski. During the summer months, at Three Mile Bend in the park, you may come across young athletes spiralling through the air and landing with a splash in the pool. They are in training for free-style skiing competitions in the winter.

Red Deer & District Museum
www.museum.red-deer.ab.ca
4525 47A Ave., 403.309.8405
Explore the history of the Red Deer area. Once you've looked at the exhibits, you may want to take a historical walking tour of the old town. Ask at the museum for more information and a brochure to guide you.

Fort Normandeau
32nd St., west of Hwy. 2, 403.347.7550

This is a reconstruction of the original fort, which was built in 1884. It features an interpretive centre with displays and demonstrations that tell the story of the Natives, freighters, settlers and militia who used the site. This is a great place for a picnic.

Kerry Wood Nature Centre
www.city.red-deer.ab.ca/kerry
The numerous trails in this area offer a good opportunity to watch migratory birds, and you can learn more about birds and other aspects of the natural history of the area in the interpretive centre.

David Thompson

Everywhere you travel in B.C. or Alberta, it seems David Thompson was there before you. Thompson, born in 1770, was a tireless explorer, surveyor and map-maker who sought to find a route through the Canadian Rockies that would lead to the Pacific Ocean. He first arrived in Rocky Mountain House in 1800 and explored west on behalf of the North West Company for several years after that, but it was not until 1807 that he made the journey over Howse Pass into what is now British Columbia.

He did make it to the Pacific via the Columbia River, arriving in 1811.

David Thompson made many more journeys into the States and through western Canada, employed by the International Boundary Commission. His maps were the best contemporary maps of the Canadian west. He died near Montreal, destitute, in 1857.

Where's the Beef?

Beef on the hoof

Beef on a plate

Just about everywhere in Alberta! In this province, beef is taken very seriously indeed. Nearly 60% of Canadian beef comes from Alberta. It's one of the icons of the province — cattle grazing on the open rangeland against a backdrop of snow-capped peaks make a pretty potent image. One of the most common bumper stickers in Alberta even reads

"I Love Alberta Beef". The reverence for good red meat is enough to make a vegetarian think twice about moving here.

The good news is, the beef lives up to the hype. Maybe it's the excellent grazing, or the wholesome barley feed, but Alberta does produce some of the world's most tender and delicious beef.

The Prince of Wales Hotel above Upper Waterton Lake in Waterton Lakes National Park

The David Thompson Highway

West of Red Deer, Highway 11 leads back into the Rocky Mountains, joining up with the Icefields Parkway at Saskatchewan River Crossing. This route begins in the prairie farmlands and gradually becomes more and more majestic, a highlight being Abraham Lake, a man-made lake of an incredible turquoise hue. Too cold for swimming, it is nonetheless a lovely sight.

The highway passes first through Sylvan Lake, a charming small beach resort, and then Rocky Mountain House, somewhat ill-named as it is still a good long way from the Rockies. (They are, however, visible from here).

The National Historic Site at Rocky Mountain House
403.845.2412
A pleasant place to have a picnic or while away an afternoon. The interpretive portion of the site tells the story of the fierce battle between the North West Company and the Hudson's Bay Company for supremacy over the fur trade, and the effects of the battle on the settlement of the west. Rocky Mountain House has been settled for over 200 years, and was used as a base for exploring the Rockies as well as a fur trading post. Be sure to wander some of the trails that lead down the river and imagine what life was like here a few centuries ago.

Alberta South

Southwest of Calgary is some of the prettiest country in Canada. Rolling rangeland framed by the peaks of the Rockies will make you wish you knew something about cattle so you could buy a ranch and settle in to enjoy the ever-changing landscape.

A visit to southern Alberta should include stops in Waterton Lakes National Park, the Crowsnest Pass area, Head-Smashed-In Buffalo Jump, and Lethbridge.

Waterton Lakes National Park

This stunning park, set in the very southwestern corner of Alberta, was founded in 1895. One hundred years later it was designated a UNESCO World Heritage Site, along with its sister American park, Glacier National Park. Together, they form the world's first International Peace Park.

Native peoples (the Kutenai and Blackfoot, primarily) had used the Waterton area for many thousands of years by the time the first white explorer, Lt. Thomas Blakiston, a disaffected member of the Palliser expedition, arrived on the scene in 1858. For decades after this, it remained largely uninhabited, save for a few hardy souls. Some of those — Kootenai Brown and Frederick Godsal — were instrumental in the creation of the reserve that became a national park (Canada's fourth) in 1911.

Attractions in Waterton

Red Rock Canyon Parkway
This 17-km drive leads to the aptly named Red Rock Canyon, a colourful gorge. Stop along the way at the interpretive panels that highlight Native use of the area before the white men arrived. This is a great place for a picnic.

Cameron Falls
This 10-metre-high step with a double waterfall is one of Waterton townsite's popular sights. It can be reached by car or on foot from the village.

Akamina Parkway to Cameron Lake
A 16-km drive along this parkway leads to Cameron Lake at the base of Mount Custer. Rent a canoe or paddleboat to explore the lake (no motorboats are allowed), or take the lakeside trail. Learn about the life of the surrounding forest at the interpretive centre.

Prince of Wales Hotel
This grand old hotel commands an unrivalled view of Upper Waterton Lake from its bluff above town. It has been declared a National Historic Site. Even if you are not staying at the hotel, stroll the grounds, and wander into the lobby to take in the view.

Waterton Shoreline Cruises
403.859.2362
One of the most popular activities in the park is the two-hour international boat cruise that goes along Upper Waterton Lake into the States. There is a half-hour stop at Goat Haunt on the Montana side. You can stay longer here, or go on a hike from here, and catch a later boat back.

Waterton Lakes Golf Course
403.859.2114
This lovely course was designed by Stanley Thompson in 1929 and still impresses with its grand scenic layout. Costs here are much more reasonable than at the other courses he designed, in Banff and Jasper.

Take a hike in Waterton

Enjoy some fresh air and beautiful views from any one of these easy walks in the Waterton area:

- **Lower Bertha Falls** (2.9 km one way). Enjoy a great view of Upper Waterton Lake while hiking to a pretty waterfall past blow-downs and avalanche paths.
- **Cameron Falls** (3.2-km loop from town). This is less of a hike than a walk, since most of the walk is through town, but it's scenic nonetheless, with access to the lake and to the falls.
- **Bear's Hump** (1.2 km one way, with lots of elevation gain). Gain an excellent vantage point over the townsite and the lake on this short, steep one.
- **Cameron Lake** (1.6 km one way). This nice flat walk goes along the lake through an evergreen forest dotted with wildflowers.
- **Red Rock Canyon** (900-m loop). Stroll up the canyon to see some of the oldest, and certainly the most colourful, rock in Alberta.
- **Bison Paddock** Viewpoint (300-m loop). See where the prairie meets the mountains — and possibly sight a bison or two into the bargain — but stay in your car when driving through the paddock, for safety's sake.

Kootenai Brown

One of the mythic figures of the old west, Kootenai Brown (born John George Brown in Ireland in 1839) roamed widely before settling down in the Waterton area in 1878. He had been in India with the British army, followed the gold rush to B.C., and ridden for the Pony Express. He had several run-ins with Native groups — once reputedly taking an arrow out of his own back after an unfortunate encounter with a band of Sioux led by Sitting Bull — and spent several years hunting and trapping in southern Alberta, before settling down near Waterton. He lobbied hard for the establishment of Waterton as a national park, and when the reserve was eventually set up, he became its first warden. His grave is alongside the road at the entrance to Waterton townsite.

High Level Bridge at Lethbridge

Near Waterton, heading west, the landscape is one of prairies, foothills and the Rockies growing ever closer. In Pincher Creek, one of the windiest places in the province, there is a majestic series of windmills dotting the landscape. Get near the windmills to hear the immense power of the wind, but remember the mills are on private property, so please don't trespass. Also in Pincher Creek, visit the Kootenai Brown Pioneer Village at 1037 Beverley McLachlin Dr. (Tel. 403.627.3684). See Kootenai Brown's house and 15 other heritage log and clapboard buildings filled with historical artifacts from the turn of the 20th century.

If you're in the area over a summer weekend, be sure to visit the Great Canadian Barn Dance in Hillspring, about 30 minutes from Waterton (Tel. 403.626.3407; toll-free: 800.661.1222).

On a Friday or Saturday night, this 40-acre resort features the fun of a barn dance and country beef dinner in a real barn. Daytime activities include fishing, canoe rentals, and horseshoes.

Cardston

Remington Alberta Carriage Museum
www.remingtoncentre.com
623 Main St., 403.653.5139
The second biggest carriage museum in the world, after one in Lisbon, this sprawling facility is an excellent stop on the way south to Waterton Lakes. Hourly tours are available, as are frequent carriage rides around the grounds. In June, Remington Day features heavy horse pulls and other activities. Younger visitors can blow off some steam at the children's discovery park.

Cardston Temple
348 3rd St. West, 403.653.1696
Rising abruptly from the prairie, with the Rockies as a dramatic backdrop, this imposing building dominates the view in the Cardston area. It was the first Mormon

Church sacred site to be opened outside of the U.S., in 1923. There is a visitor centre here, but non-Mormons are not permitted in the temple.

Lethbridge
The Blackfoot had lived in the Lethbridge area for many years before the fur traders, whisky traders, and NWMP arrived. Eventually it was the rich seams of coal in the area that spurred the settlement of the city of Lethbridge. Once the railway came through in the early 1880s, it offered an economical way to ship the high-grade coal to other parts of the country, and the coal-mining industry really took off. The wave of settlement that followed the railway came to southern Alberta, and the new settlers began to farm and ranch. Today agriculture is a major industry, the coal mines now commemorated by plaques along the river valley bottom.

Visitors to Lethbridge can enjoy a variety of cultural offerings, including a symphony orchestra, a summer theatre, and other musical and theatrical performances throughout the year. Whoop-Up Days and Rodeo takes place in late August. This traditional exhibition features a pro rodeo, chuckwagon races, a midway, and a range of baking, crafts, livestock and other displays. It lasts for five days, and offers plenty of fun for all.

Attractions in Lethbridge

Fort Whoop-Up
www.fortwhoopup.com
In Indian Battle Park,
403.329.0444

The park is the site of the last battle between any Native tribes of North America — a battle between the Cree and Blackfoot, fought in 1870. Today the park offers a self-guided tour and other facilities. Fort Whoop-Up is a replica of the fort built in 1869 by American traders of whisky and guns in Lethbridge. The fort now houses interpretive displays and recreations of life in the whoop-up days.

Helen Schuler Coulee Centre
North end of Indian Battle Park, 403.320.3064
This centre offers self-guided nature walks on a variety of trails in the coulee beside the Oldman River, an interpretive centre, and plaques

explaining Lethbridge's colourful coal-mining history. It's also a great place to get up close and personal with the High Level Bridge, a marvel of engineering and one of Lethbridge's most memorable sights. At 1.8 km long, it's the highest and longest steel railway bridge in the world.

Nikka Yuko Japanese Gardens
www.japanesegarden.ab.ca
7th Ave. and Mayor Magrath Dr., 403-328-3511
A tranquil and beautiful place for a walk, these five traditional Japanese gardens symbolize the friendship between Japan and Canada. Kimono'd hostesses (not all Japanese) lead visitors

through the gardens on the half hour, or you can stroll around at your own pace. Open May to October.

Sir Alexander Galt Museum
www.galtmuseum.com
Western end of 5th Ave. S off Scenic Dr., 403.320.4528
This museum, located in a handsome historical building, explores both the coal mining and farming history of the Lethbridge area. Sir Alexander Tilloch Galt (1817-93) was a Father of Confederation. His coal mining company was an early economic driver in Lethbridge.

Southern Alberta Art Gallery
www.saag.ca
601 3rd Ave. S., 403.327.8770

Rodeo!

Rodeo is a classic western sport. While some people object to its apparent cruelty to the animals involved, the events in a rodeo reflect things that do happen on a ranch. A visit to a small-town rodeo can be a fascinating experience. In addition to the rodeo events such as barrel racing, bull riding, calf roping and steer wrestling, there is usually an agricultural exhibit, crafts, baking competitions, and a midway — the ingredients of a real old-fashioned country fair. Some of the rodeos to be found around Alberta are:

- **Coleman**, April
- **Leduc**, May
- **Innisfail**, June
- **Ponoka**, June
- **Medicine Hat**, July
- **Pincher Creek**, August
- **Olds**, August

Lethbridge Area Day Tour

Spend a day around Lethbridge exploring the varied attractions of southern Alberta. Start with a visit to the Alberta Birds of Prey Centre in Coaldale (Tel. 403.345.4262). Just ten minutes east of Lethbridge, this fascinating facility rescues wild birds and rehabilitates them for release into the wild. The birds on display are all native to southern Alberta and Canada, including the endangered species being bred in captivity. Visitors can experience all aspects of the work that goes on at the centre — for example, there are almost always baby birds to be fed — and can learn more about endangered birds.

Drive east along Hwy. 4 to Taber and pick up some corn. Taber corn is famous throughout Alberta for its sweetness and flavour. Turn south onto Hwy. 36 and head to Warner,

home of Devil's Coulee Dinosaur and Historical Museum (Tel. 403.642.2118). See the first dinosaur nesting site found in Canada, complete with embryonic babies. The museum also features paleontological and heritage displays.

Continue past Warner to Milk River and then 32 km east to Writing on Stone Provincial Park (Tel. 403.647.2364). This serene park features sandstone cliffs, hoodoos, grasslands, and the Milk River for paddling and swimming. The name comes from the Blackfoot rock carvings and paintings to be found throughout the park. In summer, there are free daily guided walks to the rock art, as well as interpretive programs. The North West Mounted Police had an outpost here from the late 19th century, and the 1885 building has been reconstructed.

The Frank Slide in the Crowsnest Pass

Discover a changing display of interesting contemporary work by Canadian and international artists.

Crowsnest Pass

The Crowsnest Pass is a series of small towns along the Continental Divide beside Highway 3. Coleman, Bellevue, Blairmore, Hillcrest and Frank were all established as centres for resource extraction, first for logging and later for coal mining. Today the area seems somewhat forlorn, with the impressive exception of the Frank Slide. Highway 3 cuts right through an enormous landslide that took place in the wee hours of April 29, 1903. Much of the tiny town of Frank was in the path of the slide, and 70 people perished. Accounts of this event often seem to include a list of how much, how long, how deep and how wide the rockfall is. Reports vary; everything from 75 million to 91 million tons of rock has been quoted. However, no matter how many numbers you read, nothing prepares you for the sight of this completely devastated area.

To drive through this area is to grasp the incredible power of nature to alter human life. Coal miners toiling deep underground managed to dig their way up to the surface, where they found their world in turmoil. The rocks had fallen across the CPR line and train service was disrupted for days while the townspeople tried to dig out. Remarkably, the coal mine was back in operation within a few weeks.

Visit the Crowsnest Pass in mid-July, when the annual Rum Runner Days take place. (The area used to be a major centre for contraband booze from the States.) The big event is Thunder in the Valley, a massive fireworks exhibit that takes place on the Saturday night.

Attractions in the Crowsnest Pass

Frank Slide Visitor Centre
www.frankslide.com
Hwy. 3, 403.562.7388
Anyone driving through the spooky landscape of the Frank Slide area will be intrigued by the displays at the Frank Slide Visitor Centre. There is also a wealth of information and displays on the

Mormons

The Church of Jesus Christ of Latter-day Saints was begun by Joseph Smith in 1830. After claiming to have received divine instruction, he set out the 13 Articles of Faith, which are the basis of the church today. The church shares many of the Christian beliefs but adds some extra elements, including belief in the Book of Mormon as the word of God. The family is extremely important to Mormons, who have an immense genealogical database in Salt Lake City, Utah.

An interesting Mormon belief (one that contrasts with the more familiar "till death do us part") is that marriage lasts even beyond death if the ceremony is performed in a Mormon Temple. Contrary to popular belief, Mormons do not practice polygamy. Strict observers eschew coffee and tea (and even chocolate), alcohol, tobacco and illegal drugs.

The Mormon faith is very strong in southern Alberta, and the Cardston Temple is just the most visible evidence of this faith.

Musical Ride of the NWMP at Fort Macleod Museum

Head-Smashed-In Buffalo Jump

history and daily life of the area around the turn of the 20th century. Outside, a short trail winds around the rock slide.

Leitch Collieries
www.frankslide.com
Hwy. 3, 403.562.7388
Leitch Collieries, now a provincial historic site, is the ruins of a mine and series of coke ovens. A self-guided tour can be especially atmospheric just at twilight. This was the first wholly Canadian-owned coal mining operation.

Bellevue Mine Tour
www.frankslide.com
Hwy. 3, 403.564.4700
This tour offers a sure cure for any job related dissatisfaction. Don a miner's hard hat and lantern and take a fascinating guided tour into the Bellevue Coal Mine. Listen as the tour guide explains a typical miner's day — each task worse than the last — and breathe deeply of the fresh air as you exit the mine.

Fort Macleod
Fort Macleod was established in 1874 as the first home of the North West Mounted Police, after their 800-mile journey west. The town of Fort Macleod today still has a real frontier feel to it, with its wide streets and flat-fronted buildings. In fact, the downtown is a provincially designated heritage area with over 30 historic buildings to discover, and is quite a pleasant place to stroll around.

Attractions in or near Fort Macleod

Fort Macleod Museum
www.nwmpmuseum.com
219 25th St., 403.553.4703
Costumed interpreters re-enact life as it was around the

The North West Mounted Police

After the Canadian government's purchase of Rupert's Land from the Hudson's Bay Company in 1870, the west had been infiltrated by American whisky traders and was in some disarray. In 1873, Parliament passed an act to create a national police force that would establish order there. By July 1874, the first detachments of the North West Mounted Police began the long journey on horseback west from Manitoba. A few stayed in Saskatchewan to set up there, but the majority continued on towards Alberta and Fort Whoop-Up, the most notorious trading post. When they arrived, the NWMP found the fort largely abandoned, and set about building a permanent post at Fort Macleod.

Over the next years, treaties were signed with the Cree and Blackfoot. The NWMP continued to build forts and to extend their influence over the area, making it safer for settlement. They also kept a watchful eye on the men who poured in to build the Canadian Pacific Railway.

turn of the 20th century in a replica of the original fort in downtown Fort Macleod. In summer there is a daily musical ride (of the North West Mounted Police, so don't expect the current Mountie uniform to make an appearance). Learn about the colourful history of the NWMP.

Head-Smashed-In Buffalo Jump Interpretive Centre
www.head-smashed-in.com
Hwy. 785, 403.553.2731
This superb site was declared a UNESCO World Heritage Site in 1981. It is a monument to the Blackfoot people and their way of life, and is probably the best-known buffalo jump in the world. The Blackfoot had no horses until the mid-1700s. Prior to that, they

hunted buffalo on foot, involving all members of the clan in the process of chasing the buffalo over a cliff to their death. The museum is built into the hillside, blending into the prairie, and is explored from the top down. The buffalo hunt and many other facets of Blackfoot life are explained.

Medicine Hat
Anyone arriving in Alberta along the Trans-Canada Highway will pass by Medicine Hat in the South Saskatchewan River Valley. The name comes from a battle fought between Cree and Blackfoot Indians, in which the Cree medicine man lost his headdress and the Blackfoot won the battle.

Medalta Clay Products Interpretive Centre
www.medalta.org
703 Wood St. SE, 403.529.1070
Medalta Potteries, established in the early 1900s, was the first Western company to ship finished goods back to the east. It enjoyed a heyday in the 1930s when its china was used on all the railways. Today visitors can explore the Clay Products Interpretive Centre and see the "Great Wall of China" featuring a range of Medalta products.

World's Tallest Teepee
Located on the highway, this teepee is a legacy of the 1988 Winter Olympics. Made of steel, it weighs in at 200 tonnes and is 20 storeys high. A stop here allows you to take a self-guided tour of Saamis archeological site, where a buffalo camp was located in the 16th century.

Provincial Parks near Medicine Hat

Dinosaur Provincial Park features colourfully eroded badlands.

Near Medicine Hat, two excellent parks offer very different experiences. Cypress Hills Interprovincial Park is to the southeast, within both Alberta and Saskatchewan. These rolling hills are the highest point between the Rockies and Labrador. Mixed forest and grassland make up this park, which is home to a variety of wildlife. Enjoy the outdoor activities available and learn about the turbulent history of the area on an interpretive hike.

To the northwest, near Brooks, is Dinosaur Provincial Park. This site was declared a UNESCO World Heritage Site in 1979 for its vast deposits of 35 fossilized dinosaur bones from 35 species — more than anywhere else in the world. The rugged badlands in this area are extensive and impressive, although much of the park is off-limits to casual visitors. The best way to experience the park is to participate in the official interpretive program, though there are some self-guided trails as well. The Royal Tyrrell Museum has a field station here, and offers bus tours and guided hikes into the restricted areas. You can also participate in Royal Tyrrell dig programs, helping to extract bones from the fossil beds.

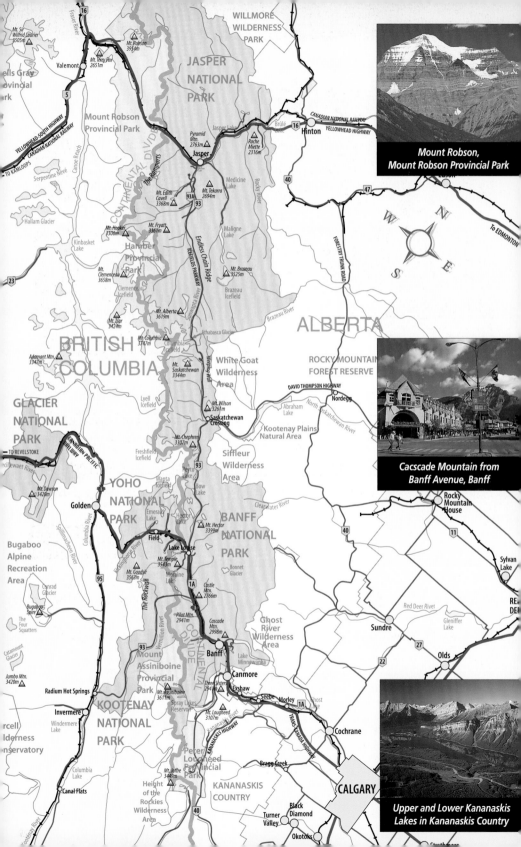

Mount Robson, Mount Robson Provincial Park

Cacscade Mountain from Banff Avenue, Banff

Upper and Lower Kananaskis Lakes in Kananaskis Country

Canadian Rockies

Aerial view of Mt. Assiniboine and Lake Magog

The Canadian Rockies are justifiably world-renowned as a magnificent wilderness preserve. Millions of visitors arrive every year to view the icons of Canada: Lake Louise, Moraine Lake, and the Icefields Parkway. Despite this enormous influx of people, it is very easy, once you step off the beaten path, to find solitude in the mountains. No matter if you are not a hardened backcountry hiker — anyone with a reasonable amount of fitness can enjoy a walk in the area that will instill a sense of the importance of wilderness to the human soul.

The national parks of Banff, Yoho, Kootenay and Jasper comprise the heart of this sublime wilderness and are the easiest areas for most visitors to reach, although the area in which they are contained stretches a vast distance. Together with the neighbouring B.C. provincial parks of Mount Assiniboine, Mount Robson, and Hamber, these seven mountain parks form a UNESCO World Heritage site.

Many histories of the area begin with the settlement by white people, though there is evidence that Native peoples travelled through the area as early as 12,000 years ago. The most recent Native peoples to live in or pass through the Rockies were the Kutenai and the Stoney, who were very familiar with the area. The Stoney began to settle in the foothills in the 18th century. Their original homeland was on the prairies, but in the face of white encroachment ever further west, they began to

Top Ten Sights in the Canadian Rockies

If you only see ten things in the mountain parks, these are the ones not to miss. These natural sights are all easily reached by car, with only minimal walking required:

1) Lake Louise
2) Moraine Lake
3) Takakkaw Falls
4) Spiral Tunnels
5) Emerald Lake
6) Peyto Lake
7) Bow Lake
8) Athabasca Glacier
9) Mt. Edith Cavell
10) Sinclair Canyon

move into the mountains.

After the Natives, the first person known to have seen the Rockies was Anthony Henday, an explorer for the Hudson's Bay Company, who met with a Native group in 1754 near present-day Red Deer. Explorers like Alexander Mackenzie and David Thompson were the first non-Natives to spend extended amounts of time in the Rockies, in the early 1800s. The North West and Hudson's Bay companies continued to head further west into the wilderness, in search of furs.

The Canadian Pacific Railway was the catalyst for the further exploration and eventual development of the Canadian Rockies, especially the Banff and Lake Louise area. The first white person to see Lake Louise was Tom Wilson, in 1882, who was working with the railway surveyors. He was guided to the lake by a Stoney named Edwin Hunter.

In 1883, when the railway tracks were pushing their way through the Rockies, three railway workers were exploring the area near Siding 29 (the site of present-day Banff). They stumbled upon a hot spring bubbling out of the lower slopes of Sulphur Mountain. The canny fellows immediately realized the commercial potential of such a site and took out a title to the land surrounding the spring.

They quickly became embroiled in the first land disagreement in the park's history, as their title was taken over by the federal government and the hot springs became the property of the

Top Things to do in the Canadian Rockies

Hiking

Horseback riding

To really experience the mountains, the best thing to do is go out and play in them. These activities are available in most of the communities through the Rockies, on both the Alberta and the B.C. sides. Ask at local information centres for recommendations on the best outfitters and places to go.

Summer:
1) Hiking
2) Rafting
3) Biking
4) Camping
5) Horseback riding
6) Wildlife watching
7) Fishing
8) Golf

Winter:
1) Downhill skiing or snowboarding
2) Cross-country skiing
3) Dogsled tours
4) Snowshoeing
5) Skating
6) Sleigh rides
7) Tobogganing

Downhill skiing

Cross-country skiing

Cascade Mountain rises behind the town of Banff.

Canadian people. This was the beginning of Rocky Mountains Park, established in 1887, the first national park in Canada and only the fourth in the world at the time. Later, in 1930, it became Banff National Park.

William Cornelius Van Horne, the president of the CPR, realized early on that there was immense potential for tourism in the wilderness. Famously quoted as saying, "If we can't export the scenery, we'll import the tourists," Van Horne proceeded to build several lodges to house visitors to the Rockies, who would naturally arrive by CPR train. The Banff Springs Hotel, opened in 1888, is the most grandiose and lasting result of Van Horne's vision for tourism.

Settlers began to arrive in Banff, drawn to the scenery and to the opportunity to make a good living. Mining was one way of earning a dollar, but many early Banff residents worked in the tourist sector, just as they do today.

Banff

Banff is the most famous settlement in the Rockies. At present, the future of the town in the heart of Canada's first national park is much debated, though its past is storied and full of glamour. Modern Banff is still a small town with only 8,000 permanent residents, but the feeling of the town, especially in summer, is that of a much bigger place. Banff Avenue, the main street, is full of tourists exploring the shops, enjoying lunch or a beer on patios, and admiring the scenery. Cascade Mountain appears to rise straight out of the east end of the avenue — a sight that is captured by thousands of cameras daily.

The town of Banff is a logical place to begin an exploration of the area. There is plenty of accommodation, lots of shopping, and a wide range of restaurants. Compact and easy to walk around in, the townsite is more easily enjoyed without a car, although for exploration outside town, having a car allows much more freedom and flexibility. The local "Happy Bus" runs regularly, for a minimal fee, to all the major hotels (many of which are within blocks of downtown anyway).

Attractions in Banff

Banff Gondola
www.banffgondola.com
Sulphur Mountain,
403.762.2523
One of the most popular attractions in Banff, the gondola whisks visitors up to an altitude of 2,281 m (7,486 ft.), to a lookout near the top of the mountain. Intrepid folks can walk the path that goes higher up to a stone weather station, named in honour of Norman Bethune Sanson, who hiked the trail over 1,000 times in his life to record weather observations.

On a clear day, the 360-degree panorama from Sulphur Mountain is absolutely stunning. A restaurant offers a good lunch buffet (or a cup of tea and a brownie) — an excellent excuse to spend some time up there soaking in the view.

Upper Hot Springs
www.parkscanada.gc.ca/
hotsprings
Sulphur Mountain,
403.762.1515, Canada toll-free
800.767.1611
Just next door to the base of the gondola are the Upper Hot Springs, so named to distinguish them from the original hot springs discovered in 1883, which are further down the mountain at a site called the Cave and Basin.

The Upper Hot Springs offer a chance to bathe in the

warm, steamy water, with a fabulous view of Mt. Rundle and the Spray Valley. A spa also offers massage and hydrotherapy. At the entrance to the springs, you might notice an odour of sulphur, but once you're in the water, the smell is not apparent. It's a good idea to take off any silver jewelry, as it will tarnish instantly in the steam. If you've forgotten your bathing suit, you can rent a vintage bathing costume so you can take a dip.

Cave and Basin

www.worldweb.com/
ParksCanada-Banff/cave.html
311 Cave Ave., 403.762.1566
The Cave and Basin is now a National Historic Site that explains the birth of Canada's first national park. The cave was the discovery of three CPR workers, who noticed steam rising from a vent in the mountain, and descended on a rope to investigate. There is a wonderful stone pavilion and pool at the site, but sadly, the pool is no longer open for bathing. A splendid boardwalk meanders through the runoff from the hot springs, with plaques explaining the unique natural phenomena found there.

The Fairmont Banff Springs Hotel

www.fairmont.com
Spray Ave., Banff, 403.762.2211
Probably Canada's most famous hotel, this towering stone edifice rises up along Spray Avenue a little way out of downtown. The Springs, as the locals call it, is a village unto itself, with a dozen restaurants, numerous shops, and a luxurious spa, as well as over 600 rooms. The view

The Fairmont Banff Springs Hotel and Bow Falls

Take a bite out of Banff

All these restaurants are stalwarts of Banff and will offer you a memorable dining experience:

- **The Beaujolais**, 212 Buffalo St., 403.762.2712 – if you want to splurge on fine French cuisine in a somewhat snooty atmosphere
- **Joe Btfsplk's**, 221 Banff Ave., 403.762.5529 – a 50's style diner with loud decor and great burgers
- **Earl's**, 229 Banff Ave., 403.762.4414 – part of a western restaurant chain, Earl's offers a mix of cooking styles and consistently good food — and amazingly perky wait staff
- **Giorgio's Trattoria**, 219 Banff Ave., 403.762.5114 – delicious and reasonably

priced Italian cuisine
- **Bumper's**, 603 Banff Ave., 403.762.2622 – They proclaim: "If you haven't been to Bumper's, you haven't been to Banff", and their steak and other meaty dishes are pretty good
- **Wild Bill's Legendary Saloon**, 201 Banff Ave., 403.762.0333 – generous portions of Tex-Mex food, real cowboys, and line dancing
- **The Grizzly House**, 27 Banff Ave., 403.762.4055 – decor that's stuck around 1975 (be warned; smoking is allowed everywhere in the restaurant), but a real experience for fondue — try exotic rattlesnake or alligator, or more usual fare

Minnewanka – "Lake of the Spirits"

Lake Minnewanka

Lake Minnewanka is the largest lake in the Canadian Rockies. The Stoney name means "lake of the spirits". The drive to the lake is a pleasant loop affording several gorgeous views of mountains and water. By stopping at all the points of interest, you can easily spend a half-day or more in this area.

Bankhead
Now a ghost town, Bankhead was set up in 1903 by the CPR. The railway needed a steady supply of coal and wanted to establish its own coal mine at the base of Cascade Mountain. The town thrived on mining, with a population of 1,000 souls at its peak — more than neighbouring Banff. By 1922, however, only 19 short years after its inception, the mine closed due to labour unrest and market instability, and the town was dismantled. Many buildings were moved to Banff or Canmore. Today all that remains are some foundations in the open meadows, an eerie reminder that all human settlement is transitory. This is a lovely spot to take a stroll and enjoy a picnic. Interpretive plaques explain the once-bustling community, yet it's still a stretch to imagine the Bankhead that was.

Lake Minnewanka Boat Tours
www.minnewankaboattours.com
403.762.3473
On a sunny summer day, there is no more pleasant trip than a boat tour of Lake Minnewanka. The glass-enclosed boats cruise several times a day to the end of the 24-km long lake, where the mountains abruptly end, and one can see the foothills and prairie clearly through Devil's Gap.

The immense mountains that surround the lake make for majestic views in every direction. Bears are sometimes spotted from the boats, and bighorn sheep and bald eagles are common sights. During the tour, on the way out, a running commentary provides insight into the history of the lake, and on the way back visitors can enjoy the views in silence (though the guide is always available to answer questions).

Johnson Lake
Enjoy a picnic, a short walk or a swim at this pretty little lake, which is the local swimming hole in summer months. Fishermen have good luck here, too.

Cascade Pits
Despite its rather unattractive name, this area is a great place to while away a summer afternoon, with man-made ponds, firepits with plenty of firewood, and a place for barbecues.

from the deck over the golf course and the Bow River is magnificent. An inexpensive way to enjoy the view is to go in late in the afternoon and order a cocktail in the Rundle Lounge. Guided tours of the hotel are available and offer a wonderful glimpse into the glamour of the early days, when visitors arrived after long train journeys with trunks full of formal clothes and spent the entire summer.

The Banff Springs Snail

This unique mollusc lives in the five mineral springs on Sulphur Mountain, and is not found anywhere else in the world. The Banff Springs snail (physella johnsoni) was discovered in 1926. It is well adapted to living in the harsh environment of the springs, with temperatures from 30-36° C (86-96° F), and lots of sulphur and other unpleasant minerals. In 1997, it was listed as a threatened species due to its rapidly declining numbers.

The snails are quite small, the largest being the size of a corn kernel. Unlike other freshwater snails, their shells coil to the left instead of the right. It's easy to see how, over the years, people have inadvertently stepped on them, disturbed their eggs, or otherwise interrupted their life cycle by disturbing their habitat. If you do see snails, please do not touch them.

This creature's existence is a testimony to the health of the springs, and, more widely, of the national park, and every effort is being made to save it from extinction.

The Whyte Museum of the Canadian Rockies

www.whyte.org
111 Bear St., 403.762.2291
The Whyte Museum offers a permanent display of the history of the Rockies, featuring lots of interesting black and white photographs and other memorabilia. There are also rotating exhibits that vary widely, from contemporary Tibetan art to historic botanical watercolours. The Whyte is a great place to learn about the settlement of Banff, while taking one of its historic walking tours or heritage homes tours. The archives are impressive, with an extensive collection of photos, books and journals that illuminate the social history of the area.

The Luxton Museum of the Plains Indian

http://collections.ic.gc.ca/luxton
1 Birch Ave., 403.762.2388
This museum offers a look at a culture whose arrival in the area long predates that of the white folks who settled Banff. The many artifacts and displays illuminate the daily lives of the Plains Indians (including the Blackfoot Confederacy, the Tsuu T'ina and the Stoney) as well as the effects of contact with European settlers. Events like the buffalo hunt, as well as spiritual beliefs, are also explained. Norman Luxton (1874-1962), the museum's founder, had a long and cordial relationship with Natives in the area and for many years was the organizer of Banff Indian Days.

The Banff National Park Museum

www.worldweb.com/Parks
Canada-Banff/museum.html

SuperGuide Recommendations: Banff, Canmore & Lake Louise

Upper Hot Springs in Banff

If you only have a day in Banff, Canmore and Lake Louise (poor you!):

1) Pick up a lunch-to-go in Canmore at Crazyweed Kitchen or Bella Crusta
2) Banff National Park: Tunnel Mountain Drive
3) The Fairmont Banff Springs Hotel
4) Sulphur Mountain Gondola
5) Picnic lunch at Johnston Canyon
6) Drive the 1A Highway to Lake Louise (watch for bear jams)
7) Moraine Lake
8) Lake Louise
9) Dinner at Baker Creek

If you have two days:
Day 1
1) Spend a morning exploring Canmore, with its charming galleries and shops
2) Spend the afternoon in Banff (Tunnel Mountain Drive, Banff Springs Hotel, Sulphur Mountain Gondola)
3) Stroll Banff Avenue and do some shopping

4) Take a walk along the Fenland Trail
5) Dinner in Banff
6) Upper Hot Springs after dinner (they're open late and it stays light until 11 p.m. in summer)

Day 2
1) Drive Mount Norquay
2) Take the boat cruise on Lake Minnewanka
3) Drive the 1A Highway to Lake Louise
4) On the way, take a short hike at Johnston Canyon
5) Moraine Lake – rent a canoe to get onto the water
6) Lake Louise – stroll around the lake

If you have three days:
Day 3
1) Take a short hike in the morning (see recommended hikes box on page 93)
2) Horseback ride in Canmore, Banff or Lake Louise
3) Or take the Lake Louise sightseeing lift in the morning
4) Explore Yoho National Park: Takakkaw Falls, Emerald Lake, Spiral Tunnels, Field

91 Banff Ave., 403.762.1566
This museum was declared a National Historic Site for its architecture and its displays, which hearken back to a different era of natural interpretation. It features a wide array of wild animals that succumbed to the taxidermist's art. The building itself, built in 1903, is a lovely log structure with an appealing design inside and out, but the animals are so real as to seem a little creepy. (Note: The building was closed in August 2002 due to structural concerns and will remain closed until it can be shored up. It is slated to reopen in the summer of 2003.)

Canada Place
Park Administration Building, 403.760.1338
This interactive museum explores Canadian heritage through the theme of "Canada: its land and people", with four loosely-connected

sub-themes: Connecting Canadians, Protecting Our Heritage, Leaving Our Mark, and Canada Touches the World. This new exhibit is high-tech and lots of fun for kids, and informative for adults as well.

Canadian Ski Museum West
Cascade Plaza, 317 Banff Ave.
While strolling around the mall, you will see many artifacts and displays illuminating the colourful history of skiing in Banff, from 1890 to the present.

Scenic Drives Around Banff

Bow Falls
Just below the Banff Springs Hotel is a road leading to Bow Falls and the Banff Springs Golf Course. Bow Falls is not a high waterfall, but the volume of water pouring over the rocks is quite impressive, especially in early summer when the runoff is at its peak. A loop road runs the length of the fabled Banff Springs Golf Course — take a drive along

here and admire the incredible scenery, or keep an eye out for elk. The course has been a favourite haunt of elk for many years, though the park wardens are now using aversive methods to try to keep them away.

Tunnel Mountain Drive
Start at the eastern entrance to the townsite and follow Tunnel Mountain as it climbs past the campground and past some excellent vantage points of the Bow Valley, the golf course, Mt. Rundle, and then the Banff townsite. Continue to Surprise Corner to see one of Banff's most-photographed sights, then descend the hill into the heart of downtown Banff.

Vermilion Lakes
Vermilion Lakes, at the western edge of town between the railroad tracks and the Trans-Canada Highway, is a series of three shallow lakes framed by jutting Mount Rundle and the Fairholme Range to the east. This area is a common haunt of elk and mule deer (part of the area is closed in spring to protect elk cows and their calves) as well as bald eagles and the odd bear. While this

---

Shopping: Banff

The main activity in the town of Banff does seem to be shopping, and it can be a good place to find a bargain, given the low Canadian dollar and the lack of provincial sales tax. If you're after quality outdoor gear, there are some excellent stores in Banff that can outfit you completely. Here are the main places to browse:

- Banff Avenue Shops
- Cascade Plaza
- Bear Street
- Sundance Mall
- Harmony Lane
- Clocktower Mall
- The Fairmont Banff Springs Hotel

Most scenic dining in Banff, Canmore & Lake Louise

1) The Timberline Lodge overlooking Vermilion Lakes, Banff
2) Top of Sulphur Mountain Gondola, Banff
3) Banff Springs Golf Course
4) Canmore Golf Course
5) Sherwood House patio, Canmore
6) Summit Café, Canmore
7) Top of Lake Louise sightseeing lift (lunch and dinner only)

Best places for a drink in Banff

1) Rundle Lounge overlooking the Bow River in the Banff Springs Hotel
2) Margaritas at the Magpie
3) Guinness (or any of 31 other beers on tap) at St James' Gate
4) By the fireplace at the Rose and Crown
5) Martinis at the Aurora

Banff Special Events and Festivals

Banff is host to many athletic and special events and festivals over the course of the year:

May: Mountain FunFest
In early May, Banff can still feel very much like a ski town, with excellent spring skiing at Sunshine Village and Lake Louise. Mountain FunFest, a family event that takes place in the townsite, offers a wide range of activities and performances to attract skiers and non-skiers alike. The intent is to showcase Banff's cultural and natural heritage and history while capturing some of its current energy as well. Everything from guided walks to packhorse racing to a big street dance is on the agenda.

June: Banff Citizens' 10 km and 4 km Race
This running race happens every year on Father's Day. The scenic course goes along the Bow River towards Sundance Canyon.

July 1: Canada Day
Activities include an afternoon parade down Banff Avenue, family events throughout the day, and fireworks at dusk.

July: Banff Arts Festival
During this three-week period in midsummer, a whole range of performers is showcased, from Aboriginal dancers to Shakespeare in the Park. It's organized by the Banff Centre, and most of the events take place on the Centre's various stages.

September: Melissa's Mini Marathon
www.melissasroadrace.com

A Banff tradition for several decades, Melissa's is always a sellout race with over 4,000 competitors. There is both a 10-km and a 22-km race. The highlight for many racers is being able to run right along Banff Avenue, with all traffic stopped.

October: Ekiden Mountain Run
A running event inspired by Japanese races, the Ekiden is a marathon relay in five legs that takes place around Tunnel Mountain and the Banff Centre.

October: Wordfest
www.wordfest.com
This celebration of the written and spoken word takes place at the Banff Centre. It's a lively event, featuring well-known novelists, poets, and other literary types from Canada and abroad.

Banff Mountain Festivals

The Banff Centre hosts many of the events of the Festivals.

Banff Mountain Festivals
These three overlapping festivals take place every year around the end of October. Together they form a celebration of mountains and the mountain lifestyle, and attract renowned climbers, writers, speakers and performers from all around the world. It's possible to purchase a passport for all three festivals, inclusive tickets for all events of only one festival, or to pick and choose among the speakers and events, attending even single presentations.

Banff Mountain Summit:
Three days of lectures, performances, seminars, and exhibitions with a mountain theme. Thought-provoking, fascinating, and inspiring.

Banff Mountain Book Festival:
Three days of readings, speakers, seminars, signings and literary award presentations, all inspired by the mountains of the world. Humour, insight and damn good writing are the hallmarks of this festival.

Banff Mountain Film Festival:
This festival highlights the exploits of the world's adventurers with diverse subjects about expeditions, climbing, and remote cultures. A must for armchair travellers.

Take A Hike in Banff

Mt. Rundle rises above the Vermilion Lakes.

While the townsite of Banff is charming, it's a wonderful idea to head out on a little walk near town to appreciate the surrounding views more fully. For a more complete description of the trails, see Altitude's *Walks and Easy Hikes in the Canadian Rockies*. Here are some places to get in touch with nature near Banff:

Fenland Trail (1.5-km loop). This flat trail goes through the woods near the impossibly pretty Forty Mile Creek, emerging on the Vermilion Lakes road. The trail is closed in late spring, as this is where the mother elk calve.

Bow River Trail. Start at the bottom of Wolf St., near the canoe docks, and take a leisurely stroll along the river until the trail stops a few blocks past the bridge. You can come back the same way or walk along Buffalo St. to admire the large riverside homes.

Tunnel Mountain (1.8 km one way). A short but steep climb to the top of the mountain, which affords beautiful views over town and the Fairholme Range. The "Tunnel" of the name refers to an overeager CPR surveyor who intended to blast right through this small mountain. For your own safety, please stay on the official trail here, as you will come to some dangerous cliffs if you venture too far off the path.

Hoodoos (500 metres one way). Along Tunnel Mountain Drive, this trail leads to some interesting rock formations and splendid views over the Bow Valley.

Bankhead (1.1-km loop). This tranquil path leads through the ghost town of Bankhead near Lake Minnewanka.

Johnson Lake (2.4-km loop). An easy trail around the lake, offering lovely views of Mount Rundle and Cascade Mountain.

Stewart Canyon (1.7 km one way). Park at Lake Minnewanka and follow the wide trail at the end of the parking lot. It mean-

ders through the woods, ending up on a bridge overlooking the canyon and the clear, deep blue-green water. The trail continues past the bridge to the left, following the creek along the canyon, but eventually becomes indistinct.

Sundance Canyon (5.1 km one way). A longer trail that begins at the Cave and Basin and continues along the Bow River into Sundance Canyon, where there is a lovely waterfall. The first section is paved, making it a popular choice for rollerbladers and people with strollers.

Marsh Trail (500-metre-loop boardwalk). This interpretive walk also begins at the Cave and Basin and offers good birdwatching, as well as a chance to learn about the endangered Banff Springs snail, which lives in the hot springs here.

Sulphur Mountain (5.5. km one way). If you're feeling fit and frugal, take this trail to the top of Sulphur Mountain to take in the amazing views. Be prepared for heckling from those in the gondola passing overhead as you make your way up the steep switchbacks, but enjoy the last laugh as you get a free ride back down!

Johnston Canyon (1.1 km to the first waterfall, 2.7 km to the second). A 20-minute drive from Banff along the Bow Valley Parkway, Johnston Canyon is one of Banff's most popular hikes, and for good reason. The trail along engineered catwalks follows Johnston Creek into the canyon, passing two beautiful waterfalls along the way.

appears to be prime moose habitat, moose are actually very rare in Banff National Park. Take a slow drive down here at dusk and admire the reflections if the lakes are calm.

Mount Norquay Road

Take a drive up this curving road towards the parking lot for Ski Banff @ Norquay. Before you come to it, you will see the "bare spot" lookout above town. There is a very good chance of spotting bighorn sheep here, and the views are magnificent.

Culture

Surprisingly, Banff is not all about the outdoors. In fact, it is an excellent place to take in a range of thought-provoking cultural experiences. The major venue is the Banff Centre, but a few smaller galleries are fun to browse in.

The Banff Centre

www.banffcentre.ca
107 Tunnel Mountain Dr., Box office 403.762.6301
The Banff Centre is a unique facility in Canada, encompassing learning, leadership development, mountain culture and the arts. Established over 70 years ago, the Centre is a place where artists of all kinds come to hone their craft, and it's also a busy conference centre. Bow Valley residents can get their cultural fix here without having to drive to Calgary. Year-round, the Centre offers a wide range of innovative programming on several stages, from dance to theatre to world-beat concerts and more mainstream classical and popular music. It's a true mountain gem.

Balanchine Dancers performing at the Banff Centre

Walter Phillips Gallery

Glyde Hall, The Banff Centre, 403.762.6281
This gallery is an interesting place to view contemporary art in many media. A wide range of art is also on display in other locations throughout the Banff Centre — take a stroll through the public buildings to enjoy some.

Canada House

201 Bear St., 403.762.3757, toll-free 800.419.1298
A commercial gallery featuring a wide range of paintings and sculptures, many with a mountain theme. This is a great place to browse.

Winter in the Rockies

While many activities, such as rafting and horseback riding, are not available in winter, the winter season is a wonderful time to visit the Rockies. The mountains capped with snow are almost painfully beautiful against the clear blue winter skies, and the dry air makes cold temperatures a lot more pleasant. Ski season is a busy time of year, but the hordes that throng to Banff in

summer are not in evidence over the winter, and the whole pace of the town is more relaxed and easygoing.

Some years may offer, early in the winter before the snow falls, the most memorable skating you will ever experience. Vermilion Lakes, Johnson Lake, and Two Jack Lake (and sometimes Lake Louise) freeze perfectly glassy and flat. You can look through the ice and see the fish and grasses growing on the bottom through at least a foot of ice. Do not venture out until the ice has frozen completely, for obvious reasons. Skates can be rented in town for very reasonable rates.

Later in the season, public skating is available all winter long on the Bow River below Bow Falls and at Lake Louise.

There are three ski hills in Banff National Park: Lake Louise, Sunshine Village, and Ski Banff @ Norquay. All offer a wide variety of terrain to suit everyone from rank beginners right through to expert skiers. In this day of Disneyfied resort villages, the experience of skiing in the national parks is not to be

Winter at Lake Louise

missed. From the tops of the lifts there is nothing but pristine wilderness and immense amounts of snow as far as the eye can see. It is sublime.

There are also plenty of places to cross-country ski. Head to Canmore for the most challenging terrain at the Nordic Centre, home of the 1988 Olympics and featuring over 70 km of trails. In Banff, there are several trails near the Banff Springs Hotel and golf course. Lake Louise has the Moraine Lake road and Highway 1A, which are closed to vehicle traffic in winter. Rent some skis and give it a try — being out in the snowy woods on skis is a wonderful feeling.

Winter is a great time to enjoy indoor pursuits too: visit a spa, explore the shops in each mountain community, take in the museums. Banff has a movie theatre and waterslides if the weather is really uncomfortable.

One of the simplest pleasures in the mountains in winter is to visit the hot springs at night, whether in Banff or Radium, or even the outdoor hot tub at your hotel. Soak in the hot water as steam rises all around you, and so much the better if it is snowing at the same time or if the stars are shining. It really doesn't get much better than this.

Lake Louise

Surely one of the most beautiful sights in the world, Lake Louise is also one of the most popular places in the Rockies. On any given summer day the atmosphere is like a mini-United Nations, with visitors speaking many languages, snapping photos, and taking in the majestic view of the Victoria Glacier overhanging the impossibly blue-green water. It is a powerful sight despite the busyness. Be sure to spend a little time here — take a walk to the end of the lake and enjoy all the vantage points along the way. It's also possible to rent a canoe for a pleasant hour of drifting over the lake. A visit earlier in the day is recommended for better photography and to avoid the bulk of the crowds.

When Tom Wilson first set eyes on the lake, in 1882, he called it Emerald Lake, but a few years later the lake was rechristened in honour of Louise Caroline Alberta, the daughter of Queen Victoria and wife of Canada's Governor General. (Her name is the source of the province's name as well.) The reaction of the Stoney, who had known Lake Louise as "the Lake of the Little Fishes", is not recorded.

The CPR built the first, rather rustic, lodge here in 1890. It has undergone many additions and transformations over the years, but has always been a retreat for wealthy mountain-lovers. At time of writing, a major conference centre is being constructed behind the Chateau. This has been controversial, but the end result is that the hotel and conference centre are being built and run in a very environmentally aware and sensitive way, in order to have as minimal an impact as possible on this precious site.

Attractions in Lake Louise

The lake is certainly the main attraction here. Those inclined to take a look through the imposing Fairmont Chateau Lake Louise, perched at the side of the lake, should be aware that the upstairs portions of the hotel, including the lobby and picture window areas, are reserved for hotel guests.

Moraine Lake

Just down the road from Lake Louise is the turnoff for Moraine Lake, which is nestled in the Valley of the Ten Peaks. This splendid lake is another must-see in the Rockies, offering more intense blue-green water and a gorgeous setting. Again, take

Canadian Rockies

Bears

Grizzly bear sow and cub

Black bear

No animal stimulates the imagination of visitors to the Rockies more than the bear. While wolves and cougars live in the national parks as well, they are more elusive and unlikely to show themselves. Bears, however, are a common sight along the highways of the national parks, and many visitors are lucky enough to spot either a grizzly or black bear from the safety of their vehicles.

While many people believe bears to be endangered species, both the black bear and grizzly bear are thriving in the Canadian Rockies. They do face real threats to their environment from encroaching development and other interaction with humans, not least from drivers on the roads that lead through the parks. However, their numbers in the wilderness areas of Alberta and B.C., including the national parks, are quite healthy at this time.

Grizzly bears tend to be more feared than black bears,

but the fact is that most bears of either kind prefer to be left to their own devices and only rarely attack humans. Bears are omnivores and will eat almost anything they can find, but the majority of their diet is plant-based.

The difference between a black and grizzly bear is not always easy to spot. Not all black bears are actually black and not all grizzly bears are grizzled. The most prominent feature on a griz is the hump at its shoulders, which makes the bear look taller at the shoulder than at the rump. Grizzlies also have a "dished" face, with a nose that is distinct from the forehead, whereas a black bear's nose comes straight from its forehead in an unbroken line. Finally, a grizzly has more of a ruff under its chin than a black bear. If you are close enough to a grizzly, you might notice that its claws are pale in colour and frighteningly long.

Bear Jams
A bear jam occurs when a number of cars have pulled over to side of the road to observe a bear. It can happen amazingly fast on a busy summer day — all it takes is one car, and then everyone else pulls over to see what they stopped to look at, and before you know it, dozens of cars have stopped. If you do spot a bear, please use caution when pulling over to avoid a collision.

Many people, when seeing a bear feeding alongside the highway, get so excited that they lose their common sense. They will get out of their car and try to approach the bear to take a better picture, or simply to watch the bear more closely. This is a very bad idea, for two reasons. First, it is dangerous. It's just not smart to approach a wild animal that is much bigger than you and could easily kill you if it wanted to. Second, it is dangerous for the bear. The more accustomed it becomes to humans, the more it loses its fear. It may start coming closer and closer to humans and eventually be labelled a "nuisance bear", with a high probability of being relocated from its home range and eventually being destroyed.

So please, for the sake of the bears, do not get out of your car when you see one. Do not attempt to approach or feed them. Even if there is a massive bear jam, and it seems all those around you are ignoring these warnings, use caution when around bears, if not for your own sake, then for theirs.

How about avoiding bears?

When hiking, people generally wish to avoid seeing a bear. Without the protection of a car around them, people feel more vulnerable. While the following precautions are no guarantee of safety, they can offer some peace of mind in bear country:

Make lots of noise. Generally the bear does not want to see you, either, so be sure to give plenty of advance warning. Sing, talk loudly, holler once in a while, clap your hands. Those bear bells sold in many shops in the Rockies are cute souvenirs, but will not do much to alert a bear to your presence.

If you see signs of recent bear activity, leave the area.

When camping, use the food cache sites or lockers provided in the backcountry, or lock everything away in your car. This includes anything with any kind of a scent, from your toothpaste to your barbecue.

Colourful poppies and the turquoise-blue water of Lake Louise

Take a bite out of Lake Louise

From gourmet to more down-to-earth fare, try any of these Lake Louise gems:

- **Laggan's Mountain Bakery and Delicatessen**, Samson Mall, 403.522.2017. This bustling little shop serves up an incredible array of home-baked treats and sandwiches, along with excellent coffee. The wait is worth it at this local institution.
- **Peyto's Café at the Lake Louise Alpine Centre**, Village Rd., 403.522.2200. Even those who can afford to spend more would do well to check out this restaurant. Unpretentious and cozy, with huge servings of hearty fare in a relaxed setting, this is a wonderful place any time of day.
- **Deer Lodge**, 109 Lake Louise Dr., 403.522.3991. Fine dining in a historic lodge dating back to 1921 — this is a place to splurge on memorable Rocky

Mountain cuisine in an intimate setting.
- **Lake Louise Station**, Sentinel Rd., 403.522.2600. Dine in the old train station at Lake Louise, which has been lovingly and tastefully restored. For a more memorable experience, have your meal in one of the restored railway cars.
- **Brewster's Dance Barn**, Lake Louise Dr., 403.762.5454. Saturday nights only, the dance barn offers an authentic western experience where you can learn to two-step after a hearty beef barbecue dinner. Nowhere else will your meal make its entrance on a pitchfork! Lots of fun.
- **Post Hotel**, Village Rd., 403.522.3989. Not the place to show up in your sweats after a day of hiking, this gem of a restaurant features 4-diamond dining at its finest, along with a 28,000-bottle wine cellar.

Take a Hike around Lake Louise

Moraine Lake and the Valley of the Ten Peaks

This is an area that deserves more exploration to be fully appreciated. Several short walks make it easy for the visitor to take in some fresh air and fantastic scenery.

Lake Louise shoreline (1.9 km one way). You will not find solitude on this walk, which goes to the "Back of the Lake", a popular mountain-climbing spot, but you will enjoy incredible scenery. Stop and enjoy the views at numerous points along the way.

Plain of Six Glaciers (5.3 km one way). Again, solitude is not the name of the game on this trail, but the stunning views and teahouse at the top make this hike well worthwhile. Be sure to take water and wear sturdy boots. Continuing past the Back of the Lake, the trail begins to climb through a glaciated landscape, with the lake and Chateau becoming ever smaller. From the trail you can see the six glaciers, including a much closer view of the Victoria Glacier.

Lake Agnes (3.4 km one way). While short, this hike is steep, and will take longer than you think! Climbing through thick woods, the trail leads past the small, green Mirror Lake, and on to Lake Agnes, a lovely small lake surrounded by imposing mountains. Photo conditions are best here in the morning due to the way the sun moves. Be sure to reward yourself for the hike with a treat from the teahouse (June to October only), but watch out for the critters that might be interested in sharing: cute little Columbian ground squirrels and cheeky whisky-jacks (grey jays).

Moraine Lake shoreline (1.5 km one way). Stroll to the end of the lake, being sure to stop along the way to take in the ever-changing landscape and mood. Be sure not to miss the Rockpile, a short interpretive trail right near the parking lot, which grants you some elevation and great photo opportunities.

Lower Consolation Lake (2.9 km one way). This hike takes you past the outlet of Moraine Lake through a forest and an alpine meadow to a beautiful little tarn. The trail is often restricted to groups of six hikers or more, due to extensive grizzly activity in the area. (There has never been a recorded grizzly attack on a group of six or more people). If your party is smaller than that, there is a system in place where you can sign on with another group to get the required numbers. The rule is strictly enforced; don't try to get around it.

Larch Valley (3.2 km one way). Again, often restricted to groups of six or more, this hike leads through alpine meadows surrounded by mountain peaks, though the views are hard-won through some stiff uphills. Always scenic, this hike is best in early fall, when the larch trees turn golden before losing their needles.

The Three Sisters near Canmore

time here to stroll to the end of the lake, to rent a canoe, or to enjoy a treat at the café of Moraine Lake Lodge. (Note: the road to Moraine Lake is open from June to October only. In winter it is a cross-country ski trail, closed to traffic.)

Sightseeing lift
Lake Louise is one of the most famous ski destinations in North America, offering astounding views and one of the longest seasons around. In summer, the Friendly Giant chairlift operates for sightseeing purposes, going halfway up the front face of the ski hill

to some lovely alpine terrain with stunning views over the Bow Valley, Lake Louise and surrounding peaks. Visit the interpretive centre to learn more about the area and how it is a grizzly bear magnet. This is a good jumping-off point for several walks and hikes, and there is a restaurant with a great terrace.

For such a small place, Lake Louise yields up several treasures for shopping and dining. Samson Mall, near the Trans-Canada Highway, has a wonderful bookstore and outdoor gear store, a small grocery store and several gift shops. The Fairmont Chateau Lake Louise has a wide selection of shops in its lower concourse.

Canmore
Built on coal mining, the town of Canmore was for many decades a well-kept secret — for most, at best, a gas stop on the way to Banff, about 20 minutes down the highway. Since it hosted the cross-country ski and biathlon events for the 1988 Winter Olympics, Canmore has gradually evolved into a very charming town with great appeal. Many visitors now use Canmore as a base from which to explore the neighbouring national parks and Kananaskis Country.

As with many of the Rockies communities, the real attraction in Canmore is the huge range of mountain activities. However, it is also a fun place to shop, with plenty of unique stores along Main Street and Bow Valley Trail (where most of the hotels are located). Many artists and

---

Take a bite out of Canmore

Try these local favourites for good food in a relaxed atmosphere:

- **Sherwood House Restaurant & Pub**, 838 8th St., 403.678.5211. At this distinctive log cabin at the end of Main Street, you can choose from a selection of Rocky Mountain specialties, from trout to venison. Excellent pizza as well.

- **Sinclair's**, 637 8th St., 403.678.5370. In a handsome wooden building, this intimate restaurant takes ordinary ingredients and gives them a fresh and innovative twist. There is an extensive wine list.

- **Crazyweed Kitchen**, 626 8th St., 403.609.2530. Unusual and delicious, but has very limited seating. Open for lunch and early dinners only at time of writing.

- **Zona's**, 710 9th St., 403.609.2000. In an old house with a very cozy feel, this restaurant's adventurous menu that will please anyone who appreciates fine food.

- **Chez Francois**, 1604 2nd Ave., 403.678.6111. Don't let the location (in a Best Western hotel) fool you — this French cuisine is exquisite, with an emphasis on fish and other seafood.

Fore! Golf in the Rockies

Golf at the Canmore Golf Course

If you look up "Canadian Rockies" in any golfer's dictionary, the definition is "spectacular mountain golf". Between Kananaskis Country and Jasper are seven world-class golf courses, where it can be difficult to concentrate on your game because the scenery is so breathtaking. Play a round at any of these courses — you won't be disappointed:

- **Kananaskis Golf Course** (two 18-hole courses) 403.591.7272
- **Kananaskis Ranch Golf** (9 holes) 403.673.2700 (May through October only)
- **Canmore Golf Course** 403.678.4785
- **Silvertip Golf Resort** 403.678.1600
- **Stewart Creek Golf Course** 403.609.6099
- **Banff Springs Golf Course** 403.762.4654
- **Jasper Golf Club** 780.852.6090

Take a Hike Near Canmore

Grassi Lakes

Canmore is a great place to go for a walk or hike. Here are a few suggestions:

Riverside trails. Canmore is blessed with a good trail system along the Bow River. You can take as short or long a stroll as you wish, and the trails are flat and well-graded enough for baby strollers. The views here are as lovely as anywhere in the Rockies.

Grassi Lakes (1.75 km one way). Above the town of Canmore, with wide-open views over the valley, this is one of the best hikes in the area. Along the way is a memorable waterfall, and the hike culminates at two pure green cold springs. The cliffs above the lakes, which are part of an ancient marine reef, are a popular place for climbers.

Heart Creek (2 km one way). This walk is a wonderful choice on a hot summer's day, following Heart Creek into a cool canyon. A hidden waterfall is at the end of the hike: heard but not seen. An ideal short walk for families.

Grotto Canyon (2.5 km one way). Follow this canyon to a waterfall that runs year-round. Keep an eye out for pictographs that are painted onto the cliff walls. The age of these drawings is unknown, but they are probably at least several hundred years old.

Two more demanding climbs in the Canmore area are **Mount Lady Macdonald** and **Ha Ling Peak** — both half-day (or longer) trips that top out high above Canmore. If you undertake one of these, you are likely to have rubbery legs by the end, but also a magnificent sense of accomplishment.

artisans live and work in the community, and their work is displayed in several excellent galleries. Canmore is also a terrific place to stock up on outdoor gear and to get groceries before heading into the parks.

Hollywood North

Canmore has been discovered in a big way recently by the movie industry. The town has stood in for numerous other locations (often Alaska) in these recent movies. Have a Canmore film festival one night — while the plots may not stay with you forever, the scenery just might.

Legends of the Fall (1994) – Brad Pitt, Anthony Hopkins, and Aidan Quinn (filmed near Canmore on the Stoney reserve)

Last of the Dogmen (1995) – Barbara Hershey and Tom Berenger

The Edge (1997) – Anthony Hopkins, Alec Baldwin, Elle Macpherson

Wild America (1997) – Jonathan Taylor Thomas and Devon Sawa

I'll Be Home for Christmas (1998) – Jonathan Taylor Thomas

Mystery, Alaska (1999) – Burt Reynolds and Russell Crowe

John Q (2002) – Denzel Washington, James Woods, Robert Duvall

Snowdogs (2002) – Cuba Gooding Jr. and James Coburn

Open Range (for release in 2003) – Kevin Costner, Robert Duvall and Annette Bening (filmed near Canmore on the Stoney reserve)

Attractions in Canmore

Canmore Nordic Centre
403.678.2400

This provincially-run facility is a magnificent legacy from the Olympics, with over 70 kilometres of trails winding below the eastern peaks of Mount Rundle. In summer, the centre provides a spectacular place to mountain bike, offering wide, easy trails for beginners (rentals and lessons are available) and very challenging singletrack for experts. In winter, it is used for cross-country skiing, again with a range of trails to suit all abilities. It sees frequent use both summer and winter as a competitive venue, so on weekends there is often a chance to see some action (as well as participate). There is a free disc (Frisbee) golf course set up here in the summer.

Canmore Festivals and Special Events

Canmore has a good number of festivals and special events happening throughout the year:

January: Winter Festival Celebrate winter with 10 days of fun, featuring in- and outdoor events, anchored by the Rocky Mountain Ski Marathon.

May: Children's Festival www.canmorechildrens festival.com Children of all ages will be delighted by these two days of fun and imagination.

July: Canada Day Parade People come from all over to enjoy the special feeling of small-town Canada Day festivities. The parade is a highlight, with Mounties, marching bands, and the magnificent mountain backdrop at both ends of Main Street. Festivities carry on all day long, and into the evening.

July: 24 Hours of Adrenalin www.24hoursofadrenalin.com The Canmore Nordic Centre plays host to this mountain bike extravaganza — a relay race and festival all in one that's been called the Woodstock of mountain biking.

August: Folk Festival www.canmorefolkfestival.com A tradition for over 25 years, this festival features three days of music from all over the world, in a family-friendly atmosphere.

Labour Day: Highland Games www.discovercanmore.com/highlandgames This is a full day of Scottish events, from sheepdog trials to heavy sports, with a liberal helping of bagpipe bands and highland dancing.

September: Rocky Mountain Half Marathon www.cause.ca/marathon Hundreds of runners turn out for this race, which is run on mountain trails and throughout the town on one of the most scenic courses anywhere.

October: Festival of Eagles Birdwatchers and other nature lovers will appreciate this event, which celebrates the annual migration of the golden eagles that pass high above Canmore in early October.

Canmore Centennial Museum

907 7th Ave., 403.678.2462
This small museum is devoted to the social and geological history of the community. It's staffed by volunteers and open limited hours, but it's a good introduction to the area.

NWMP Barracks

609 Main St., 403.678.1955
The oldest surviving police barracks in Alberta, this small building tells the story of how the North West Mounted Police came to Canmore in 1892. A tearoom offers tea, lemonade and treats through the summer, and the gardens behind the barracks are a lovely place for a picnic.

Jasper

The town of Jasper is smaller and less crowded than Banff, but it offers similarly striking mountain scenery and activities. The town was first settled by whites in 1810, but was little more than a fur-trading outpost and base for exploration until the railway made its way through at the end of the 19th century. For a time, two railways were making tracks for Jasper, but the Canadian National Railway won out. Jasper is still a railway centre, and the only major destination in the Alberta Rockies reachable by regular passenger train. (Service to Calgary and Banff was stopped in the late 1980s.) Jasper is a popular destination for Edmontonians, who regularly make the 3.5-hour drive into the town to play in the mountains.

Things To Do in Jasper

As with all the mountain communities, Jasper is a place where you can enjoy many different outdoor activities and attractions. Once you have explored Jasper and area, take the scenic drive one hour west to Mount Robson Provincial Park in B.C. to see the highest peak in the Canadian Rockies.

Attractions in Jasper

Jasper Tramway

www.jaspertramway.com
Whistlers Mountain Road, 780.852.3093
Take this tramway 2,500 metres up Whistlers Mountain for a superb view over the Jasper townsite and the surrounding mountains. If you're feeling energetic, you can hike another hour or so to the very top of the mountain. You may well see and hear hoary

Maligne Canyon

marmots, the "whistlers" for whose piercing cry the mountain is named.

Maligne Canyon

A spectacular gorge located along the Maligne Road, this is a fascinating place to learn

---

Take a bite out of Jasper

Much of the dining is found along Patricia and Connaught Drive, mingling with the majority of the shops in Jasper. There are plenty of interesting places to eat — try some of these:

- **Bear's Paw Bakery**, 4 Cedar Ave., 780.852.3233 – amazing freshly baked treats
- **Mountain Foods and Café**, 606 Connaught Dr., 780.852.4050
- **Fiddle River Seafood Company**, 620 Connaught Dr., 780.852.3032
- **Papa George's**, 406 Connaught Dr., 780.852.3351 – one of the oldest restaurants in town, still serving excellent food

- **Sorrentino's Bistro Bar**, located in the Chateau Jasper, 96 Geikie St., 780.852.5644 – Italian food in a charming atmosphere, with striking large paintings of local sights gracing the walls
- **Becker's Gourmet Restaurant**, 780.852.3535 – inspired gourmet meals with a casual flair
- **The Fairmont Jasper Park Lodge**, 780.852.6052 – several dining outlets, with everything from light and casual fare in Meadows to four-diamond award-winning cuisine in the Edith Cavell.

Take a Hike in Jasper

Spirit Island on Maligne Lake

As with all the mountain communities, Jasper offers a wonderful selection of short hikes and walks:

Old Fort Point (4.5-km loop). Starts with a steep climb, but continues in a gradual descent from meadows overlooking Jasper townsite and Pyramid Mountain. Lovely in the fall when the aspen have turned a golden colour.

Path of the Glacier (1.6-km loop). Up the hill at Mt. Edith Cavell, this walk is one of the most interesting in the area, traversing a harsh landscape scoured out by the Angel Glacier and culminating at a chilly milk-green lake fed by the glacier. Dress warmly, as there is often a wind here. If you're lucky, you may see an avalanche or a piece of the glacier fall into the lake.

Cavell Meadows (3.8 km one way). Branch off from the Path of the Glacier trail after a short while to head into these meadows, which are perched on top of an area once covered in ice. In summer, there is a lovely array of wildflowers and a great view of the Angel Glacier.

Annette Lake (2.4-km paved loop). There is a wheelchair-accessible path around this small lake, which is a popular swimming hole in summer. There is no outlet from the lake — the water disappears underground, as it does from the better-known Medicine Lake.

Maligne Canyon (0.8-km loop). Follow the paved trail to discover the depths of Maligne Canyon. If you feel like a longer hike, it's possible to continue as far as the sixth bridge over the canyon.

Maligne Lake (3.2-km loop). Follow the trail to the Schaffer Viewpoint, where the exploration of the lake by Mary Schäffer's party in 1908 is described.

Pocahontas (1-km loop). Add this short walk to a visit to the Miette Hot Springs for a full day of exploration and enjoyment. The remains of the old mining town that lasted only 11 years are scattered about.

The Whistlers (1.4 km from top of tramway; 9.3 km if you choose to hike up the whole way). On a clear day you can see Mt. Robson, the highest peak in the Canadian Rockies, from the top of Whistlers Mountain. On regular days you can see an amazing array of peaks and valleys from here.

Valley of the Five Lakes (4.6-km loop). Discover five lakes of varying shades of blue and green in this pretty walk that leads through pine and aspen woods.

Lac Beauvert (4-km loop). Near the sprawling Jasper Park Lodge, the paved trail circles the lake and passes by part of the celebrated Jasper Park Lodge golf course. It's not a wilderness trail, but you might spot waterfowl and other wildlife.

about the power of water. This limestone canyon is as deep as 50 metres in some places, and the river rushes along impressively at the bottom. In winter the waterfalls freeze, creating a fantastical icy wonderland. Several bridges cross over the canyon, allowing for good views below. A teahouse is open in summer months.

Medicine Lake

Between Maligne Canyon and Maligne Lake, this is a bit of a mystery lake, as the water levels fluctuate throughout the year due to underground drainage. Sometimes there is no water at all, but when there is, it's another gorgeous photo opportunity.

Maligne Lake

Located an hour's drive from Jasper townsite, Maligne Lake is one of the world's largest glacial lakes, and one of the prettiest sites in the front country of Jasper National Park. There is a popular boat cruise here that goes out to Spirit Island, a small and picturesque spot of land near the end of the lake. You can also rent a canoe or sea kayak to paddle these clear blue-green waters at your own pace. Several hiking trails begin here, and in winter this is a great place to cross-country ski.

Mt. Edith Cavell

The highest mountain visible from the townsite of Jasper, Mt. Edith Cavell looks as if it's been tilted onto its side. A drive up the winding road leads to stunning views of the mountain. Continue for a walk in the alpine meadows near the Angel Glacier to a small milky-green lake.

Mary Schäffer

An intriguing woman, Mary Schäffer (b. 1861) was a widow from a wealthy Philadelphia family, who, in her forties, made several four-month long trips into the wilds of the Rockies north of Jasper with her colleague, Molly Adams. The determined women reached Maligne Lake in 1908, with the help of guides Sid Unwin and Billy Warren, and with directions from Samson Beaver, a Stoney chief. This was a considerable achievement, and one that had defeated several other parties.

In 1911, Schäffer went back to survey Maligne Lake. An accomplished writer, photographer and watercolourist, she published an account of her travels, *Old Indian Trails of the Canadian Rockies* (reprinted in 1980 as *A Hunter of Peace*), which brought her some fame.

Schäffer married Billy Warren in 1915, and settled in Banff, where she died in 1939.

Mary Schäffer with Billy Warren

Jasper Festivals and Special Events

Jasper has a number of festivals taking place throughout the year.

January: Jasper in January
This multifaceted event means two weeks of fun for the whole family. Come to ski, stay a few days, and experience some of the activities and events scheduled to celebrate winter.

August: Jasper Heritage Folk Festival
www.jasper.ca/folkfestival
Every odd year on the August long weekend, Jasper hosts a folk festival celebrating all forms of world music. There is plenty to see and do, as well as wonderful music to delight the senses.

May: Jasper Festival of Music and Wine
This weekend offers a truly inspired combination: musicians from all over the world performing at unique venues around Jasper, and a series of wine tastings. Seminars on both wine and music take place throughout the weekend.

August: Jasper Indoor Professional Rodeo
This is a weekend of country-and-western competition and fun. If you've never been to a smaller rodeo, the atmosphere here will be a real treat.

October: Jasper Root Romp
People come in from all over to challenge themselves on the trails in this tough 10-km race.

Num-Ti-Jah Lodge sits on the shore of Bow Lake.

Miette Hot Springs

www.parkscanada.gc.ca/
hotsprings (May to October)
780.866.3939, toll-free
800.757.1611

These are the hottest springs in the Canadian Rockies. Located within the Fiddle River valley, they are a lovely place to soak and relax. Hiking trails nearby and a restaurant make this an ideal place for a stop between Jasper and Edmonton. Be sure to stop at Punchbowl Falls and the Ashlar Ridge viewpoint on the drive in.

Jasper Yellowhead Museum & Archives

400 Pyramid Lake Rd.,
780.852.3013

Learn about Native history, the fur trade and other elements of Jasper's history at this small museum.

The Den

105 Miette Dr., 780.852.3361

In the basement of Whistler's Inn, this extensive taxidermy display has one of every mammal found in the Canadian Rockies (and a few that aren't, like a pronghorn antelope from southern Alberta). It's a small but fascinating exhibit.

Lake Edith and Lake Annette

In summer, both lakes are popular for swimming, picnics and hiking.

Pyramid Lake and Patricia Lake

Follow Pyramid Lake Road to these two handsome, small lakes. Boat rentals are available at Pyramid Lake, while fishing, hiking and picnics are popular at both sites.

Icefields Parkway

One of the most celebrated drives in North America, the 230 km-long Icefields Parkway connects Lake Louise and Jasper. It traverses a massive wilderness, broken only by a few outposts along the way. In summer it is heavily travelled by visitors for its astounding mountain scenery and opportunities to spot wildlife.

Take the whole day to travel the parkway. There are many stops of interest, a chance to get onto the Athabasca Glacier, and some short but stupendous walks and hikes to be taken. Bring a picnic, warm clothes, and lots of film. Gas and food are available at a few spots.

Parts of this route were an ancient Native trail, but for many years after Banff and Jasper were settled by whites, this area was almost completely impassable, used only by trappers, surveyors and truly adventurous tourists on guided trips. The first person known to have followed the entire route of what is now the Icefields Parkway was Jim Brewster, in 1904.

The first road through the area was built in the 1930s, a Depression-era make-work project. Gangs of workers began in Jasper and in Lake Louise and worked towards each other, meeting up at the "Big Bend" below the Columbia Icefield. The road has not changed substantially since the 1960s, and still follows the spine of the Continental Divide.

Beginning from the Lake Louise end of the parkway, here are the major points of interest along the way. (Recommended travel guides: *The Canadian Rockies: An Altitude SuperGuide* and *The Canadian Rockies Access Map*, both by Altitude Publishing.)

Hector Lake

The first stunning lake along the parkway, ringed by forest with a huge mountain backdrop.

Crowfoot Glacier

An excellent photo opportunity, especially early in the day. Not so long ago, the glacier had three distinct "toes", hence the name. Only two remain, but their blue colour and stunning location on the cliffs above Bow Lake make this a worthwhile stop nonetheless.

Bow Lake

The source of the Bow River and one of the loveliest sights in the Rockies, this lake is a recommended place to stop and take a walk or hike (see hike descriptions below). The red-roofed lodge by the lakeshore is called Num-Ti-Jah Lodge — stop in for a coffee or a browse in the gift shop.

Num-Ti-Jah Lodge

www.num-ti-jah.com
This handsome log and stone building was begun by the Simpson family in 1937. This fulfilled a vow of Jimmy Simpson, a mountain guide and outfitter who camped at Bow Lake in 1898, and who for several decades thereafter dreamed of building a place there. The lodge offers rustic accommodation — no phones or TV in the rooms, which are comfortable and cozy — splendid food, and outdoor activities summer and winter. With its distinctive red roof, it has become something of an icon of the Rockies. Be sure to book well in advance if you want to stay here.

Bow Summit

At 2,067 m (6,780 ft.) this is the highest point of the parkway. An alpine meadow stretches for some distance on either side of the pass.

Take a hike on the Icefields Parkway

Athabasca Glacier from Wilcox Pass

While driving the Icefields Parkway is a magnificent experience in itself, the beauty of the area is even more awesome on foot. Take a short walk or hike to feel it for yourself.

Parker Ridge (2.4 km one way). One of the finest short hikes in the Rockies, allowing relatively speedy access to an alpine meadow. At the top are wonderful glacier and mountain views.

Athabasca Glacier (2 km one way). Park on the same side of the road as the glacier to walk to its toe. The trail is rough, but it's fascinating to see how the ice has receded over the past century.

Wilcox Pass (4.5 km one way). This hike begins with a steep climb that does eventually level out to offer astounding views of the Athabasca Glacier and surrounding mountains. The pass is found in an alpine meadow.

Sunwapta Falls (short). Walk a few hundred feet to view these thunderous falls threading through a limestone canyon. The trail continues past the main falls to more rapids and falls downstream, which are less busy with visitors and very pretty.

Athabasca Falls (short). Follow the trail to these impressive falls that tumble 23 metres through a canyon, with the backdrop of Mt. Kerkeslin above the Athabasca River.

Peyto Lake

Park at Bow Summit and take the short walk to the viewpoint overlooking Peyto (pronounced "Peetoe") Lake far below. This lake has one of the most pronounced colours of any in the Rockies, and its distinctive shape and mountain backdrop are truly captivating.

Mistaya Canyon / Howse Pass

Stop here and take a brief (but somewhat steep) walk to a bridge overlooking the Mistaya canyon, which has been deeply eroded by the effects of water.

Saskatchewan Crossing

The road branches here — Highway 11, the David Thompson Highway, leads east, past some superb mountain scenery and the stunning Abraham Lake, to Rocky Mountain House and Red Deer. Continue north on 93 to reach Jasper.

Weeping Wall

The valley is narrow here, and to your right is the massive cliff face known as the Weeping Wall for its many cascading waterfalls. In winter this is a world-renowned ice climbing location, and the view of the Wall is even more beautiful with the falls all frozen and glistening.

The Big Bend

Here the road begins to climb in earnest en route to the Columbia Icefield. Around this area are a number of impressive waterfalls (Panther Falls, Bridal Veil Falls) and an expansive view back towards the southern part of the parkway. Be sure to stop at both viewpoints.

Icefield Centre

Be sure to stop here, where the glaciers come down nearly to the road in a harshly beautiful landscape. The Icefield Centre has a series of interpretive displays about glaciers and the area.

Brewster Snocoach

www.brewster.ca/attractions/icefield.asp
Take the opportunity to ride the Snocoach, a specially designed vehicle that climbs right onto the Athabasca glacier. It offers a unique perspective on the area, as well as a chance to walk in safety on the glacier ice high above the roadway.

Tangle Falls

This very pretty braided waterfall is visible from the road. People clamber around on the rocks near these falls, and it's a delightful spot to stop for a few minutes.

Stutfield Glacier

An impressive double glacier that covers 900 m (2,950 ft.) of cliffs. It's a lovely sight, though difficult to photograph properly.

Mountain Goats

Mountain goats

Mountain goats (*Oreamnos americanus*) are goat-antelopes that live in the mountains of western North America. They are the most agile creature in the Canadian Rockies, and can often be seen standing comfortably on windswept rocky cliffs where most other animals can't go. This is their protection from predators of all kinds. Their only threat is from golden eagles, who can sometimes swoop down on baby goats and carry them off.

Mountain goats are often seen along the roadways in the Jasper area, licking the mineral salts. In summer they tend to look rather ragged, as they are shedding their warm winter coats. Male and female mountain goats look very similar as both have horns, unlike their bighorn sheep cousins.

Like all wild animals, mountain goats need to be allowed to exist in peace. Please do not approach them or try to feed them.

Goat Lookout

As the name implies, this is a likely place to spot shaggy white mountain goats, which cling to the side of the cliff, licking the mineral salts from the earth. There is also a sweeping view of the Athabasca Valley and the peaks around it.

Kananaskis Country

This area, west of Calgary in the eastern slopes of the Rockies, is less well-known than Alberta's national parks, but is an area of stunning mountain scenery that offers a wide range of outdoor activities. It is a collection of provincially managed lands under various degrees of protection. Some areas are reserved for hikers and other nature lovers, the two major recreation areas being along Highway 40 in the valley of the Kananaskis River, and along Highway 742 (the Smith-Dorrien Trail) in the Spray River Valley. Other areas of Kananaskis are used for logging and oil and gas extraction, and some are open to off-road vehicles.

Previously used for centuries by Native nomadic bands, the Kananaskis Valley was first settled by whites determined to extract its natural resources, coal and timber. German prisoners of war were housed here during WW II, but for many years after that it was an area largely undeveloped for outdoor pursuits, used mainly by Albertans.

In 1988, Nakiska ski hill sprang to the world's attention as the venue for the downhill ski events of the

Take A Hike in Kananaskis Country

Barrier Lake off Highway 40

There are many appealing hikes and walks to discover in Kananaskis Country. Listed here are a few along Highway 742 (the Smith-Dorrien Trail) and several along Highway 40.

Watridge Lake (3.8 km one way). This pleasant walk along forestry roads leads to Watridge Lake, a small, blue-green lake that's an excellent picnic and fishing spot. If you are interested in adding a short distance to the hike, you can see the karst spring, which bursts out of the side of Mt. Shark in a torrent.

Tryst Lake (3 km one way). A beautiful small lake nestled under a striking peak. This hike is best in fall, when the larches are in golden glory.

West Wind Pass (3 km one way). This hike, while not difficult, does involve quite a bit of elevation gain, but the view from the top is worth it. You can see over Wind Valley towards the Bow Valley, and back along the peaks and lakes of the Spray Valley.

Barrier Lake (600 m one way). Follow the trails along this beautifully blue man-made lake to a viewpoint overlooking it.

Wedge Pond (600 m). A short walk around a small, picturesque lake that is a popular fishing hole.

Eau Claire (900-m loop). Stroll though the forest and learn about the logging history of the area on this pleasant self-guided walk.

Canadian Mount Everest Expedition Trail (3 km one way). This route skirts Upper Kananaskis Lake, rising gradually to a viewpoint offering great views over the lake.

Ptarmigan Cirque (2.2 km one way). You will climb a fair bit on this short hike in the Highwood Pass region, but your efforts will be rewarded with splendid views and a colourful alpine meadows filled with wildflowers in July and August.

Take A Hike in Yoho

Takakkaw Falls

Takakkaw Falls (600 m). An easy paved walk along the Yoho River to the base of the falls. You can clamber up the rocks for some way to get closer to the water, but be prepared to get wet from the mist, and do take care on the slippery surfaces.

Emerald Lake (4.8-km loop). This walk around the lake goes through some remarkable vegetation that is totally different on the two sides of the lake. The dry side (the far side from Emerald Lake Lodge), while not exactly a desert, gets much less moisture than the wet side. Both sides have plenty of vegetation, including colourful wildflowers.

Leanchoil Hoodoos (1.6 km one way). This trail, while short, gains plenty of elevation in order to get to the upper viewpoint of these wonderful rock formations. There is also a lower viewpoint that will save your legs if you don't want to climb the whole way.

Wapta Falls (2.3 km one way). A lovely 30-metre-high waterfall along the Kicking Horse River. The hike goes through the forest to come out at a viewpoint above the falls, then continues down to the bottom. Stop off at the midpoint for the best view.

Sherbrooke Lake (2.8 km one way). A steady climb through a flower-filled forest leads up to this delightful lake ringed by mountains.

Laughing Falls (4.6 km one way). This longer walk leads to several branch waterfalls before the main falls and campground. This is an ideal hike for beginning backpackers, as well as a great family day hike. The falls have a very strong flow and are quite impressive.

Winter Olympics. Today, superb summer and winter activities are the main attraction here. There are two ski hills, Fortress Mountain and Nakiska, offering excellent skiing in the winter. In summer, hiking, rafting, horseback riding, golf, climbing and mountain biking are some of the favourite activities in Kananaskis.

At the very least, a three-hour loop drive from Canmore will give you a taste of the magnificent scenery of the area, but if possible, plan to spend more time and get in an activity or two. Be sure to stop at the Kananaskis Lakes, which are very beautiful and much less busy than the lakes in the national parks. Both Upper and Lower Kananaskis Lake are too cold for swimming, but they are wonderful for fishing, boating, picnicking and walking around.

Yoho

Yoho, a small national park, begins where Banff National Park ends, along the Trans-Canada Highway west of Lake Louise, in British Columbia. Some of the most sublime scenery in the world is to be found here, among the 28 peaks over 3,000 m (9,800 ft.). Most visitors take a day to explore the easily accessible sights of Yoho — the "Rock Walls and Waterfalls" that inspire the park's official theme.

Takakkaw Falls

Thundering falls over 250 metres high, these are a truly magnificent sight, especially in early summer when the melt from the unseen glacier above is at its peak. (Note: The road to Takakkaw Falls is closed from October to June, and even in summer is not passable by RVs, due to an amazingly steep switchback section. Those travelling in RVs and trailers must park at the entrance to the road and be shuttled up the hill.)

Emerald Lake

A jewel of a lake first named in 1882 by Tom Wilson, the first white man to see Lake Louise (which he also christened Emerald Lake, confusingly enough). The café here is a wonderful place for a summer lunch.

Natural Bridge

Carved by the Kicking Horse River, this limestone arch over the river could be used as a bridge, though given the turbulence of the water below, you might not want to try (and in any case are prevented from doing so by protective fences).

Spiral Tunnels

The Spiral Tunnels are an incredible feat of engineering, allowing trains to descend the "Big Hill" at a manageable pace. The original grade of the track laid in 1884 was a dangerous 4.5%. Early trains faced a very real danger of gathering too much speed and derailing on the way down, and on the way up a great number of locomotives were needed to push even a small train uphill. Once the tunnels were built, in 1909, the safety of the line was much greater, with a more acceptable grade of 2.2%. Today, a viewing platform allows visitors to watch as trains snake their way through the tunnels. A long train can be seen at

both ends and seems to be going in separate directions.

The Burgess Shale

This highly significant fossil field is a UNESCO World Heritage Site, located high above the town of Field in Yoho. The

vast numbers of fossils here were formed about 505 million years ago in the Middle Cambrian period, when the ancient creatures were buried by periodic mudslides. Many millions of years later, when the mountains were created,

Lake O'Hara

Lake O'Hara

Those who live in the Rockies, or who come here year after year, speak of the Lake O'Hara area with special reverence. This area is one of sublime mountain beauty that really does outshine all others in the Canadian Rockies.

Several members of the Group of Seven spent time here painting the landscape, which has inspired artists for decades. Most visitors may not have a paintbox in hand, but will be equally inspired by the area and the wide range of hiking trails available.

Located some 13 km up an access road off the Trans-Canada Highway, the lake features a lodge and a campground, as well as an Alpine

Club of Canada hut, for those who wish to stay and explore the area for a few days. It is possible to come in for a day of hiking, but access is restricted to those who take the shuttle bus or who choose to slog in on foot. This restricted access protects the fragile alpine environment. If you want to hike in this area, be sure to book your bus access three months in advance by calling 250.343.6433 (March through October only). There are hikes for all abilities here, and sometimes it's enough to sit near the lake and soak it all in — Lake O'Hara is not necessarily for hardcore hikers alone.

the fossils were transported to their current position high on the ridge.

The fossil beds are not open to the general public, but it is possible to take a guided hike with the Yoho-Burgess Shale Foundation (Tel. 250.343.6006) to see them. They offer two hikes — one a strenuous 10-hour trip to the Walcott Quarry, the other a more moderate 6-hour hike to the trilobite beds.

Field

This small community huddled at the base of Mt. Stephen offers some good dining and memorable gift shops. There are B&Bs here, but not much else in the way of accommodation. Field is,

however, a wonderful place to start a longer exploration of Yoho.

Kootenay

Established in 1920, Kootenay National Park was a joint effort of the B.C. government (which donated the land) and the federal government (which built the road that was the first highway to cross the Rockies). Today, a drive through Kootenay reveals splendid mountain scenery, which ends abruptly at the southwestern edge of the park at Sinclair Canyon, near Radium Hot Springs, as the Columbia Valley unfolds. As with the rest of the Rockies, driving through this landscape offers ample rewards,

but getting off the road and onto the trails — and in this case, into the pools — enhances the experience even more.

Radium Hot Springs

www.parkscanada.gc.ca/hotsprings
Hwy. 93, 250.347.9485
The largest of the Canadian Rockies hot springs, Radium's pool is nestled below the highway, cradled by large cliffs that rise up on either side of the highway at Sinclair Canyon. There is a hot and a cool pool here as well as a plunge pool, and spa and massage services are also offered. Bighorn sheep are very frequently seen in the area — please do not feed them.

Take a hike in Kootenay

Friends of Kootenay offers guided walks on selected days through the summer, or you can take to the trails on your own and discover the area at your own pace.

Fireweed (1-km loop). This fascinating short walk leads through the regenerating forest around Vermilion Pass that was scarred by a huge fire, started by a lightning strike, in 1968. Interpretive plaques explain how fire is a natural process that is necessary for forest growth. To walk through this area now, with its profusion of flowers and reburgeoning trees, is a pleasure indeed.

Stanley Glacier (4.2 km one way). This is a longer hike that has some elevation gain and some serious scenic rewards at the end. Climb through the woods (again, regenerating af-

ter the Vermilion Pass burn, and with lots of colourful wildflowers) and enter the hanging valley with Stanley Glacier at its end. A colossal cliff with another icefall/waterfall beckons across the valley, and hoary marmots make their home in the rocks around here.

Marble Canyon (800 m one way). This trail crosses Tokumm Creek seven times, culminating in the waterfall that tumbles 39 metres into a deep plunge pool. The rock that makes up the canyon walls, though not strictly marble, is beautifully layered.

Ochre Beds and Paint Pots (1 km one way). The Paint Pots are some of the prettiest pools to be found in the Rockies, their reddish hues a far cry from the usual blues and greens. The Natives who passed

through the area used the colours from the Ochre Beds for body paint and to decorate their teepees.

Dog Lake (2.7 km one way). Climb through the forest sprinkled with wildflowers — look for the distinctive western wood lily in early summer — to this lake edged with marsh. You may see wildlife along the way, since everything from coyotes to bears is known to frequent the area.

Juniper Trail (4.6-km loop). Hike this loop for views of the Columbia Valley. This hike, striking for how different it is to the Rockies only a few kilometres distant, is well worth the up and downhills. Walk back from the hot springs along the sidewalk through the towering walls of Sinclair Canyon.

Harrison Lake

Canal Flats, Columbia Valley

Little Shuswap

Bald eagle

British Columbia

Orchard near Naramata on Okanagan Lake

T he original inhabitants of this region, going back thousands of years, were Native tribes who lived off the bounty of the land and sea. The coastal nations, in particular, enjoyed easy access to food, which allowed them the leisure time to create wonderful art in the form of carvings, jewellery, and dance.

Spanish explorers first sighted Vancouver Island back in 1774, but it was the English, and the Hudson's Bay Company, who eventually established permanent settlements and colonized the island, while trading for fur with the locals. British Columbia was established as a colony in 1858, and the rush of fortune seekers to the goldfields of the Fraser Valley that same year contributed to the growing population in the new colony.

In 1871, after Prime

SuperGuide Recommendations: British Columbia Interior

1) Fort Steele Heritage Town near Cranbrook
2) Hell's Gate Airtram on the Fraser River
3) Eagle Express Gondola at Kicking Horse, Golden
4) Look for Ogopogo in Lake Okanagan
5) Rent a houseboat and cruise the Shuswap
6) Discover artsy Nelson
7) Take a tour of the small towns of the Kootenays
8) Whistler Village
9) Okanagan wine tour
10) Drive the "Meadows in the Sky" road in Revelstoke

Minister John A. Macdonald promised to link it to the rest of Canada by a transcontinental railway — British Columbia, which by then included Vancouver Island — joined Canada as a province. The Canadian Pacific Railway was completed in 1885, the ceremonial "Last Spike" being driven at Craigellachie, near Revelstoke, B.C.

Today, B.C.'s economy rests on resource extraction — primarily forestry products and mining, with the second-biggest industry being tourism. The province has an incredibly diverse range of landscapes for visitors to discover, offering towering mountains in the east, arid semi-deserts in the Okanagan, and in the west, coastal vistas and rain forests. While many visitors to British Columbia head straight for Vancouver, Whistler or Victoria, the interior of the province is well worth a visit. Those with a keen sense of Canadian history will find the route along the Trans-Canada Highway particularly interesting, as it follows the ambitious route of the Canadian Pacific Railway, the completion of which united the country.

Several main areas of B.C. will be covered in this chapter, moving from east to west. The route along the Trans-Canada Highway from Yoho National Park to Vancouver (including the Coquihalla Highway) is one section. The southeastern part of the province, from the Crowsnest Pass along Hwy. 3 to Vancouver (including Hwy. 93 south) is another, the Okanagan is a third, and Whistler and the Sunshine Coast is the fourth.

Columbia River Wetlands, near Golden

(Vancouver and Vancouver Island have separate chapters of their own, and the Rockies are covered in the preceding chapter.)

The Trans-Canada Highway

Golden

Golden is the first town beyond Yoho National Park. It is

Major A.B. Rogers

Also known as "Hell's Bells" Rogers for his colourful language and personality, A.B. Rogers was the American-born engineer and railway surveyor hired by the CPR in 1881 to devise a route through the Canadian Rockies. He was a tough little man with a huge mustache, and he drove his men hard in the search for this route. It took several attempts to find a suitable one.

Imagine slogging for days on end through the deep forest over high passes, without much idea where you are going, and being disappointed when an apparent route turns out to be a false one. Rogers had this happen several times before he finally became convinced that the pass that now bears his name was the only way through the Selkirk Mountains. The railway soon came through, with the first passenger train only four years later.

The CPR presented Rogers with a cheque for $5,000 for finding the route. He had it framed and refused to cash it, stubborn to the last.

Major A.B. Rogers

an outdoor enthusiast's paradise with a whole range of mountain activities to be enjoyed. The new resort at Kicking Horse has breathed new life into this former logging town in winter, with an aggressive marketing campaign to promote the ski hill. There is still little in the way of tourism development in Golden at present, which will delight those who come to play in the outdoors, and are not interested in glitzy resorts.

Visitors come here for the wonderful activities, which range from mountain biking to tandem paragliding and scenic air tours by small plane or helicopter. A good time to visit is in May, during the Birds & Bears Festival. This is a celebration of the animals that make their home in the Golden area or migrate through in spring.

Attractions in Golden

Eagle Express Gondola at Kicking Horse
1500 Kicking Horse Trail, 866.754.5425
Take in the astounding view from the top of the Dogtooth Range, with views over the Rockies, Purcells and Selkirks. Have a wonderful meal up there as well, in the Eagle's Eye restaurant.

Columbia River Wetlands
Visit Reflection Lake or Moberly Marsh for great views of the Columbia River Wetlands, home to more than 265 bird species and lots of other wildlife.

Golden Golf Club
250.344.2700, toll-free 866.727.7222
Enjoy a round on this scenic but not terribly difficult 18-hole course.

Glacier National Park
This park was established in 1886, and is home to Rogers Pass, the path chosen by the CPR through the mountains, and now also a long climb and descent by car along the Trans-Canada Highway. The drive through Rogers Pass is a testament to the determination of first the railway and later the road engineers. It ascends beneath the shadows of fantastically steep mountains through what is still a daunting, though gorgeous, wilderness. It also passes through numerous sheds and tunnels designed to protect winter travellers from the frequent deadly avalanches that occur here.

Several hiking trails, from short leg-stretchers to longer day and multi-day hikes, offer visitors a chance to get into this sublimely wild landscape. Ask at the Rogers Pass Centre for information on shorter day hikes if you don't intend to venture into the backcountry. The centre also offers interpretive displays about the history of Rogers Pass. Look for the low shed with the sod roof.

Mount Revelstoke National Park
This exquisite small national park, right near the town of Revelstoke, was created in

Take a Hike in Glacier National Park

Hikers in Glacier National Park, with Mt. Sir Donald behind

Hemlock Grove Boardwalk (600 m one way). Discover an old-growth hemlock forest on this short trail, which is wheelchair accessible.

Abandoned Rails Trail (1.2 km one way). Follow the old rail path on a self-guided tour between the summit of Rogers Pass and the Visitor Centre.

Loop Brook Trail (1.6-km loop). Learn the story of how the railway was pushed through Rogers Pass.

Glacier House. Take a short walk past the ruins of this former grand CPR hotel, which closed in 1925.

1914 after considerable lobbying by the local residents, who enjoyed day trips up to the alpine meadows and wanted a road built to the summit to make such outings easier.

The 25-km long "Meadows in the Sky" road was completed in 1927 and is a popular drive for visitors to the area who wish to see the astonishing flowers blooming in the brief mountain summer. There are ten hiking trails to discover here, and most are easily accessible from the Trans-Canada Highway, which runs through the park.

Revelstoke

Revelstoke is a small town with a strong sense of its history. Its roots lie in logging and in the CPR, both of which still drive the economy today. Mining was important for a briefer period after gold was discovered further north. Today, most visitors to Revelstoke come to enjoy the splendid mountain scenery and activities in nearby Mount Revelstoke and Glacier national parks.

A morning can be well spent in Revelstoke exploring the charming downtown around Grizzly Plaza, host to a farmers' market every summer Saturday morning, and discovering the excellent Revelstoke Heritage Railway Museum. Other attractions in the area include the enormous Revelstoke Dam, the 18-hole golf course, and several nearby hot springs.

Revelstoke Heritage Railway Museum

www.railwaymuseum.com
719 Track St. W., 250.837.6060, toll-free 877.837.6060

Revelstoke's Grizzly Plaza

Take a Hike in Mount Revelstoke National Park

Mt. Revelstoke National Park boasts remarkable wildflower displays.

Skunk Cabbage Boardwalk (1.2 km one way). This trail meanders through a swamp that is home to beavers, muskrats and big skunk cabbages (which can get a little smelly late in the summer!).

Meadows in the Sky Trail (1 km one way). A paved trail through a subalpine meadow at the top of Mt. Revelstoke. The long drive up is almost as lovely as this walk, which is at its best from mid-July to September.

Balsam Lake Trail (1.2 km one way). This short walk winds around a pretty lake and through fields of flowers. Go further up the Eagle Knoll Trail for some amazing panoramic views.

Giant Cedars Boardwalk (500 m one way). A short walk amongst trees up to 800 years old.

The Last Spike at Craigellachie was driven by Donald Smith.

This museum tells the story of the Canadian Pacific Railway, without which Revelstoke would almost certainly not exist. Even today, many jobs in the town rely on the railway yards. The museum has a splendid collection of displays related to the building and running of the railway, as well as several railway cars to explore inside and out.

Revelstoke Dam
250.814.6600
Just 4 km outside the city, this enormous dam on the Columbia River offers free tours to visitors in summer, as well as year-round displays about hydroelectric power.

The Enchanted Forest
Hwy. 1, 250.837.9477
This unusual attraction features a nature path and gardens, self-guided swamp tours, and a host of "jolly fairy folk" figurines. It is open from mid-May until late September.

Three Valley Gap
This large hotel west of

Revelstoke on Three Valley Lake features a ghost town with over 20 heritage buildings and a nightly stage show in summer.

Craigellachie
This is the site where, on November 7, 1885, the ceremonial "Last Spike" was driven by Donald Smith, Lord Strathcona, to mark the completion of the Canadian Pacific Railway. There is a cairn here, and a nice little picnic area. Trains still pass frequently, but there is no sign of the gold spike used for the occasion and photo op so long ago.

Sicamous
A busy little town known as the Houseboat Capital of Canada, this is an excellent place to rent a houseboat for several days or a week of cruising Shuswap Lake with a group of friends. If you don't have that much time, take one of the daily two-hour cruises aboard the MV *Phoebe Ann*, or take the longer six-hour cruise that goes to the Narrows, a fascinating little

floating village and mini-mall along the lake.

Salmon Arm
This small town on Shuswap Lake is known for its outdoor activities, especially lakeside ones. Summer is busy here, especially in August, during the Roots and Blues Festival. This excellent three-day outdoor festival features a ton of well-known performers from all over Canada, with a healthy sprinkling of international music and craftspeople. Call 250.833.4096 for information.

Another interesting time to visit Salmon Arm is in October, when over two million salmon fight their way 29 km a day up the Fraser and Thompson rivers to spawn in the Adams River. Visit Roderick Haig Brown Provincial Park, west of Salmon Arm, to learn more about this phenomenon and see it for yourself.

R.J. Haney Heritage Park and Museum
751 Hwy. 97B, 250.832.5243
Learn about the past of the Shuswap region as explained through displays and restored buildings.

Kamloops
Kamloops is situated more or less in the centre of B.C., either on or near most of the major routes that pass through the province, so most visitors will pass through it unless they take the southern route along Hwy. 3. The city lies at the confluence of the North and South Thompson rivers, and its name, from the Shuswap *kahmoloops*, means "meeting of the waters."

During the 1860s gold rush, some Overlanders reached Kamloops by rafting down the Thompson River, but today most visitors arrive by more conventional means — car or railway. Kamloops is where ranching country begins, and the area around the city is arid and semi-desert.

Historically, Kamloops developed around the fur trade, mining, logging and ranching. Some of these activities continue today, but the area is also developing as a tourism destination and as a high-tech hub (along with Kelowna to the south). A good time to visit Kamloops is in August, when a pow-wow is held just outside town. This is an athletic and beautiful gathering.

Other visitors will enjoy the Kamloops Cattle Drive (see www.cattledrive.bc.ca). This is a chance to take part in a real cattle drive — a six-day journey that begins at a specific ranch and crosses the grasslands to Kamloops. Beginners are welcome to participate, and all is provided in the registration fee.

Attractions in Kamloops

Secwepemc Museum & Heritage Park
www.secwepemc.org/museum.htm
335 Yellowhead Hwy., 250.828.9801
On the site of a 2,400-year-old winter village, this interpretive centre illuminates the way of life of the Secwepemc (Shuswap) people, who are native to the area around Kamloops. Visitors can go through a reconstructed winter village or take in musical and theatrical presentations.

Kamloops Museum & Archives
207 Seymour St., 250.828.3576
Learn about the history of the area, from Native culture through to the fur-trading era (Kamloops was founded by the North West Company as a fort and trading post), with an emphasis on social history. The archives and photographs here are especially good.

Kamloops Art Gallery
www.galleries.bc.ca/kamloops
101 - 465 Victoria St., 250.828.3543
Visit this gallery to enjoy work by contemporary Canadian artists, with a special focus on those from western Canada. Located in a brand-new building, itself a work of art, this is one of the largest galleries in the B.C. interior.

Kamloops Wildlife Park
www.kamloopswildlife.org
Hwy. 1 east of Kamloops, 250.573.3242
Discover more than 70 species of exotic and native animals, as well as gardens, a children's area, and a miniature train ride. The local area's desert-like qualities make the exotic animals seem more at home than they do in most Canadian zoos.

Spirit of Kamloops Steam Railtours
www.kamrail.com/index.html
#6 - 510 Lorne St., 250.374.2141
This trip on a 1930s vintage railway car, departing from the restored train station, is a must for train buffs.

Wanda Sue
www.wandasue.bc.ca
250.374.7447
From late June through late September, take a two-hour narrated cruise on the Thompson River on this sternwheeler. The Wanda Sue was built by a local man, George Slack, in his front yard. (It's very seaworthy, though!)

Western Canada Theatre
250.374.5483
This company produces a lively range of theatre, mixing

Gold Fever — The Cariboo Gold Rush

In 1858, word spread of the discovery of gold on the Fraser River, and within months thousands of gold seekers from several nations were on their way into the B.C. interior. The California gold rush had ended not long before, and people were eager for the next big strike. Not all that much gold turned up in the Fraser, but the prospectors kept moving upriver, and in 1862, Billy Barker struck gold on Williams Creek, far north. The town of Barkerville grew to over 10,000 people within a year.

Towns along the more southerly route up to the Cariboo, even those as far south as Yale, benefited from the steady stream of prospectors heading north. The Cariboo Wagon Road was begun in 1862, and travel to the goldfields became much easier than in the early days of slogging through the brush. However, the Cariboo gold rush began to wane only a few years later.

Salmon

To spawn, salmon return to the stream in which they were born.

These delectable fish are visible everywhere in B.C.: in Native art, in the ocean, and far inland. Long an amazingly abundant source of food for Natives, today there are far fewer salmon due to overfishing and the obstruction of their traditional rivers. However, the sight of the annual salmon run is still something magnificent to watch.

Salmon are born in freshwater lakes and rivers, and then move to the ocean (sometimes a journey of several thousand kilometres) to live for several years, after which they return to the same stream where they were born,

to spawn and die. The journey they make back home usually takes place in the fall to early winter. The fish labour back along the same thousands of kilometres — upstream this time — turning a bright red colour along the way. Other animals such as eagles and bears feast on the spent salmon.

B.C. salmon — whether coho, chum, chinook (king), sockeye, or pink — is a true delicacy, especially when freshly caught. The best place to eat salmon is on the coast and around the islands, where the fish are caught in the deep sea.

well-known award winners with more offbeat offerings. They work from both the Pavilion and the Sagebrush theatres; the latter is home to the Kamloops Symphony Orchestra.

Leaving Kamloops and heading west, travellers have several ways to reach Vancouver. The fastest route is the Coquihalla Highway, a high-speed toll road that also incorporates some scenic elements. If you have more time, following the Trans-Canada is a more interesting route, both historically and for the range of things to see along the way.

West of Kamloops on Hwy. 1, the landscape becomes dry and baked-looking, with a real Wild West feel. Cache Creek is a small junction whose major attraction is the Historic Hat Creek Ranch at Hwys. 97 and 99 (Tel. 250.457.9722). The ranch is located on the original Cariboo Wagon Road, where so many hopeful prospectors made their way north in search of riches. More than twenty historic buildings make up this ranch, which was once a stop and staging area for the B.C. Express stagecoach line.

Lytton

Now a quiet, small town at the confluence of the Thompson and Fraser rivers, Lytton was historically a large Native settlement where the salmon were astoundingly plentiful. The first white people to arrive were (naturally) the explorers of the Hudson's Bay Company. (The Thompson River is named for David Thompson.) Lytton now proclaims itself to be the Rafting Capital of Canada, and this is an excellent place to start a rafting trip of a half-day to many days' duration.

Hell's Gate Airtram
www.hellsgateairtram.com
Hwy. 1, 604.867.9277
The evocative name "Hell's Gate" was inspired by Simon Fraser's journals after he journeyed down the Fraser River in 1808, but this area was not officially named until 1913, after a landslide during the building of the Canadian National Railway.

At its narrowest point, the gorge is 35 metres wide, with 900 million litres of water pouring through it every minute. At this point it is

Ginseng — B.C.'s *other* lucrative cash crop

Anyone driving through the B.C. interior along Hwy. 1 will pass ginseng farms, with their strange-looking black tents that protect the plants from the sun. Ginseng root is much in demand in Asian markets and is becoming increasingly popular in the west as a remedy for various troubles and as a general pick-me-up.

Growing ginseng is a potentially lucrative endeavour, but one that requires patience and hard work. The plants need to be shaded, as their natural habitat is deep forest. It takes four years for the plants to mature for harvest. They are then either refrigerated or dried immediately. Since the second planting on the same soil is not thought to be as potent, farmers often plant other crops such as alfalfa and oats where ginseng once grew.

Fraser River Canyon near Lillooet

Simon Fraser

An intrepid fur-trader and explorer, Simon Fraser (1776-1862) became a partner in the North West Company at the age of 25. His mandate was to expand the territory for the company by crossing the Rockies and setting up relationships with the Natives in British Columbia. In central B.C. he founded, between 1805 and 1807, Fort McLeod, Fort St. James, Fort Fraser, and Fort George (now Prince George). He was then assigned the task of finding a route to the Pacific. He set out in May 1808 with a group of about twenty men including two Native guides, to follow what was thought to be the Columbia River to the sea. It turned out to be another river entirely — the one now known as the Fraser River. The journey took 36 days to complete and covered some incredibly dangerous rapids through the Hell's Gate area.

Simon Fraser

On to Vancouver

Fort Langley National Historic Site

After Harrison Hot Springs, the Fraser River valley is broad and peaceful, but there is a sense that this agricultural way of life can't continue in the face of continued expansion of the city. The Trans-Canada moves along past numerous localities that have become bedroom communities for Vancouver. Here are some of the local attractions worth a look.

Kilby Store and Farm,
Harrison Mills
215 Kilby Rd., 604.796.9576
Learn how life was in the 1920s at this recreated store and farm, which features costumed interpreters.

Minter Gardens
www.mintergardens.com
52892 Bunker Rd., Rosedale, 604.792.3799
This is one of B.C.'s most beautiful show gardens, with eleven themed gardens on over 32 acres of land.

Trethewey House Heritage Site
2313 Ware St., Abbotsford, 604.853.0313
This lovely Arts and Crafts-style house has been restored to its 1920s-era splendour. Learn about the history of the area, and explore the grounds.

Bridal Veil Falls Provincial Park, a short and steep trail leads to the base of the falls. This is a great place to walk or have a picnic.

Fort Langley National Historic Site
23433 Mavis Ave., Langley, 604.513.4777
On the site of a 19th century Hudson's Bay Company fort, reconstructed buildings illustrate daily life at the fort and illuminate facets of the local fur trade. It was here in 1858 that B.C. was proclaimed a crown colony of England.

almost completely invisible from the road, so the cable car is the only way to see the churning water below. Amazingly, salmon make their way up this stretch of the river every year, and there are exhibits explaining their progress and the concrete fish ladders that have been installed to make things easier for them.

Yale

Yet another town that has seen busier days, Yale is now a tiny settlement (pop. 200) that was once a gold-rush boom town, considered for the provincial capital. Gold made the town's fortunes — at its peak it had a population of 20,000 — and the construction of the CPR extended its life. The railway's existence erased Yale's importance as a transportation hub, and the town faded away.

Hope

Established as a fort in 1848 by the Hudson's Bay Company, at the strategic confluence of the Fraser and Coquihalla rivers, Hope is still a meeting place today. Three highways now converge here: Highways 1 and 3, and the Coquihalla.

Today there are several attractions in Hope. The town promotes itself as the Chainsaw Carving Capital of the World — well, somewhere had to be — and there are indeed some very innovative chainsaw carvings to be seen, with an astonishing level of detail and skill, done by a local carver. Christ Church, built in 1861, is the oldest church in B.C. still on its original site. The Hope Slide, which is visible from the road, occurred in 1965 when Johnson Peak collapsed, burying Hwy. 3 in up to 79 metres of rock and debris.

Harrison Hot Springs

Located at the base of the Cascade and Coast ranges, Harrison Hot Springs was built around tourism, but has still managed to keep its charm. Harrison Lake is one of the largest lakes in B.C. and the site of the World Championships of Sand Sculpture, which take place every Labour Day weekend. The hotly contested championships involve five days of competition for $40,000 in prize money. The sculptures — truly intricate works of art — stay up until Thanksgiving weekend. If you're visiting in July, take in the Harrison Festival of the Arts, which features a number of musical performances and many other events for all ages. For more information, call 604.796.3664.

Visit the public hot pools on Hot Springs Road at the Esplanade for a scenic dip.

The Kootenays

(including Highway 93 South & the Crowfoot Highway)

Invermere / Windermere Valley

The Invermere area is well-known to Calgarians for the warm waters of Lake Windermere, which is a real summer playground. This is a fine place to get in some beach time, to go waterskiing or jet boating, and to take in the crowds. You will not find much solitude on this lake

Fort Steele

Sam Steele

The legendary superintendent of "D" Division of the North West Mounted Police, Sam Steele (1849-1919) was a massive mustachioed man with a barrel chest. He joined the NWMP at the very beginning and participated in the Great March West of 1874. After setting up forts in Alberta, he was sent west in 1887 from Fort Macleod with a small contingent of troops to establish order in the Kootenay region. The thriving gold rush there was causing the usual troubles, including tension between settlers and Natives — two Kutenai had been accused of murdering two white miners. As police magistrate, Steele weighed the evidence and released the Natives.

Time and again in his career with the NWMP, he demonstrated both firmness and fairness that defused

A young Sam Steele

tensions in volatile situations and usually resulted in justice being served. After he left the Kootenays, he ended up in the Yukon in the heart of the Klondike gold rush, again to restore order. Eventually he resigned from the NWMP and went to fight overseas.

unless you're lucky enough to be staying with someone who has property here, but the beach scene is a lot of fun. Around the area you can find hiking, golf, mountain biking, rafting, fishing, and many other mountain activities.

Panorama Mountain Village
Recently developed into a world-class ski resort with plenty of on-slope accommodation (think Whistler on a smaller scale), Panorama is open all summer for many mountain activities, from biking to golfing to rafting.

Fort Steele Heritage Town
www.fortsteele.bc.ca
9851 Hwy. 93/95, 250.417.6000
This is a reconstructed turn-of-the-20th-century settlement. Fort Steele was founded in 1864 as Galbraith's Ferry. It was a major boom town by the late 19th century as a provisions stop for gold prospectors, and later on for silver, zinc and lead miners. In 1888, it was renamed Fort

Steele in honour of Sam Steele, the legendary NWMP superintendent. However, once nearby Cranbrook was chosen as the route for the British Columbia Southern Railway, Fort Steele went into a steady and irreversible decline.

Today visitors can explore more than 60 restored, reconstructed or original buildings. Costumed interpreters carry out daily tasks such as blacksmithing, bread-baking and ice-cream making. Clydesdale-drawn wagon rides and steam train rides are available through the summer months. There are special events at Fort Steele throughout the year, most with a heritage or historical theme.

Sparwood
A small town almost entirely dependent on coal — there are five mines in the area — Sparwood is home to the world's largest dump truck, visible from Hwy. 3. Visit the open pit coal mine above town to learn more about today's mining industry.

Fernie
Fernie has become one of western Canada's most-hyped ski destinations, justifiably famous for its incredible 9-metre annual snowfall. Until 1998, the ski hill was a favourite of Calgarians — it's only a three-hour drive — but was not so well known elsewhere. When Resorts of the Canadian Rockies acquired the ski hill and began pouring millions of dollars into renovations and infrastructure, an explosion of development hit the base of the mountain.

Extensive marketing for the ski hill has increased public awareness of the destination, but the visitation tends to be concentrated in the area at the base of the mountain, leaving the downtown core to be explored by those in search of something more authentic. It's also much quieter in the summer months, which means better rates on accommodation. While the scenery may lack the grandeur of the Canmore-Banff-Lake Louise area, there are a great deal of summer outdoor activities to choose from.

Fore! Golf in the Invermere Area

There are over a dozen courses to try. These 18-hole courses are all challenging and very scenic:

- **The Springs at Radium**
  250.347.6200
- **Windermere Valley Golf Course** 250.342.3004
- **Fairmont Hot Springs Resort** (2 courses)
  800.663.4947
- **Greywolf at Panorama**
  250.342.6941
- **Eagle Ranch Golf Course**
  250.342.0820

Canal Flats Project

Near the end of the 19th century, an enterprising Englishman named William Adolph Baillie-Grohman devised a plan to link Columbia Lake to the Kootenay River by means of a canal. The idea was to open up the area along the Kootenay River for agriculture and create a north-south corridor linking Golden to Montana. He managed to raise the funds to do this, and the canal was opened in 1889. Unfortunately, there was little traffic. One boat went through in 1894, and the second boat that attempted to pass (in 1902!) got stuck in the lock, essentially ruining the entire canal. By this time, Baillie-Grohman had long since returned to Europe. Remnants of the doomed canal project are still visible today.

Cranbrook

The major town and service centre of the Kootenays, Cranbrook is surrounded by loveliness, though the town itself feels somewhat workaday. Kutenai people were the original historical inhabitants, and Cranbrook was developed in the wake of the discovery of gold and other minerals. Once the town was selected as a stop on the CPR line, it became the transportation and shipping hub for the region, a role it still fills today.

A great time to visit Cranbrook is in July, when Sam Steele Days take place. The five-day party celebrates the life and times of Sam Steele, with a parade, fairgrounds, a rodeo, concerts, and fun family events.

The Cranbrook Pro Rodeo takes place in August at the Wycliffe Exhibition Grounds and features heated competition in all the usual events.

One of Cranbrook's best attractions is the Canadian Museum of Rail Travel, on Hwy. 3/95 (Tel. 250.489.3918). It houses a collection of restored vintage railway cars and accoutrements from the Trans-Canada Ltd., a luxury train built, unluckily, just before the Great Depression. Photo archives and a large model railway round out the exhibit.

Kimberley

The "Bavarian City of the Rockies", Kimberley is a charming little town where the fire hydrants are painted like little people (complete with lederhosen and dirndl skirts). The main street has been turned into the Plaztl, a pedestrian market that is a pleasure to stroll while browsing the shops, most of which are housed in Bavarian-style buildings. Be sure to get a photo of yourself with Happy Hans, Kimberley's ski and suds-loving mascot, and to see Canada's largest cuckoo clock, which also has a Happy Hans emerging on the hour.

Kimberley's history is in mining, and until 2001 a lead and zinc mine sustained the town's economy. Today visitors can ride the Bavarian City Mining Train from downtown to the Mine Interpretive Centre to learn about this massive mining operation.

The train continues around Kimberley Alpine Resort, a blossoming ski resort in winter. There are also numerous summer activities, including a family fun park with a giant slide, go-karts, bumper boats and mini-golf. You can also ride the chairlift to get into the alpine area and see some terrific views. Mountain bikers can take the chair up and then enjoy an exhilarating ride back down to the base.

Creston

A small town surrounded by lush orchards and mountain peaks, Creston is a gardener's dream. Stop in at one of the fruit and vegetable stands along the way to pick up produce as fresh as it gets. Try to time a visit during the May long weekend, when the orchard blooms are at their peak and the town celebrates its annual Blossom Festival, with activities all weekend.

Dancers in the Platzl in Kimberley

Attractions in Creston

Creston Valley Wildlife Management Area
www.crestonwildlife.ca
Off Hwy. 3, 250.402.6900
This protected site is a wetland haven for millions of migratory birds. Over 250 species have been sighted here, and one of the world's largest osprey populations resides here. Visit the interpretive centre to learn about the area, or take a guided walk along the dikes or a canoe

Duck Lake, near Creston

ride through the wetlands to see more.

Kootenay Candle Company Tours
1511 Northwest Blvd., 250.428.9785
Stop in here to see how pure candles are made, and pick up a few for the folks at home.

Columbia Brewery Tours
1220 Erickson St., 250.428.9344
The celebrated Kokanee beer is produced here. There are daily tours, along with tasting afterwards. Be sure to wear closed-toe shoes for the tour.

Kimberley Festivals and Special Events

Kimberley hosts some fun festivals and events every summer:

July: Kimberley International Old Time Accordion Championships
July: JulyFest features tons of family activities and events for five days in late July
September: Kimberley International Folk Festival

Gateway Ostrich Ranch
4628 36th St., Canyon (just south of Creston), 250.428.4000
Drop in to see a 400-pound rooster (male ostrich) at the largest ostrich ranch in B.C. Ostrich is known to be a healthy meat and the rest of the bird is also very useful. Learn about these amazing birds and pick up some ostrich meat or other products, like the fabulous skin-care products available in the gift shop.

Upon leaving Creston, there are two ways to get to Nelson, one of the most attractive small cities in British Columbia. The more scenic route follows Hwy. 3A up the eastern shore of Kootenay Lake and crosses over on a free ferry — the world's longest — from Kootenay Bay to Balfour, and then continues to Nelson. Alternatively, you can go through Salmo and climb over a high pass to arrive in Nelson slightly more quickly. There is more of note along the previous route, which is described here.

Glass House
250.223.8372
En route from Creston to Nelson, you will pass a house constructed of bottles — embalming fluid bottles, to be precise. This attraction is both bizarre and charming, and worth a stop to explore the grounds and house.

Crawford Bay
Crawford Bay is home to a number of artisans and craftspeople, many of whom welcome visitors to their studios. Kootenay Forge (Tel. 250.227.9466, toll-free 877.461.9466) is well-known for their hand-forged home accessories. The North Woven Broom Company (Tel. 250.227.9245) makes brooms by hand in a charming log barn. Barefoot Handweaving (Tel. 250.227.9655), in a straw-bale building by the lake, makes one-of-a-kind woven items. Be sure to visit Fireworks Copper and Glass, and the Forge and Furnace Gallery, also along the same stretch of Hwy. 3A.

Crawford Bay is also home to a small-scale but very fun three-day, somewhat hippie-ish music festival known as the Starbelly Jam. It takes place in July.

Yasodhara Ashram
Kootenay Bay, 250.227.9224
This beautiful retreat will make anyone want to take up yoga. Stroll around the grounds or browse the book-shop, and make plans to come back for a real retreat at this calm and lovely place.

Nelson
A collection of colourful wooden buildings nestled

against the western side of Kootenay Lake against the Selkirk Mountains, Nelson is a thriving and charming small city that is well worth a visit. There are numerous artists and craftspeople living and working in the area, as well as plenty of organic farmers and back-to-the land types, giving the place a bit of a millennial hippie air. With some justification, the town calls itself both the "#1 Small Arts Community in Canada" and the "Heritage Capital of B.C."

Like so many other places in B.C., Nelson has a long history of Native settlement, but it was not founded as a city by white settlers until 1897. The explorers of both the Hudson's Bay and North West companies passed through the area in the early 1800s, and a brief flurry of gold mining began in 1876. It was the discovery of silver and copper that formed the town and created the first rush of wealth and settlement.

Over 350 Victorian-era buildings are listed as heritage buildings. Some are private homes, and others are open to the public. The medieval-style courthouse (1903) is of particular interest, as it was designed by Francis Rattenbury, the architect who designed the Empress Hotel and the Parliament Buildings in Victoria. Stop in at the Visitor Information Centre to get a map, and set out on a self-guided walking tour. There is also a driving tour that allows you to pass by the private homes and admire their exteriors.

Attractions in Nelson

Nelson Mining Museum
215 Hall St., 250.352.5242
Learn about the history of mining in the area and explore the rock, mineral and crystal collections.

Nelson Museum
www.museum.kics.bc.ca
402 Anderson St., 250.352.9813
More mining history, as well as artifacts illustrating daily life in Nelson throughout the years.

Streetcar #23
This restored historic streetcar runs along the waterfront from Lakeside Park to the town centre.

Farmers and Artisans Market
Every summer Saturday morning, this is the place for fresh organic produce and other food and craft items.

Lakeside Park
Hit the beach here and have a picnic, or rent a boat to cruise the lake.

North of Nelson, further up the lake, are several small towns that are worth the detour. The drive itself is spectacular and most people will not mind doubling back. However, it is possible to continue north to Revelstoke and Hwy. 1, or to make a one-day circle tour that includes Nakusp and returns to Nelson.

Ainsworth Hot Springs
250.229.4212, toll-free 800.668.1171
Stop in for a dip at these natural springs inside a cave that borders Kootenay Lake. The water inside the cave is about 40-42°C (104-107° F), but there is also a large pool, with splendid views, where the

Canada's #1 Small Arts Community

In keeping with its artsy traditions, Nelson has several galleries to discover and studios to visit. Be sure as well to check the calendar of the Capitol Theatre (see www.capitol theatre.bc.ca). Originally built in 1927 as a cinema, this restored heritage theatre now hosts live theatre and music, with several performances a month.

Nelson has an opera company, the Nelson Community Opera, and twice a year these talented performers present selected operatic pieces, accompanied by the Nelson Chamber Orchestra.

As well, there are several cultural festivals throughout the summer:

July: Streetfest
www.streetfest.bc.ca
Street performers hit the town for three hectic days of performances, crafts, and community spirit at this excellent festival.

August: Summer Songfest
www.nelsonsongfest.com
Daily vocal performances, for two weeks in late August

July and August:
Nelson Artwalk
During the summer months, experience various galleries and artists' work in downtown Nelson. Exhibits change every month.

Kaslo

water has been cooled to a more comfortable 35-38°C.

Kaslo

By the shores of Kootenay Lake, Kaslo is one of the prettiest small towns in B.C., despite its lumber and mining origins. Like so many other places in the province, Kaslo was a bustling city for a brief period during the silver-mining boom, and has now faded back to peace and quiet. A great time to visit is on the first weekend in August, during the Kaslo Jazz Festival, a three-day lineup of jazz and blues performers (with a few surprises) against the scenic lake and mountain backdrop.

The major attraction in Kaslo is the SS *Moyie* National Historic Site (Tel. 250.353.2525). The oldest surviving paddle steamer in North America, launched on Kootenay Lake in 1898 and retired in 1957, the *Moyie* is open as a tourist attraction, though it no longer plies the waters. It's a very interesting look at the steamer era, filled with displays and artifacts from the time when the boats

were the major link between communities.

Sandon

In 1892, a silver boom caused Sandon to blossom. It was the first fully electrified town in B.C., and more than 5,000 people called it home. The silver ran out, and the town went bankrupt in 1920. Today it is almost a ghost town, reached by a gravel road with astounding views. Visit the original Silversmith Power Plant for a tour (daily in summer, other times by appointment at 250.358.2247).

Another fascinating attraction in Sandon is the Steam Railway Exhibit — a restored railway car housed near the old K&S Railway Station. (The station is a replica of the original, which burned down in 1980). Hard as it is to imagine today, there were once competing railway lines battling to reach Sandon. This story is interpreted at the City Hall and museum. Start a scenic walk along the old narrow-gauge railway that affords some stunning views of mountains, glaciers, wildflowers, and an old mine.

New Denver

A tiny town on Kootenay Lake, New Denver also has a silvery past, but mining is no longer a mainstay of the economy. Today visitors can revisit the boom days at the Silvery Slocan Museum, 6th Ave. (Tel. 250.358.2201), and explore the mining, logging, transportation and social history of the area.

New Denver is the location of the Nikkei Memorial In-

ternment Centre, 306 Josephine St. (Tel. 250.358.7288). This museum commemorates the shabby treatment of Japanese Canadians during the Second World War. Thousands of people were uprooted and relocated to internment camps, their assets seized (and in many cases never returned). The internment camp in New Denver has been maintained as a monument to this shameful episode in Canadian history. There is a Japanese garden at the centre.

Just outside of New Denver, a stunning viewpoint over Slocan Lake is well worth the stop and the brief walk.

Nakusp

North of New Denver (and requiring a return trip along the same route unless your travel plans include continuing north to Revelstoke) is Nakusp, a charming small town on Upper Arrow Lake at the base of the Selkirks. The major attraction here is Nakusp Hot Springs, a nicely-maintained pair of pools near the lake (Tel. 250.265.4528). Visit the Nakusp Waterfront Japanese Garden to enjoy a lakeside stroll at this picturesque location.

The small Nakusp and District Museum, 92 6th Ave. NW (Tel. 250.265.0015) displays artifacts dating from the paddlewheeler era, as well displays on logging, transportation and mining history.

Castlegar

Leaving Nakusp to rejoin Hwy. 3, the next stop is in Castlegar. From here there are several small towns with various attractions.

Castlegar is an excellent location for outdoor activities, but what sets it apart from most other Kootenay towns is its Doukhobor heritage. Today visitors can learn about this interesting Russian Christian sect on a visit to the Doukhobor Village Museum, 112 Heritage Way, Castlegar (Tel. 250.365.6622). The Doukhobors settled in this region in 1908 and lived here for several decades. The museum highlights elements of their culture and way of life, with about 1,000 artifacts on display. Spinning and weaving displays are presented throughout the summer.

Zuckerburg Island Heritage Park, 7th Ave. and 8th St., Castlegar, is a pleasant place to spend an afternoon. Across a small suspension bridge, this park features a number of eclectic items ranging from a Native pit house to a Russian Orthodox onion-dome chapel.

Trail

Located south of Castlegar, Trail is home to the largest lead and zinc smelter in the world. It is not possible to tour the mine itself, but there is an excellent interpretive centre downtown, which explains the processes that happen at the mine. In early May, Silver City Days celebrate the silver-mining history of the town.

Rossland

Just past Trail is Rossland, a community known for its excellent skiing at Red Mountain, and mountain biking in summer. Rossland's mining history is in gold, and Le Roi mine is where most of it was extracted. Take a tour into the mine (which is no longer functioning) and try your hand at gold-panning. The adjacent museum has mining artifacts and mineral samples to admire and to buy.

Rossland Historical Museum also explains mining, as well as many other facets of life in the area, including a display on skiers (Nancy Greene was raised here) and other Canadian athletes.

Osoyoos

Returning to Hwy. 3, the scenery remains pretty and mountainous all the way west towards Osoyoos, although the towns along the way are fairly small. The views begin to change and become decidedly desert-like before Osoyoos.

Located on Osoyoos Lake in the very southern part of the Okanagan Valley, Osoyoos is just about in the United States. The surrounding area is a true desert, with only 25 cm of rain per year, and the weather is so warm that bananas can actually be grown successfully. One of the most interesting attractions is the Desert Centre, on Hwy. 97 north of town (Tel. 250.495.2470, toll-free 877.899.0897). Here visitors can learn about Canada's only desert, and the unique animals and plants that live here, by walking the boardwalk through this eco-

Doukhobors

This dissident group originated in Russia as early as three hundred years ago, with two simple precepts: love God, and love your neighbour as yourself. The name, in translation, means "Spirit Wrestler". These people were persecuted in Russia for their anti-militaristic stance and their rejection of the Russian Orthodox Church. In an effort to settle the North-West Territories, the Canadian government invited them to immigrate to Canada and live communally according to their motto of "Toil and Peaceful Life".

More than 7,400 Doukhobors sailed to Canada in 1899, settling in Assiniboia and Saskatchewan in the North-West Territories. When their refusal to swear an oath of allegiance in fear of military service led to their homestead entries being cancelled, they followed their leader, Peter V.

Central dom of the village

Verigin, to southern B.C. They arrived in the Kootenays in 1908 and began farming successfully, prospering in the rich lands around the Columbia River in the Castlegar area. Their communal lifestyle began to disappear in the 1930s, but there are still descendants of those Doukhobors living in the area who speak Russian and preserve their traditions of peace, activism and holistic living.

Vineyards line a hillside near Osoyoos.

Wine in B.C.

B.C.'s wineries produce a wide range of award winning wines.

B.C. has some of the best climate in Canada for growing grapes — perhaps that's why the province has led the continent in wine consumption for years. There are some wineries on Vancouver Island and in the Gulf Islands, but the majority of the wine produced in B.C. is from the Okanagan. Oliver, a tiny town in the southern part of the valley, is home to more than half these vintners.

A wide variety of excellent wine is produced in the Okanagan. Chardonnay, Pinot Gris, Gewürztraminer, Pinot Blanc and Riesling are the major whites, while reds include Pinot Noir, Merlot, and Cabernet Sauvignon.

Be sure to enjoy some of these fine wines, or better yet, tour a few vineyards to learn more. There are several festivals throughout the year celebrating wine. The Okanagan Fall Wine Festival is the biggest, but there is also an icewine festival in January, a Spring Wine Festival in May, and a summer festival in August. Call 250.861.6654 for more info on the festivals.

logically sensitive area and checking out the displays inside the centre.

Other visitors may prefer to bask at the beach, for the waters of Osoyoos Lake have an average summer temperature that is very comfortable to swim in.

Keremeos

An attractive little town in the Similkameen Valley, Keremeos is known for its long growing season and its wonderful orchards. This is an excellent place to visit in summer and fall when the produce is at its freshest, and it's also gorgeous in spring when the orchards are in bloom. Visit the Grist Mill & Gardens, Upper Bench Road (Tel. 250.499.2888), for a pleasant stop. This flour mill, which dates from 1877, has been lovingly restored and is now an interpretive centre. The mill still functions and it's possible to purchase flour made on-site with some of the original machinery, from wheat grown on the acres surrounding the mill. There are some extensive heritage gardens and orchards as well — altogether it's a lovely place for a walk and a picnic.

Highway 3 cuts right through scenic Manning Provincial Park, climbing almost 1400 metres to Allison Pass. This is a great place to view wildflowers, even from the car. Stop off to walk the Rhododendron Flats Trail, where in early summer you can see these showy flowers in bloom. If you're visiting in July, try the Rein Orchid trail, a 500-m trail that passes by many beautiful orchids and some beaver ponds.

The Okanagan

The Okanagan region has one of Canada's warmest climates, and is known for its extensive orchards, award-winning wineries, and warm lake. Visitors flock here in the summer for the lake sports and festive atmosphere, and usually stock up on peaches, cherries, plums, and apples, as well as berries and other produce, to take home.

Okanagan Lake

Historic O'Keefe Ranch

www.okeeferanch.bc.ca
Hwy. 97, 250.542.7868
At over 20,000 acres, the O'-Keefe Ranch was once among the largest cattle ranches in B.C. It was built in 1867, and is now a historic site with many preserved and restored buildings. Visit the O'Keefe mansion to see how the family lived during the Victorian era. On the first weekend in August, the ranch hosts the Cowboy Festival and Wild West Show — a celebration of the Wild West life, featuring cowboy poets, trick shooting, stagecoach holdups and many other events.

Okanagan Opal

www.opalscanada.com
7879 Hwy. 97, 250.542.1103
The Klinker commercial-grade precious opal deposit was discovered near Vernon in 1991. Visitors can come and dig their own opals here by hand. There is a daily dig fee and whatever you find, you get to keep, up to 2.5 kg of material. Be sure to call in advance to see what you need to bring to enjoy your day to the fullest. Or stop into their gift shop to pick up jewellery or specimens.

Vernon

A charming city at the very top of Lake Okanagan, Vernon has a more relaxed pace than some of the other centres in the Okanagan Valley, while still offering excellent beaches and lake activities. The downtown, with its historic buildings and shady streets, is very pleasant to explore. Kalamalka Lake Provincial Park, just south of town, has an exceptional beach.

Silver Star Mountain offers summer chairlift access to hiking and biking trails, as well as guided trail rides. There is a disc (Frisbee) golf course here as well. Call 250.542.0224 for information.

Vernon has a brand-new state-of-the-art cultural centre and multiplex with a wide variety of performances and events such as hockey games to take in. Call 250.549.7469 for the current schedule.

Kelowna

Located on the shores of Lake Okanagan, Kelowna is the major city in the B.C. interior. With its mild climate, extensive recreational opportunities, and emerging arts and culture scene, this is a very pleasant place to spend a few days. Be sure to keep an eye out for Ogopogo, the creature said to live in the lake.

Natives lived in this area for many centuries before 1859, when a mission was founded here by Oblate Father Pandosy. He planted the first apples and grapes in the region, but could not have foreseen the rosy future of commercial fruit-growing in the area. Within a few decades many orchards were up and running.

Today Kelowna is a very busy summer destination with a wide range of attractions and activities. Take a scenic orchard drive in early May, when the blossoms are at their peak, along Benvoulin, KLO or Casorso roads. A good time to visit is in July, when the annual regatta and Mardi Gras take place around the downtown and lakeside area.

In September, the Dragon Boat Festival (www.kelownadragonboatfestival.com) features races, musical entertainment, and a family area on the lake.

Attractions in Kelowna

Knox Mountain Viewpoint
Drive to the top of Ellis Street to take in a beautiful view of the valley and the lake.

Okanagan Valley Wine Train
250.712.9888,
toll-free 888.674-TRAK
This train tours through the wine and orchard area surrounding Kelowna and includes a meal and entertainment.

Kelowna Art Gallery
www.galleries.bc.ca/kelowna
1315 Water St., 250.762.2226
This gallery features the work of contemporary Canadian artists, as well as some historical works.

Wine in Kelowna

There are plenty of vineyards to explore right in and around Kelowna. It's a good idea to take a tour if you are going to be sampling lots of wines. There are several knowledgeable local tour operators who would be more than happy to do the driving for you!

- **Calona Vineyards**
  250.762.9144,
  1125 Richter St.
- **Cedar Creek Estate Winery**
  250.764.8866,
  5445 Lakeshore Rd.
- **House of Rose Winery**
  250.765.0802,
  2270 Garner Rd.
- **Mission Hill Family Estate**
  250.768.7611,
  1730 Mission Hill Rd.
- **Quail's Gate Estate Winery**
  250.769.4451,
  3303 Boucherie Rd.
- **St. Hubertus Estate Winery**
  250.764.7888,
  5225 Lakeshore Rd.
- **Summerhill Estate Winery**
  250.764.8000,
  4870 Chute Lake Rd.
- **Slamka Cellars Winery**
  250.769.0404,
  2815 Ourtoland Rd.
- **Pinot Reach Cellars**
  250.764.0078,
  1670 Dehart Rd.

Fore!
Golf in the Okanagan

The mild climate of the Okanagan means it's possible to play golf almost every month of the year. These golf courses all offer at least 18 holes of challenge and beauty.

- **Predator Ridge Golf Resort**
  Vernon, 250.542.3436
- **Okanagan Golf Club**
  Kelowna, 250.765.5955
- **Gallaghers Canyon Golf & Country Club**
  Kelowna, 250.861.4240
- **Harvest Golf Club**
  Kelowna, 250.862.3103
- **Kelowna Golf & Country Club**
  Kelowna, 250.762-2531
- **Kelowna Springs Golf Club**
  Kelowna, 250.765.4563
- **Mission Creek Golf Club**
  Kelowna, 250.860.3210
- **Sunset Ranch Golf & Country Club**
  Kelowna, 250.765.7700
- **Shadow Ridge Golf Club**
  Kelowna, 250.765.7777
- **Shannon Lake**
  Westbank, 250.768.4577
- **Ponderosa Golf Course**
  Penticton, 250.768.7839

Wine and Orchard Museums
1304 Ellis St., 250.868.0441
Located in the historic Laurel Packing House, a long wooden shed, these two museums give an admirable introduction to the area and its main economies.

Kelowna Museum
www.kelownamuseum.ca
470 Queensway Ave.,
250.763.2417
Explores the natural and Native history of the Okanagan, as well as the pioneers and early ranching and fruit farming.

Geert Maas Sculpture Gardens
www.geertmaas.org
250 Reynolds Rd., 250.860.7012
See one of the largest collections of bronze sculpture in Canada, many of them created by this Dutch-born artist, at this outdoor gallery, which is open daily from May through October.

Kelowna Land & Orchard Co.
www.k-l-o.com
2930 Dunster Rd., 250.763.1091
This working apple orchard is a delightful attraction, with daily hayride orchard tours, a petting zoo, and of course a farm market selling apples and apple products. They also grow many other fruits, but the dozen or so apple varieties are the heart of this large operation.

Culture
Kelowna has a burgeoning cultural scene. Check out these venues and companies to see what's happening around town.

Rotary Centre for the Arts

421 Cawston Ave.,
box office: 250.763.1849,
toll-free: 866.689.2177
This brand-new facility is the new home of the arts in Kelowna, featuring theatre, studio and workshop space, with many performances and special events taking place on a regular basis.

Kelowna Community Theatre

1375 Water St.,
box office: 250.762.2471,
toll-free: 866.689.2177
This handsome space is the home of both the Sunshine Theatre and the Okanagan Symphony Orchestra (Tel. 250.763.7544). The orchestra presents over forty performances around the Okanagan during its September–May season.

Sunshine Theatre

www.sunshinetheatre.org
250.763.4025
Kelowna's professional theatre company produces several entertaining plays every year. It is also responsible for producing the Kelowna Comedy Festival in late July (www.kelownacomedy festival.com; 250.763.4025). This festival features free performances as well as ticketed events.

Shakespeare Kelowna

www.shakespearekelowna.com
250.470.1818
This is a community Shakespeare company that offers up the Bard with a twist. Their summer production takes place on the Island Stage in Waterfront Park.

Viva Musica Opera

Viva Musica Opera has produced several operas and operettas in recent years, and are responsible for staging the Mozart Festival (www.okanaganmozart festival.com; 250.762.3747), which takes place in July.

Leaving Kelowna and heading further south, Hwy. 97 follows the western shore of Lake Okanagan, offering excellent views of the lake and surrounding area.

Westbank, just outside of Kelowna, blends right into the outskirts of the larger city. One of B.C.'s best-known and most awarded vineyards is here: Mission Hill Family Estate, 1730 Mission Hill Rd. (Tel. 250.768.7611). Visitors can take a tour to see how wine is made, sample some wines, admire the Mission-style architecture, or enjoy a picturesque picnic.

Peachland and Summerland, the next two communities, offer more beaches, orchards and recreational opportunities. In Summerland, hop aboard the Kettle Valley Steam Train, 18404 Bathville Rd. (Tel. 250.494.8422, toll-free 877.494.8424). Learn about the history of the railway and of the area on this two-hour ride through lush orchards above Lake Okanagan.

Penticton

Located between two lakes, Okanagan and Skaha, Penticton is a beautiful small city known by triathletes and climbers all over Canada, if not the world. It's the host of Canada's Ironman competition, which takes place every

Kelowna and Lake Okanagan

year in August, as well as the location of Skaha Bluffs, a popular and challenging climbing spot. Visitors with an interest in neither of these activities will still find plenty to see and do in Penticton, with its wineries, cultural scene, and lakeside activities.

A highlight of Penticton is the historical SS *Sicamous* (1099 Lakeshore Dr. W., www.sssicamous.com; Tel. 250.492.0403), which is the largest remaining original steam paddlewheeler in Canada. Built in 1914, she plied the waters of Okanagan Lake for only 22 years, but now serves as a museum of the steam era.

Walk part of the Kettle Valley Railway — there is plenty of access to it around Penticton, and the views are superb.

A good time to visit Penticton is in early August, when the Peach Festival takes place. This five-day revel includes peach-pie eating contests, a parade, a Miss Penticton pageant, concerts and family events. Call 800.663.5052 for information.

Kettle Valley Railway

The Kettle Valley Steam Railway is a historic way to take in the scenery.

Built in the early part of the 20th century to link the southern interior of B.C. to the coast, this railway turned out to be one of the most expensive ever built, due to its challenging route along the Coquihalla River. It was considered at the time to be essential, as American miners were taking away enormous amounts of the silver being mined in the Kootenays in the late 1880s and 1890s. There was a real threat that if a railway was not built to keep the wealth in Canada, this portion of the country could be taken over by the U.S.

By 1916 the Kettle Valley Railway linked Vancouver to Nelson, passing through Hope, Princeton, Summerland, Penticton, and a multitude of tiny towns in the very southernmost part of the province. It was always expensive to run, and eventually, with more roads and air travel becoming more common, the railway was shut down and the tracks torn up. Today there is only a 16-km section of track remaining, but there are 600 km of railbed to be explored. It's a popular cycling and hiking route.

Icewine

A sweet dessert wine, icewine is created from grapes that have frozen on the vine. It is now produced in Canada in both the Niagara and Okanagan regions, and requires a very special set of circumstances. First, there must be an extended period of frost to freeze the grapes hard, and then they must be harvested at about -8°C. This temperature allows for an extremely concentrated juice to be ex-

tracted, which is then allowed to ferment naturally for several months. It can take a whole vine to produce one bottle, which is why icewine is an expensive treat, but the flavour is well worth all that effort.

Enjoy icewine at many of the local wineries — the Okanagan is one of the world's leading producers of this delicious wine.

Whistler and Sunshine Coast

The drive to Whistler along Hwy. 99 — the Sea to Sky Highway — is almost painfully beautiful. Following Howe Sound inland towards the mountains, this road has irrefutable scenic merit. It is also very busy, narrow, and convoluted, so do drive with care, especially when the weather is poor. Be sure to stop at the scenic turnoffs to enjoy the splendid views.

Attractions of the Sea to Sky Highway

British Columbia Museum of Mining
Hwy. 99, Britannia Beach, 604.896.2233
At the site of what was once the largest copper-producing mine in the British Empire, visitors can now learn about the history of the mining industry on a mine-train tour.

Shannon Falls Provincial Park
Only a few kilometres past Britannia Beach, the huge 335-metre Shannon Falls are visible from the road. It's a short walk to the base of the falls.

Squamish
Known by rock climbers the world over for its challenging routes, Squamish is otherwise known mostly as a town you pass by on the way to Whistler. It is the entrance to the Diamond Head area of the magnificent Garibaldi Provincial Park. Those who stop in to spend time in the Squamish area will find almost unlimited outdoor recreational

opportunities and a slower pace of life than the frenetic Whistler Village can offer.

"The Chief" is a large rock outcropping near Squamish that's an extremely popular climbing spot. A hiking trail leads to the top, with excellent panoramic views of Howe Sound. It's not an easy hike, as there is significant elevation gain, but for those with sturdy knees it's well worth it.

Squamish is known as the bald eagle capital of the world, especially in late fall and winter when the salmon are spawning and the eagles can gorge on fresh fish. Many other birds are resident here as well.

West Coast Railway Heritage Park

93645 Government Rd., 604.898.9336
Take a look at numerous railcars — the largest collection in western Canada — in various stages of restoration in this 12-acre park. Take a ride on the miniature train and stroll around the station.

Whistler

Settled by whites at the beginning of the 20th century, Whistler was for many years an isolated destination, with adventure and fishing lodges, but not much else except for astounding scenery. In 1966, a ski hill was opened at "Garibaldi Whistler Mountain", with a day lodge and a few chairlifts. Twelve years later, construction began on Whistler Village, and in 1980, Blackcomb Mountain opened. Today, Whistler is considered by many to be the number one ski resort in North America. It has an im-

mense amount of varied terrain and a tons of snowfall every year, plus a bustling, if somewhat artificial, village at its base.

In summer, Whistler is still busy with holidaymakers who come to shop, dine, mountain bike, hike and golf. The Whistler Adventure Centre at the base of Whistler Mountain has lots of fun activities for

Nothing to do in Whistler? Try this list!

Outdoor enthusiasts can choose from an incredible range of activities. For more information, contact Tourism Whistler's Activity Centre at 604.938.2769.

- Aerial sightseeing
- ATV tours
- Bald eagle viewing
- Bungee jumping
- Camping
- Canoeing or kayaking
- Fishing
- Glacier skiing
- Golf
- Helicopter hiking, rafting or fishing
- Hiking
- Horseback tours
- Hummer tours
- In-line skating
- Jet boating
- Lake sports (sailing, windsurfing)
- Llama tours
- Mini-golf
- Mountain biking
- Mountaineering
- Paintball
- Sightseeing
- Swimming
- Rafting
- Rock climbing
- Tennis
- Zipline tours

The Sea to Sky Highway

Whistler Festivals and Special Events

Some of Whistler's festivals and special events include:

June: Jazz & Blues Weekend
Whistler hosts a summer weekend of great music from all over the world. There are some indoor ticketed events, but also plenty of free outdoor performances.

October: Oktoberfest
The traditional Bavarian celebration, with lederhosen, oom-pah music, and plenty of beer.

November: Cornucopia Food & Wine Celebration
This is a week-long celebration for learning about and enjoying food and wine, with culinary offerings from the region's most talented chefs, and wine from over fifty B.C. and western U.S. wineries.

Blackcomb Mountain in Whistler

kids and adults, including a luge ride, a climbing wall, a trampoline/bungee, and a trapeze ride. You can also go on a 45-minute horseback tour from here. Many people choose to ride the gondola to the top of Whistler Mountain to take in the stunning views, have a meal in the Round-

Fore!
Golf in Whistler

There are three challenging golf courses to choose from in Whistler, each impeccably groomed, designed by well-known names, and very scenic.

- **Nicklaus North** (designed by Jack Nicklaus) 604.938.9898, toll-free: 800.386.9898
- **Chateau Whistler** (designed by Robert Trent Jones Jr.) 604.938.2092 toll-free: 877.938.2092
- **Whistler Golf Club** (designed by Arnold Palmer) 604.932.3280 toll-free: 800.376.1777

house Restaurant or Steeps Grill, or to continue exploring the high alpine on foot.

Attractions in Whistler

Bear Watching
604.932.3434
There are about fifty black bears living in the Whistler area (not the village so much as the surrounding mountains). Four-wheel-drive bear-watching tours depart twice daily (May through October) with Michael Allen or other researchers. Travel up to about mid-mountain to get a look at up to a dozen bears and their dens and day beds. Learn about these animals and their foraging habits, and assist with important research that will help to protect Whistler's bears in the future.

Whistler Cooking School
www.whistlercookingschool.com
119 4295 Blackcomb Way,
604.935.1848
This cooking school offers day and evening classes under the watchful eye of culinary professionals and talented chefs from the various restaurants around Whistler. Beginners and advanced cooks can hone their skills in a state-of-the-art kitchen in the Whistler Village Centre.

Ziptrek Tours
www.ziptrek.com
604.935.0001
Tour the forest on a zipline, a series of cables and suspension bridges.

Art Galleries
There are more than half a dozen commercial galleries in Whistler, located in some of the major hotels and throughout the village.

Whistler Museum
4929 Main St., 604.932.2019
Drop in to this little museum to learn about Whistler's history, from the early days of the trappers to the present.

Brewhouse Pub
4355 Blackcomb Way,
604.905.BREW
Learn how a microbrewery works on one of their tours, Thursdays and Saturdays at 3 p.m.

Maurice Young Millenium Place (known locally as MY Place)
4335 Blackcomb Way,
604.935.8418
This new venue is host to a series of musical and theatrical performances and special events throughout the year.

Shopping and Dining
Whistler is a fun place to shop, in the three main areas of the village that are set up as small outdoor malls. Everything is pedestrianized, so there's no need to worry about traffic within the shopping areas. Whistler Village, Upper Village and Village North all offer an interesting blend of well-known international chains and independent retailers and galleries. Restaurants are scattered throughout the village and offer a wide range of dining choices. All summer long, buskers and street performers enliven the atmosphere in the village.

VANCOUVER

Horseshoe Bay

WEST VANCOUVER

Cypress Prov. Park

Capilano Canyon Reg. Pk.

Lynn Headwaters Reg. Park

NORTH VANCOUVER

Dempsey Rd.

Cypress Bowl Rd.

99

Caulfeild Marine

Upper Levels Hwy.

Drive

Passage I.

Lighthouse Park

Queens Rd.

29th St.

Lynn Valley Rd.

Lynn Canyon Park

Marine

Welch St.

Pemberton St.

13th St.

Capilano College

Mountain Hwy.

Mt. Seymour Pkwy.

Seymour Hts.

Deep C

Mt. Seymour

Dollarton

99

3rd St.

Dollarton Hwy.

Inlet C

Burrard

Inlet

Stanley Park

English Bay

SeaBus

Cates Pk.

McGill St.

Wall St.

Powell St.

7A

Hastings

Exhibition Park

Confederation Park

St.

NW Marine Dr.

Chancellor Blvd.

Jericho Beach Park

Planetarium & Museum

Parker St.

Holdon Ave.

Sperling Ave.

Curtis

University Blvd.

4th Ave.

Howe St.

BC Place Stadium

Terminal Ave.

1st Ave.

Renfrew St.

Broadway

Canada Way

Duthie Ave.

Lougheed Highwa

BURN

UNIVERSITY ENDOWMENT LANDS

U.B.C.

10th Ave.

16th Ave.

MacDonald St.

King

Arbutus St.

Burrard

Broadway

16th Ave.

Clark Dr.

Commercial St.

Ave.

7

Grandview Hwy.

J Hendry Pk.

22nd Ave.

Kingsway

BC Institute of Technology

Mascrop St.

BURNA

Marine Dr.

Foreshore Pk.

Pacific Spirit Park

SW Marine Dr.

Dunbar St.

33rd Ave.

41st Ave.

West Blvd.

VANCOUVER

Edward Ave.

Oak St.

Cambie St.

Q.E. Park

Main St.

33rd Ave.

Fraser St.

Knight St.

29th Ave.

Victoria Dr.

41st Ave.

Joyce St.

Boundary Rd.

Central Park

1A

Deer L Pk.

Deer L.

Burns Natu

Musqueam IR 2

49th Ave.

St.

Arbutus

57th

99

70th Ave.

Granville St.

49th Ave.

57th Ave.

SW Marine Drive

49th Ave.

54th Ave.

Kerr St.

Patterson Ave.

Imperial

St.

SW Marine Dr.

Edmon

20th St.

Iona Island

Sea Island IR 3

Vancouver International Airport

Mitchell I.

River Rd.

No. 7 Rd.

Fraser R. Park

Byrne

Marine Way

Rd.

STRAIT OF GEORGIA

Sea Island

Grant McConachie Way

Bridgeport Rd.

Cambie Rd.

91

Richmond Freeway

Westminster Highway

91A

Annacis I.

Westminster Highway

RICHMOND

Lafarge

Sturgeon Bank

Granville Ave.

Blundell Rd.

No. 1 Rd.

Railway Ave.

No. 2 Rd.

Gilbert Rd.

No. 3 Rd.

No. 4 Rd.

Williams Rd.

Shell Rd.

No. 5 Rd.

99

River Road

Boundary Bay Airport

Steveston

Steveston Hwy.

Finn Rd.

Woodwards Landing

FRASER

RIVER

Ladner

Lost Lagoon in Stanley Park

Westham Island Rd.

River

River Rd.

48 Ave.

64 St.

72 S

36 Ave.

VANCOUVER

Expressways

Provincial Highways

Arterial Roads

Collector Roads

Municipal Boundary

Built-Up Area

Government Area

Parks

0   2   4km

41B St.

46A St.

34 St.

33A Ave.

36 Ave.

34B Ave.

27B Ave.

28 Ave.

52 St.

56 St.

16 Ave.

Boundary Bay Rd.

12 Ave.

Robson Square

Tsawwassen IR

Tsawwassen

6 Ave.

Vancouver

Downtown Vancouver and Stanley Park

Vancouver is without question one of the world's most beautiful cities. Bordered by the Pacific on one side and the Coast Mountains on the other, the city is a shining gem set amid considerable natural splendour. On a sunny day, it's hard to imagine a better city to live in or visit.

The area around present-day Vancouver and the B.C. lower mainland/Fraser Valley has been occupied by Native people for thousands of years. The people of this region speak a language called Halkomelem and are commonly referred to as Sto:lo ("River People"). They lived well off the bounty of the seas, as well as the Fraser River, which was incredibly full of salmon, and the surrounding forests. The names of the bands, or First Nations, in the immediate vicinity of Vancouver are Musqueam, Tsawwassen, Squamish, Burrard and Coquitlam.

The first Europeans to arrive around Vancouver were Russian traders in the 1740s, followed by the Spanish explorer José Maria Narvaez, who sailed the Georgia Strait in 1791 in search of the Northwest Passage. A year later, British navigator George Vancouver sailed into Burrard Inlet. The name subsequently bestowed on the city indicates that the Spanish gave up their claim to the new area (they were more interested in finding the Northwest Passage than in settling new colonies at that time), and the British claimed it as their own in 1792. Incidentally, Captain Vancouver spent only a day here in the place that was

The Lions Gate Bridge and Downtown Vancouver light up a west coast night.

eventually to bear his name.

A bedraggled Simon Fraser was the first white man to arrive in this area by land, in 1808, after his epic journey down the Fraser River.

The Hudson's Bay Company arrived to set up a trading post, Fort Langley, on the Fraser River near Vancouver, in 1827. There, they traded fur and salmon with the Natives while discouraging widespread European settlement. For the Native groups, contact with traders had both a positive and negative effect. New tools and new wealth made it possible to spend more time on the arts, allowing for a great creative outpouring. But European diseases decimated the local population, who had no immunity to smallpox and influenza. Within a century, the Native population had dropped by 80 per cent.

In 1858, when the Fraser River and Cariboo gold rushes got underway, the area began to be more heavily settled. The gold rush was the major impetus for the proclamation of British Columbia as a crown colony. Prior to this, the borders had been fairly fluid (though always competitive) and the Hudson's Bay Company had ruled the area in a peaceful and profitable fashion, but the British were now eager to protect the natural assets of their territory. In November 1858, mainland B.C. was declared a British crown colony.

All this was happening some 50 kilometres to the east of present-day downtown Vancouver. In 1862, three Englishmen purchased land and set up a brickworks on the shore of Burrard Inlet. The brickworks eventually failed, and for many years the "Three Greenhorns" had a difficult time selling the land for development. In 1867, "Gassy Jack" Deighton set up his Globe Saloon in the same

Beaches of Vancouver

Vancouver boasts of an enormous number of public beaches, so that each neighbourhood has its own access to the sea. Most, though not all, have concession stands and lifeguards. While the Pacific Ocean waters can be chilly, these beaches are packed in summer months. Try one or two during your stay. (Be aware that clothes are optional at Wreck Beach.)

- Jericho
- Locarno
- Spanish Banks
- Wreck Beach
- Kitsilano
- English Bay
- Sunset Beach
- Second Beach
- Third Beach
- White Rock
- Ambleside
- Dundarave
- Cates Park
- Deep Cove

area, which now had several thriving sawmills. The area became known as "Gastown", and two years later was incorporated as the town of Granville.

British Columbia became a province of Canada in 1871, after the federal government promised to build a transcontinental railway that would link the country.

In 1886, Granville was incorporated as the City of Vancouver, and the burgeoning city was selected over Port Moody to become the western terminus for the CPR's transcontinental railway, basically ensuring that Vancouver would be the transportation and business capital of B.C. This was despite a massive fire that had overtaken the

city that same year, razing most of the buildings and requiring a great deal of reconstruction. The first train arrived in 1887.

Vancouver's growth has continued steadily to this day, when it now routinely tops lists of the best places to live in the world. Its profile — and population — have soared since its centenary in 1986, when it hosted Expo 86, the extremely successful international exposition.

Vancouver is best envisioned as a collection of neighbourhoods, each with its own flavour and flair. The neighbourhoods are described more fully below, in the Neighbourhoods and Shopping section.

Attractions

Attractions in Vancouver

Stanley Park
One of Vancouver's greatest blessings is Stanley Park, North America's largest city park and a true oasis near the downtown core. A visit to this park is a must for any visitor.

A day can easily be spent exploring the park, which is over 1000 acres in size. It was set aside as a reserve in 1886 by the far-thinking first city fathers of Vancouver, and officially opened in 1888. Previous to that, it had been used as a military reserve and had also been extensively logged.

Today, a network of trails — actually old logging roads — leads through the forested areas of the park and past some very old cedar and hemlock trees, some as old as 800 years. Walking through these areas feels like being in a real rain forest, a million miles from the urban environment.

The most popular walk in Stanley Park is the seawall, a 10-km paved trail that goes around the circumference of the park. The view shifts constantly along the seawall, looking first at Vancouver's bustling port, then the Lions Gate Bridge, then out to sea, and then back towards English Bay. The seawall is always busy with runners, walkers, rollerbladers and cyclists, so do be aware of who is around you to avoid any collisions.

Train buffs will enjoy a ride on the Stanley Park Miniature Railway, a replica of the CPR train that made the first transcontinental run in 1886. Horse and carriage rides are also available.

Top Things to Do in Stanley Park

1) Check out what's fishy at the Vancouver Aquarium
2) Visit the totem poles at Brockton Point
3) Take in the view of the Coast Mountains from Prospect Point
4) Enjoy some fish and chips from the concession near Lumberman's Arch
5) Run through the waterpark at Lumberman's Arch
6) Keep your eyes open for ducks, geese, raccoons and other wildlife
7) Take in the sunset over a romantic dinner at The Teahouse
8) Stop and smell the roses at the formal Rose Garden, or enjoy the colour of the Ted and Mary Greig Rhododendron Garden
9) Stroll around Lost Lagoon to see trumpeter swans and great blue herons
10) Stroll around the seawall

Joggers on the seawall in Stanley Park

Chinatown

Chinatown stretches along Pender Street between Carrall and Gore Streets, and along Keefer between Main to Gore. This lively area features excellent bargain shopping and authentic Chinese cuisine in every style imaginable. Take a 75-minute historical walking tour organized through the Chinese Cultural Centre to discover the hidden stories of Chinatown. Be sure to look for the skinniest commercial building in the world: the Sam Kee Building at 8 West Pender St. is only six feet wide.

Granville Island

Once a grubby series of warehouses and factories built on reclaimed land under the Granville Street Bridge, Granville Island began transforming itself in the 1970s into one of Vancouver's most interesting destinations. Wander around the large Public Market, with vendors selling everything from homemade pies to fish fresh from the sea, and with a liberal sprinkling of artisans and craftspeople. Buskers and entertainers perform here every day.

A stroll around the outdoor part of the market will reveal a community of artists and artisans working away, a selection of unique shops and galleries, and several performance spaces. The Kids Market is filled with shops catering to the younger set (or to those who like to buy them presents!). On a hot summer day, the free waterpark is a great place to cool down. A newly developed part of Granville Island, called "Railspur Alley", is an excellent place to watch artists and

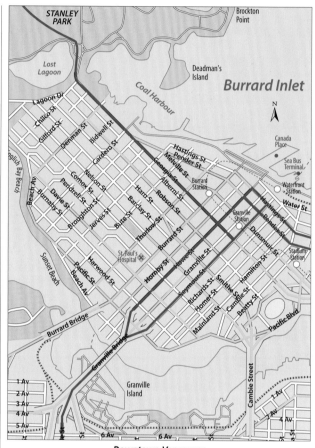

Downtown Vancouver

artisans at work.

Three unique museums in one space offer intriguing displays about Sportfishing, Model Trains and Model Ships. Call 604.683.1939 for info.

The Emily Carr Institute of Art + Design is located on Granville Island. It has several free exhibit spaces filled with students' projects that are thought-provoking and stimulating.

Gastown

The historic heart of Vancouver, Gastown hearkens back to an earlier day, with its cobblestoned streets, Victorian street

lamps, and an antique steam clock. Busy and touristy, it is a cheerful place to visit during the day, only a few blocks from Canada Place.

Science World

www.scienceworld.bc.ca
1455 Quebec St., 604.443.7443
The geodesic dome that houses Science World is a legacy from Expo 86, now converted into a fun, hands-on science museum. Aimed at children, this museum is interesting for all ages, however, and you are bound to learn a few things you didn't know. There is an OMNIMAX theatre within the dome.

Gastown, downtown Vancouver

Science World reflected in False Creek

Vancouver Must-do's

On your visit to Vancouver, be sure to try as many of these as possible, to look and feel like a true Vancouverite:

1) Run along the Seawall in Stanley Park
2) Have a coffee
3) Take the Aquabus from downtown to Granville Island
4) Have another coffee
5) Stroll along Kits Beach (dog not necessarily required)
6) Do the Grouse Grind
7) Have another coffee
8) Visit a gallery or museum
9) Enjoy seafood straight from the sea
10) Carry an umbrella
11) Go as bare as you dare at Wreck Beach
12) Take in live music any night of the week
13) Pretend not to notice if you run into a celebrity

Chinese Immigration

Vancouver is a city that has always appealed to Chinese immigrants, who have arrived in successive waves over the years. The first wave, in the 19th century, was of immigrants mainly from the southern province of Guangdong, where opportunities were few, and who came for the 1858 gold rush. Later on, Chinese men were wooed by the Canadian government and the CPR, who saw them as hard workers who did not demand too much in the way of wages and special treatment while labouring on the railway. It is said that one Chinese labourer died for every mile of track laid.

The government head tax on Chinese immigrants was $50 in 1885. It jumped to $100 in 1902, and then quintupled to $500 per person just a year later. This exorbitant tax (considering the rate of pay on the CPR was $1 per day) was meant to discourage Chinese workers already in Canada from bringing over their wives or other family members, and to prevent their arriving in great numbers once the CPR was complete.

By 1923 the government passed an act that made Chinese immigration virtually illegal — a state of affairs that continued until 1967.

Late in the 20th century, with Hong Kong about to revert back to Chinese rule, there was a new flood of Chinese immigrants to B.C. These were a far cry from the peasants who had flocked to the province earlier on; rather, they were very wealthy Hong Kong residents who wished to maintain their comfortable lifestyle.

Whatever their origin, it is certain that the Chinese immigrants to Vancouver have enhanced the city. Today there is a strong Asian influence here which makes it a delight to visit.

H.R. MacMillan Space Centre

Cruise ship at Canada Place

VanDusen Botanical Gardens

www.vandusengarden.org
5251 Oak St., 604.878.9274
Begun in 1975, these themed
ornamental gardens cover 55
acres, and are connected by
pathways and bridges. There
are more than 7,500 types of
plants and trees here, comple-
mented by outdoor sculptures
and art. Themed guided tours
are available and special
events happen throughout
the year.

Vancouver Maritime Museum

www.vmm.bc.ca
1905 Ogden Ave., 604.257.8300
This museum is devoted to all
things seafaring. Take a self-
guided tour of the restored
St. Roch, a supply ship built in
1928 that became the first
boat to traverse the Northwest
Passage in both directions.
There are plenty of marine artifacts and art on display, as
well as a "Pirates!" section and
a hands-on children's area.

Vancouver Museum

www.vanmuseum.bc.ca
1100 Chestnut St., 604.736.4431
Established in 1967, the
Vancouver Museum's distinctive shape echoes the lines of
a woven basket hat of the type
made by Northwest Coast Natives. The focus of the museum is the natural and social
history of the Vancouver region and the entire Pacific
Coast, and there is an extensive collection of Native artifacts. Changing exhibits highlight both Native themes and
more recent Vancouver happenings.

H.R. MacMillan Space Centre

www.hrmacmillanspacecentre.com
1100 Chestnut St., 604.738.7827
Several virtual reality shows, a
planetarium, and an observatory with a brand new 0.5-me-
tre telescope make this a fun
stop for families. Live demonstrations and multimedia
shows in the *GroundStation
Canada* display illuminate
Canada's role in space.

Vancouver Aquarium

www.vanaqua.org
Stanley Park, 604.659-FISH
The Vancouver Aquarium is
one of the city's most popular
attractions. It features resident beluga whales, dolphins,
sharks, sea lions, sea otters,
and many other species.
Some of the displays include
the Amazon rain forest, a jel-
lyfish display, and a B.C.
coastal environment.

The Lookout!
At Harbour Centre Tower

www.vancouverlookout.com
555 West Hastings St.,
604.689.0421
The tallest building in B.C.,
the Harbour Centre Tower is
177 metres high and offers an
excellent panoramic view of
the harbour and the city. If the
view isn't enough, you can
watch video presentations
about Vancouver and B.C. Be
sure to keep your ticket stub
— you can come back later on
to see the city lights by night.

Canada Place

North End of Howe and Burrard, right on the water
Visit Canada Place to admire
the sails of the building and
the views from the prome-
nade. This multi-purpose
building, originally the Canadian pavilion at Expo 86, now
houses the cruise ship terminal, an IMAX theatre

Vancouver Art Gallery

(see below), the Pan Pacific Hotel, and the Vancouver Convention Centre.

CN IMAX Theatre
www.imax.com/vancouver
Canada Place, 604.682.4629,
toll-free 800.582.4629
The IMAX format is becoming well-known for scenic films and documentaries. The films are shot on the largest format (70 mm) film and projected by large projectors onto enormous 8-storey screens. The format is intended to make the audience feel as if they are part of the onscreen environment, and it offers a unique filmgoing experience. Several shows are available at any given time.

Vancouver Art Gallery
www.vanartgallery.bc.ca
750 Hornby St., 604.662.4719
The Vancouver Art Gallery is located in the handsome old city courthouse that was designed by Francis Rattenbury. It has one of the best collections of Emily Carr's work, as well as a permanent collection of historic and contemporary work by many Cana-

dian painters. The visiting exhibits are always stimulating.

B.C. Sports Hall of Fame
www.bcsportshalloffame.com
777 Pacific Blvd., 604.687.5520
This intriguing museum, which will interest even those without an athletic bone in their body, pays tribute to B.C.'s athletes from the 18th century to the present. Galleries include everything from information about Native games played since long before the Europeans first arrived, to modern young sports heroes like Ross Rebagliati and Simon Whitfield.

Chinese Cultural Centre Museum and Archives
555 Columbia St., 604. 658.8880
The Chinese have a long history in Vancouver and in B.C. Many arrived during the gold rushes, while many more were brought over to work on the building of the railways. This museum features exhibits on the Chinese history in the area, from the early gold seekers to Chinese veterans who fought for Canada in both world wars.

Dr. Sun Yat-Sen Classical Chinese Garden
www.vancouverchinese
garden.com
578 Carrall St., 604.662.3207
Built completely by hand according to traditional methods, this serene park was created for Expo 86, and is the first replica of a Ming dynasty scholar's garden built outside of China. Unlike a traditional western show garden, the plants here are selected carefully and simply placed, one by one. The four elements in the garden are stone, water, plants, and architecture, all carefully placed to create an overall effect of tranquility. Take a guided tour to learn more about the garden, or simply let the ch'i of the place overtake you as you meditate on yin and yang.

UBC Museum of Anthropology
www.moa.ubc.ca
6393 N.W. Marine Dr.,
604.822.3825
This fascinating museum has an incredible array of Native artifacts stored in its innovative visible display system. It would be impossible to see everything in one day; the sheer numbers are overwhelming. The regular displays are astonishing — the craftsmanship of the coastal peoples of B.C. in sculpture, jewellery making, and weaving simply dazzles. The massive cedar bent-boxes are yet another wonder. A highlight is Bill Reid's large wooden sculpture, "The Raven and the First Men".

On the grounds are two Haida houses and several outdoor totem poles. Strolling around this section also gives

Dr. Sun Yat-Sen Classical Chinese Garden

Queen Elizabeth Park

one a full appreciation of Arthur Erickson's striking 1976 design for the museum, whose post-and-beam structure echoes those of the Northwest Coast Native peoples.

UBC Botanical Garden
www.ubcbotanicalgarden.org
6804 S.W. Marine Dr.,
604.822.9666
Five gardens on 70 acres of land offer a respite from the city. The collections include the Asian Garden, the B.C. Native Garden, the Alpine Garden (carefully managed to create blooms much closer to sea level), the Physick Garden (medicinal herbs), and the Food Garden (all food raised is donated to the Salvation Army).

Nitobe Memorial Garden
604.822.6038
Another gem on the UBC grounds, this Japanese Tea and Stroll Garden is an authentic Japanese garden created with the intent of creat-

ing harmony and tranquility. Guided tours are available; they are recommended in order to get the most out of a visit. Spring is exceptionally pretty when the cherry trees are in bloom.

Queen Elizabeth Park
Cambie St. at West 33rd Ave.
Atop Little Mountain, the highest point in Vancouver, this sprawling, 103-acre park offers great views of the city and harbour. Like the Butchart Gardens near Victoria, the area started as a quarry and today features reclaimed quarry gardens as one of its highlights. There are also many other less-visited gardens to discover within the park.

Bloedel Conservatory
604.257.8570
Located within Queen Elizabeth Park, this triodetic dome houses a lush blooming environment with plenty of exotic plants, free-flying birds and koi fish in ponds and streams.

There are three separate areas: desert, subtropical and rainforest.

Attractions in North Vancouver
Only a few minutes over the Lions Gate Bridge or the Second Narrows Bridge, you will find yourself in North Vancouver. The North Shore is where the mountains begin, and this area is famed for its challenging mountain biking, skiing and hiking so close to downtown. Not far outside the communities along the harbour is some real, rugged wilderness. This is one of the charms of the area, to be sure. North and West Vancouver boast some of the priciest real estate in Canada, but there's no cost to drive around, take in the splendid scenery, and visit the attractions.

Capilano Suspension Bridge and Park
www.capbridge.com
3735 Capilano Rd.,
604.985.7474

Take a Tour of Vancouver

You often get more out of a guided tour than you do in years of wandering around a new city. Learn some of the secrets and history of the city on one of these tours:

Harbour Cruises
www.boatcruises.com
#1 North Foot Denman St.,
604.688.7246, toll-free
800.663.1500
Take a narrated tour around Vancouver's inner harbour, or enjoy a salmon luncheon sailboat trip around Indian Arm. For the most scenic tour of all, take the Howe Sound boat/train trip.

Historic Tours
www.walkabouthistoric
vancouver.com
604.720.0006
Take a walking tour of historic Vancouver with a guide in period costume.

X-Tours
www.x-tour.com
604.609.2770, toll-free
888.250.7211
The truth is out there, and this tour of X-Files locations and other TV and movie sets will take you to it. Vancouver is known as Hollywood North for its thriving film and television industry.

Paddlewheeler Riverboat Tours
www.vancouverpaddle
wheeler.com
604.525.4465
Depart from New Westminster and travel up the Fraser River on the MV *Native*, a restored paddlewheeler. Take a full-day Gold Rush tour to Fort Langley, or enjoy a three-hour river cruise.

Totem poles at UBC Museum of Anthropology

Cherry, cherry blossom

Cherry blossoms in spring

One of the loveliest sights in Vancouver are the thousands of cherry trees that bloom in the spring. The peak month is April, though some bloom in March and others in May. Many of these trees are Japanese ornamental varieties that do not bear fruit. It's wonderful to come unexpectedly across a whole street in bloom, but to be sure of seeing some, visit the following locations:

- Stanley Park
- Granville Island
- Queen Elizabeth Park
- Burrard Skytrain Station
- Lower Mall at UBC
- Vanier Park
- Kitsilano Beach

Not for those with vertigo, this bridge has a 137-metre span, hanging 70 metres above Capilano Canyon. Once you've swayed your way across, there's lots more to look at. In the Big House, carvers work on creating totem poles, and tell visitors about the art and the meaning behind each totem. Stroll through the Living Forest and past trout ponds on an interpretive walk. The Story Centre brings to life the stories of people who settled in Vancouver long ago, and tells of the building of the bridge.

Capilano Suspension Bridge

Cleveland Dam

An outing that is much more interesting than it sounds is the Cleveland Dam. See where 40 per cent of Vancouver's water supply comes from — Capilano Lake, the picturesque reservoir created in 1954 by the building of the dam. There are several scenic walking trails around the area and a place to view the impressive spillway, as well as a salmon hatchery to visit.

Lynn Canyon
604.981.3103

Lynn Canyon Park is located in nearly 700 acres of second-growth rain forest along Lynn Creek. Visit the Ecology Centre to learn more about how the rain forest ecosystem works, then take a walk along the trails to enjoy the trees for yourself. There is a 20-storey-high suspension bridge here, as well as some pretty waterfalls and even a swimming hole. Bring a picnic and enjoy the day here amidst the striking canyon scenery.

Grouse Mountain
www.grousemountain.com
6400 Nancy Greene Way, North Vancouver, 604.980.9311

At night, all year long, you can see the bright lights of Grouse Mountain across the water from Vancouver. This is a popular ski hill in winter, offering both day and night skiing, with some excellent views of the city. In summer, too, Grouse offers plenty to see and do. The Skyride, North America's largest aerial tramway, departs every 15 minutes, taking visitors to a

viewpoint 1128 metres above sea level. Once at the top, take the chairlift that climbs even higher to 1250 metres, where the view is even more outstanding.

In summer, there is a 45-minute lumberjack show three times a day that is lots of fun to watch, as well as a "Birds in Flight" demonstration of falcons, eagles, hawks and owls. Mountain bike rentals and tours are available for those who wish to participate rather than watch.

Grouse is also home to a

Take a Hike at Lynn Canyon

Longer hikes are available, leading to more rugged areas. Check at the Ecology Centre for a map and trail description.

Twin Falls. This 40-minute loop begins at the suspension bridge and ends at the parking lot, taking in pretty Twin Falls along the way. There is plenty of up-and-down to reach the canyon floor — be prepared for some stairs.

30-Foot Pool. An easy 15-minute walk from the parking lot, this pool is a fine place to swim on a hot summer day, and the clear green water makes this worth a walk any time.

Baden-Powell Trail. This creek-side walk takes about 1 1/4 hours each way. It is part of a larger trail system that runs from Horseshoe Bay all the way to Deep Cove.

Vancouver in winter from the top of Grouse Mountain

new wildlife sanctuary called the Grouse Mountain Refuge for Endangered Wildlife. Four orphaned grizzly cubs were introduced to the area in 2001-02, and they're now making the mountain their home. Visitors can learn more about these animals by taking in an interpretive program.

Hiking trails lead higher into the alpine areas from the top of the Skyride, but Grouse is probably most famous for the Grouse Grind, a stiff, 2.9-km climb that feels like it goes straight up from the base of the mountain to the plateau at 1128 metres. This trail is the site of a yearly race in which the fastest times are around 27 minutes!

Attractions in West Vancouver

Ambleside Beach
Spend a lazy summer afternoon on one of the prettiest beaches in Vancouver, with a million-dollar view of Stanley Park and Lions Gate Bridge. Take some time to stroll a few kilometres along the seawall.

Dundarave
Enjoy lunch or a morning's browse in this charming little village along Marine Drive. Park here and walk out along the pier for some great views and photos of Vancouver, or take more time and amble along the seawall.

Lighthouse Park
An extremely photogenic spot, Lighthouse Park is the home of the Atkinson Lighthouse, a working (but not manned) tower in bold white and red. Several trails wind through the 185-acre park's old-growth forest and down to the rocks along the shore.

Bowen Island
Once on the North Shore, it is not so very far to Bowen Island. Just a short ferry ride from Horseshoe Bay, this is an excursion well worth taking. Snug Cove is the major settlement on Bowen Island, with unique galleries and shops, as well as a Sunday market. Other things to do include sea kayaking, hiking, cycling and beachcombing.

Attractions South of Vancouver
Vancouver's airport is located in Richmond, and for many visitors this is their only experience of the southern suburbs of Vancouver — Delta, Richmond, and White Rock. They are primarily residential in nature, but do offer several interesting and worthwhile options for visitors.

Delta Museum
4858 Delta St., 604.946.9322
Located in historic Ladner Village, this museum explores the history of the Delta area, beginning with the Tsawwassen people, who were the early inhabitants, through to the pioneers who dyked the area and began to farm here, and the fisheries that were an economic mainstay in the early part of the 20th century.

Reifel Bird Sanctuary
A must for bird and nature lovers, the George C. Reifel Bird Sanctuary in Delta is an 850-acre area of wetlands that is home to over 230 species of migrating birds. In November, the Snow Goose Festival celebrates the arrival of the these geese, who summer in the Arctic.

Burns Bog
www.burnsbog.org
Much more appealing than it sounds, the Burns Bog is a large undeveloped area within Delta. At 8,200 acres, this raised peat bog is the largest undeveloped urban landmass in North America. Millions of birds winter here, and the best place to view them is at the Delta Nature Reserve, in the northeastern

part of the bog. Here are pleasant, flat walking trails, some on boardwalks, from which to birdwatch, discover a beaver dam, look for man-eating plants, and toss sticks into quicksand.

Steveston Village
Richmond

A charmingly restored area where it is easy to spend a day exploring, learning, dining, and browsing among the small wooden buildings. Once a major canning centre where over 195,000 cases of salmon were packed every year, the harbour is still Canada's largest commercial fishing harbour. For locals, this is an excellent place to buy fish and seafood as fresh as it comes, right off the boats at Fisherman's Wharf. A small museum explains the area's history.

Gulf of Georgia Cannery
www.gulfofgeorgiacannery.com
12138 4th Ave., Richmond,
604.664.9009

This National Historic Site was once a flourishing canning operation. It was built in 1894 at the height of the salmon-canning years. The exhibits here tell the story of the canneries and illuminate what it was like to work in these busy, smelly, and often dangerous places.

Britannia Heritage Shipyard
5180 Westwater Dr., Steveston,
604.718.8050

This National Historic Site, also home to a cannery, preserves and celebrates the art of wooden boat building. Learn about the Japanese experience through the story of one family, the Murakamis, who used to live here.

The Atkinson Lighthouse in Lighthouse Park

Richmond is home to the second-largest Asian population in North America. Many Chinese labourers settled here after the railway was completed, working at the canneries and expanding into other industries over the decades. Add to that a substantial recent wave of immigration from Hong Kong as well as mainland China, and you have a community that is bursting with new traditions as well as old. Travelling through this area along No. 3 Road is practically like being in an Asian country, with all the Asian shops, restaurants, services and signs.

Kuan Yin Temple
www.buddhisttemple.org
9160 Steveston Hwy., Richmond, 604.274.2822

This exquisite gilt-roofed building is the largest Buddhist temple in Canada. Outside, it features beautiful gardens on twelve acres of land. Inside, it is ornate and tranquil, with lovely statues, tapestries and other decorative elements. There is Buddhist

literature in the library, for those interested in learning more, as well as weekly ceremonies and meditation classes.

Gateway Theatre
www.gateway
theatre.com
6500 Gilbert Rd., Richmond,
604.270.1812

This professional theatre features a rotating calendar of plays and musical performances.

White Rock

White Rock is a great beach destination not far from downtown Vancouver. Named for the large white rock near the sandy beach, this community enjoys plenty of sunshine and a relaxed atmosphere, making it ideal for a day excursion from the city.

Attractions East of Vancouver

East of Vancouver is another string of suburbs where there are also several interesting things to see.

Steveston Village

Burnaby

The home of Simon Fraser University and Metrotown, B.C.'s largest shopping mall, Burnaby also has some natural attractions.

Burnaby Mountain Park

Enjoy strolling around this scenic park, with its lovely rose garden and towering totem-like sculptures, known as the Kamui Mintara.

Burnaby Village Museum

6501 Deer Lake Ave., 604.293.6501

This ten-acre historical village features costumed interpreters recreating life in Burnaby circa 1925. Visit a blacksmith's shop or a Chinese herbalist. Enjoy a spin on the historic carousel, built in 1912. Special events take place throughout the year.

New Westminster

The oldest city in western Canada, founded in 1859 and once the capital of mainland B.C., New Westminster is now more a suburb of Vancouver. Visit the Irving House/New Westminster Museum, 302 Royal Ave. (Tel. 604.527.4640) for a glimpse of how things were in the old days. The Irving House is the restored house of Captain William Irving, the "King of the River". When it was built in 1864, it was lauded as "the finest, the best home of which British Columbia can yet boast." Today it is a window into the privileged world of the wealthy Victorians. The adjacent museum features photos and artifacts from the history of New Westminster.

Culture

Vancouver's lively cultural mix makes for a widely diverse artistic community, in all disciplines from performing arts to visual, literary, and media arts. The city boasts 17 dance companies, 30 professional theatre groups, more than 100 art galleries, a symphony orchestra, a ballet company, and an opera company.

The result is a city where there is always something going on, so the hardest thing can be choosing which event to attend. A good place to start is a phone call to Tickets Tonight at 604.684.ARTS. Check out some of these other venues for happenings all year-round:

Fish in a Can

Today, canned tuna and salmon are something we take for granted. However, back in 1867, when the first canning factory opened along the Fraser River, the idea of putting fish in a can was rather revolutionary. With prospectors and miners heading into the B.C. interior and later the Yukon, there was a sudden huge demand for preserved fish. By 1899 there were 47 canneries operating along the west coast, all operating at full tilt when the salmon runs came in.

Many of the cannery workers were of Chinese, Japanese or First Nations ancestry, and many women worked alongside the men, especially during the two world wars. Working conditions were difficult and wages poor, though gradually unionization improved things. The last major cannery in Steveston closed in 1992.

Orpheum Theatre

Smithe at Seymour,
604.299.9000 ext. 8050
Once the most lavish vaudeville house on the Pacific coast, the Orpheum has been restored and is now the home of the Vancouver Symphony Orchestra. It is also the host venue for many touring concerts and musical events.

Vancouver East Cultural Centre

Venables and Victoria,
604.251.1363
Once a Methodist Church, the "Cultch" is home to a wide range of innovative performing artists. On any given night you may experience theatre, dance, or a concert.

Queen Elizabeth Theatre

Hamilton at Dunsmuir,
604.669.9000 ext. 8051
This theatre, operated by the City of Vancouver, is the home of Vancouver Opera and Ballet British Columbia. A wide range of programming offers everything from ballet to musicals to rock shows.

Vancouver Playhouse

Hamilton at Dunsmuir,
604.669.9000 ext. 8052
Right next door to the Queen E, the Playhouse is the home of Vancouver Playhouse Theatre Company, Friends of Chamber Music, and the Vancouver Recital Society. This is the place to be for theatre performances and concerts.

Chan Centre for the Performing Arts

6265 Crescent Rd., 604.822.9197
Recently built on the UBC campus, the Chan Centre offers a wide variety of performances and events

Rocky Mountaineer Railtours

One of the most unforgettable excursions leaving from Vancouver is the Rocky Mountaineer, a two-day, all-daylight train trip from Vancouver to either Jasper or Banff and Calgary. (You can also take it in the other direction).

When regular passenger service along the historic route of the CPR was terminated, the Rocky Mountaineer was born, in 1990. This high-end journey allows visitors to enjoy this phenomenal railway in the utmost comfort, while enjoying excellent cuisine and educational commentary. Daytime travel means none of the scenery is missed, and an overnight stop in Kamloops allows for a fun dinner show in the evening.

The Rocky Mountaineer

This is some of the best scenery in Canada, from the churning Fraser Canyon to the ranchlands of the B.C. interior to the majestic Rocky Mountains. Wildlife is also frequently sighted along the way. No wonder this train ride is billed as "The Most Spectacular Train Trip in the World".

The King of the River

William Irving, born in Scotland in 1816, was a pioneer of riverboat transportation on the Fraser. While he is not a household name today, when he died in 1872 the newspaper was printed with a black border to show the sorrow felt by the entire community.

Irving arrived in the Fraser Valley in 1858, drawn, like so many others, by the opportunity to make money from the gold rush. Since he chose not to prospect, but instead to transport would-be miners to the goldfields, he prospered. He dominated the stern-wheeler business for over a decade. Yet when he died, his obituary claimed that "his only purpose in life seemed to be to aid in the prosperity and welfare of those around him."

In March 1880, the sternwheeler *William Irving* was launched on the Fraser by Irving's son, John, who had taken over the business upon his father's death. She plied the Fraser between New Westminster and Yale for many years, often winning races against other sternwheelers while transporting cargo and passengers.

year-round in three theatres. The building itself is lovely and the superior acoustics, especially in the Chan Shun Concert Hall, make it an excellent venue for theatre and musical events.

Arts Club Theatre
1585 Johnston St., 604.687.1644
This Granville Island institution offers live theatre all year-round — generally well-known, popular productions like *West Side Story* and *Dial M for Murder*. The productions are either at their original stage or at the Stanley Theatre, 2750 Granville St.

Firehall Arts Centre
280 East Cordova St., 604.689.0926

Sports in Vancouver

Vancouver has several professional sports teams. Check out a game or two while you are in the city.

The **Vancouver Canucks** are the city's National Hockey League team, playing out of GM Place. While the Canucks have not yet won a Stanley Cup, they are a strong team that will certainly do it someday. In the meantime, a Canucks game is always an exciting event.

The **BC Lions** are the city's Canadian Football League team, playing out of BC Place Stadium. The Lions won the Grey Cup in 2000 and continue to play a mean game of football.

The **Vancouver Canadians** are the city's Triple A baseball team, playing out of Nat Bailey Stadium in Queen Elizabeth Park. They are the farm team for the Oakland A's.

In the heart of Gastown (and actually in a restored firehall), this venue is the place to come for theatrical and dance performances reflecting Canada's cultural diversity.

Centre in Vancouver for the Performing Arts
777 Homer St., 604.602.0616
Vancouver's premier entertainment complex, the Centre (formerly the Ford Centre) is a beautiful building just to walk around in, and one that offers state-of-the-art acoustics. An eclectic variety of programming is featured from around the world, including theatre, dance and music.

In summer, there are two outdoor venues for theatre: Stanley Park and Vanier Park. Theatre Under the Stars (Tel. 604.687.0174) takes place at the Malkin Bowl Amphitheatre in Stanley Park. Productions are usually musicals and are lots of fun under the towering Douglas firs. Bard on the Beach Shakespeare Festival (Tel. 604.739.0559) takes place all summer long at Vanier Park in a series of tents with the Vancouver skyline as a backdrop. What better way to enjoy Shakespeare?

Vancouver Neighbourhoods and Shopping
A visit to Vancouver offers a chance to sink into the rhythms of the city, which has an astonishingly laid-back atmosphere for such a cosmopolitan centre. The city's neighbourhoods each have a distinctive feeling and appeal. Although there are plenty of attractions to see, often the greatest pleasure of a visit to Vancouver is walking around

the city, taking it all in, and feeling the energy.

Downtown
Vancouver's downtown is filled with large skyscrapers that glitter against the sky in the evening. Several malls are interconnected here, and there are plenty of movie theatres, and the lovely lines of the Vancouver Art Gallery. At the foot of it all, on the harbour, are the stylized sails of Canada Place.

Robson Street
This is the shopping heart of the city, with tons of trendy shops, and one corner famous for having two Starbucks kitty-corner from each other along with a competing coffee shop on a third corner. It's fun to walk along Robson, even if you're not young, wealthy, a size 2, and talking on your cell phone.

Chinatown
Vancouver has an enormous Asian population, with the second-largest Chinatown in North America after San Francisco. This area just east of downtown is a bustling commercial hub with excellent restaurants and the peaceful Dr. Sun Yat-Sen Classical Chinese Garden. On summer weekends, a visit to the Chinatown Night Market along Keefer Street is a must.

Yaletown
Yaletown is the up-and-coming area of Vancouver that's known for its smart new condominiums, upscale home-decor shops, trendy bars, restaurants and offices — all situated in restored warehouses.

Vancouver

Vancouver Festivals and Special Events

Vancouver is a city with many special cultural events and festivals. Here are some of the highlights of the annual calendar.

February: Chinese New Year 604.682.2222
Usually a month or so after the Western New Year, the Chinese New Year is a big deal in Vancouver, with its large Asian population. Celebrations include a colourful parade along Pender Street, lion dancing, firecrackers, and festivities all day at the Dr. Sun Yat-Sen Classical Garden. Other celebrations take place in Richmond, South Vancouver and Port Coquitlam.

March: Vancouver Playhouse International Wine Festival 604.872.6622
Over 150 international wineries participate in this annual week-long celebration of the grape. Events include wine tastings and winemaker dinners.

April: Vancouver Sun Run 604.689.9441
More than a race, this is an event. A staggering 42,000 runners take part in this annual run, which starts in downtown Vancouver and progresses through Stanley Park, finishing at BC Place. This is the second-largest 10-km run in the world. Elite athletes will run the course in well under 30 minutes (the course record is 27:31) but most recreational runners and walkers take on the run as a celebration of spring.

May: Vancouver International Marathon 604.872.2928
A scenic full- and half-marathon that loops around the city, attracting close to 4,000 runners. It is inspiring to watch these determined athletes on their journey.

May: Vancouver International Children's Festival 604.708.5655
A Vancouver tradition for over 25 years, the Children's Festival offers seven days of programming for children of all ages, with events, activities and just plain fun (such as the Big Hairy Deal tent, where you can dye your hair a crazy temporary colour).

June: Alcan Dragon Boat Festival 604.688.2382
Begun during Expo 86 on the waters of False Creek, Vancouver's Dragon Boat Festival has grown to become one of the largest events of its kind in North America, attracting close to 200 teams and over 100,000 spectators over the three days. Numerous entertainers and performers of many backgrounds make it a truly multicultural festival.

June: Vancouver International Jazz Festival 604.872.5200
For ten days in June, a multitude of free and ticketed performances (jazz, blues and world music) take place at over a dozen venues around Vancouver.

July: Vancouver Folk Music Festival 604.602.9798, toll-free: 800.985.8363
Three days of incredible music from all over the world at Jericho Beach Park. One of the highlights is The Collaboratory, a jam session featuring over a dozen performers from completely different musical genres.

July: Vancouver International Comedy Festival 604.683.0883
This festival takes place over ten days, adding even more festivities to Granville Island.

July: Caribbean Days Festival 604.515.2400
A free two-day party at Waterfront Park in North Vancouver, featuring excellent music, food and a multicultural parade.

July: Dancing on the Edge Festival 604.689.0691
Ten days of contemporary dance performances, featuring more than 100 Canadian and international dance troupes.

July: Molson Indy 604.280.INDY
This is one of the most popular events of the year — CART racing at speeds of up to 300 km/hr through the streets below BC Place Stadium.

July: Illuminares 604.879.8611
A one-night dusk and evening festival that features entertainment for the whole family, from a parade with giant animals and stiltwalkers to fire dancers and plenty of beautiful lanterns adorning Trout Lake Park.

July and August: HSBC Power Smart Celebration of Light 604.641.1193
Four phenomenal nights of choreographed fireworks competitions that take place at English Bay. These fireworks can be seen from many places around the city; try English Bay, Vanier Park, Kits Beach, or Jericho Beach.

Vancouver Festivals and Special Events

The Vancouver Sun Run is the second-largest 10-km race in the world.

August: Festival Vancouver
A 17-day celebration of every type of music, with over 90 concerts performed at venues around the city. Genres include choral, world music, chamber, orchestral, and jazz.

September: Vancouver Fringe Festival 604.257.0350
"Theatre for Everyone" is the theme of a fringe, and Vancouver's festival is no exception. Over 100 theatre groups and performers arrive for eleven days of challenging and entertaining theatre at many venues around the city.

September: Vancouver International Film Festival 604.685.0260
Over ten days, more than 150,000 people attend screenings of more than 300 films from fifty countries. A must for film buffs, this festival takes place at various venues.

October: Vancouver International Writers Festival 604.681.6330
An informal event on Granville Island featuring a great number of talented authors, some well-known and others up-and-coming. This five-day event celebrates the written word in all its forms.

December: Carol Ships Parade of Lights
This colourful event features a whole flotilla of boats bedecked in Christmas lights, parading along one of several routes: to False Creek, North and West Vancouver, Deep Cove, or Port Moody. Watch them depart from Coal Harbour, or join one of the commercial cruises to be part of the parade while enjoying a Yule meal and carolling.

Granville Island
Is it touristy, or is it the real Vancouver? Granville Island is doubtless a bit of both, but it's nonetheless charming to visit, with its bustling Public Market, microbrewery, and mix of boutiques, fishmongers, and marine supply stores. The area nearby, along False Creek, is surely one of the most appealing residential neighbourhoods in Canada.

Kitsilano
Named for a chief of the Squamish people who used to live here, "Kits" today is a vibrant neighbourhood filled with unique shops and restaurants along West 4th Avenue and along Broadway. The feeling of Kitsilano is strongly influenced by its more recent past as the centre of Vancouver's counter-culture and hippie life in the 1960s. Its park and beach are both lively and lovely.

Lonsdale Quay
One of the most fun ways to see Vancouver is from the water. A Seabus ride to Lonsdale Quay, in North Vancouver, offers some splendid views of the downtown core and the bustling Port of Vancouver (the biggest Pacific port in the Americas), as well as a view of the north shore approaching, with the mountains rising behind. Once you arrive at Lonsdale Quay, take some time to explore the market and the shops.

Commercial Drive
"The Drive", from First Avenue south to Twelfth, is another area that offers unique shops and unparalleled ethnic dining. It's known

153

as Little Italy, but the ethnic mix is much wider than that. Located in the east end of the city, it has some lovely neighbourhoods as well as some that are still becoming gentrified.

English Bay

With its towering condo buildings, the West End of Vancouver is one of the most densely populated areas in Canada, yet it still has a wonderful feeling about it, probably due to the proximity of the ocean and Stanley Park, and the tree-lined streets that are filled with blossoms in spring. The major streets, Denman and Davie, have a varied selection of shops and restaurants — perfect for whiling away a day of browsing and people-watching.

Kerrisdale

There are plenty of boutiques and restaurants in this upscale area located between 41st Avenue and East Boulevard. VanDusen Botanical Gardens is nearby, as is Pacific Spirit Park.

Dining

A visit to Vancouver is a gastronomical delight. With a plethora of fresh seafood and a huge range of multicultural influences (most notably Asian) the food here is fresh, innovative and tasty.

One of the chief pleasures of dining in a city like Vancouver is the wide range of multicultural restaurant choices. While many restaurants offer a fusion of culinary styles, and ethnic restaurants of every description are scattered throughout the city, here are some suggestions for neighbourhoods to sample.

Shopping in Vancouver's Chinatown

What is Dim Sum?

The Cantonese tradition of dim sum (meaning "dot of the heart", or "to touch your heart") is one of the most pleasant of Chinese dining experiences. The cuisine consists of a variety of steamed dishes, dumplings and other deep fried selections, and sweet treats for dessert. The waiter comes along with a trolley or tray full of delectable items and the diners call out their selections, which are then shared with the whole table. It's lots of fun with a group of people who have several hours to spend together — the original Sunday brunch.

Try dim sum in Vancouver at the Sun Sui Wah Seafood Restaurant, Hon's Wun Tun House, the Pink Pearl, Dynasty Chinese Seafood, Floata Seafood, and many other Chinese restaurants.

La Casa Gelato

One of the most delicious outings in Vancouver is a trip to the Casa Gelato at 1033 Venables St. (Tel. 604.251.3211). This brightly lit and decorated gelato emporium is a Vancouver institution. It has created 488 flavours to date and offers 198 flavours at any given time. Flavours include such delights as Lemon Raspberry Sorbetto and at least two dozen chocolate variations. There are also such flavour oddities as Beer, Garlic, and Wild Asparagus, as well as many exotic-fruit flavours. The gelato and sorbetto are made using only natural and fresh ingredients, and are served up in homemade waffle cones.

Take some time to decide which treat to savour. Sample a few of the flavours. If you came back every day for six months, you would just about have time to sample one of each!

Vancouver is known for its seafood.

style Chinese food in town is probably to be found in Richmond, around Yoahan Centre, President Plaza, Aberdeen Centre, Parker Place, and Fairchild Square. Of course the downtown Chinatown has plenty of excellent restaurants featuring Szechuan, Mandarin, and Cantonese cooking, as well as terrific dim sum.

The best place in town to find a unique Italian restaurant is in Little Italy, along Commercial Drive just east of downtown. (There are plenty of other ethnic restaurants along the Drive as well; it's by no means only Italian.)

Indian food is available in south Vancouver at Main and 49th Ave., the Punjabi Market. Here, you may feel as though you are in a tiny microcosm of India. Enjoy fine cuisine and shopping for Indian foods.

For Greek food, head to the intersection of MacDonald St. and West Broadway. The area around here has numerous notable Greek restaurants.

This area is also home to several sushi restaurants that feature all-you-can-eat sushi (or sushi in very large quantities) for a very reasonable sum. Fine dining it is not, but for sushi lovers this is sheer heaven.

North Vancouver is home to many Iranians, and there are several Iranian/Persian restaurants in the area.

Chinese is probably Vancouver's major standout. The city has been rated as having the best Asian dining in North America, and you could spend a lifetime discovering its Chinese fine cuisine. The most authentic down-home

Fore! Golf in Vancouver

The Vancouver area has had a recent blossoming of championship golf courses. Explore the following, all within a 90-minute drive of Vancouver, for challenging holes amid excellent scenery. Some courses are open year-round.

- **Peace Portal**
  White Rock, 604.538.4818,
  toll-free: 800.354.7544
- **Mayfair Lakes**
  Richmond, 604.276.0505
- **Meadow Gardens**
  Pitt Meadows, 604.465.5474
  toll-free: 800.667.6758
- **Morgan Creek**
  Surrey, 604.531.4653,
  toll-free: 800.513.6555

- **Northview** (two 18s)
  Surrey, 604.576.4653
- **Swan-e-Set Bay** (two 18s)
  Pitt Meadows, 604.465.9380
  toll-free: 800.235.8188
- **Westwood Plateau**
  Coquitlam, 604.552.0777,
  toll-free: 800.580.0785
- **Furry Creek**
  Britannia Beach,
  604.896.2224,
  toll-free: 888.922.9462
- **The Redwoods**
  Fort Langley, 604.882.5132,
  toll-free: 877.882.5130
- **Sandpiper**
  Harrison Mills, 604.796.1000
  toll-free: 877.796.1001

Most Scenic Dining in Vancouver

Looking for a place where the views will take your breath away? Try any of these stunning restaurants, where the food is excellent as well.

- Seasons in Queen Elizabeth Park
- Teahouse in Stanley Park
- The Observatory, atop Grouse Mountain
- The Top of Vancouver at Lookout! Tower
- Cloud 9 Restaurant, Empire Landmark Hotel
- Hart House on Deer Lake Avenue, Burnaby
- Five Sails Dining, Pan Pacific Hotel
- Beach Side Café, West Vancouver
- Raincity Grill, English Bay
- Monk McQueens, False Creek
- The Cannery Seafood House, east of downtown

The Butchart Gardens

Sea lions

Thunderbird Park, Victoria

Orca

PACIFIC

OCEAN

Vancouver Island

Brooks Bay

Vancouver Island

Ferries passing through Active Pass provide scenic transportation to and from Vancouver Island.

J ust getting to Vancouver Island can feel like a glorious adventure. Whichever BC Ferry you take from the mainland, your anticipation builds while waiting in line, and once the vessel is boarded, people jostle for the best seats from which to enjoy the views. The trip over to the Island may last only ninety minutes, but by the time the boat arrives on the other side, a holiday-like feeling has been achieved.

On a clear day, the views in the Strait of Georgia are stunning, with the Coast Mountains rising to the northeast, the snowy cone of Mount Baker hovering on the horizon to the southeast, blue waters all around, and the Island itself growing ever closer. Some travellers are lucky enough to see whales, seals, and other marine animals. If you're travelling from

SuperGuide Recommendations: Vancouver Island

1) Whale-watching boat tour
2) Visit a Gulf Island
3) Feast on a wild salmon caught only hours earlier
4) Afternoon tea in Victoria
5) Visit at least one public garden
6) View old-growth trees in Cathedral Grove
7) Pick up a piece of art made locally
8) Kuw'utsun' Cultural Centre in Duncan
9) Beachcomb in Parksville
10) Drive the scenic Malahat
11) In winter, storm-watch at Long Beach

Tsawwassen to Sidney, you will pass several Gulf Islands, while on the Horseshoe Bay-to-Nanaimo route, the islands are more distant.

Most visitors begin their trip with a day or two in Victoria, then choose to head further up the Island to do more exploring. Pacific Rim National Park is one of the biggest draws, with its wild scenery, pounding surf, and extraordinary sea adventures. The road to Pacific Rim leads through many smaller communities that have much to offer the visitor: Duncan with its totem poles, Chemainus with its murals, Nanaimo with its many outdoor activities. Another delightful place to explore after Victoria are the Gulf Islands, which have a distinct holiday flavour all their own, each island having something special to offer.

Further north on the Island, past wonderful winter skiing and the gorgeous Strathcona Provincial Park, are many tiny communities known for their incredible fishing and wildlife tours. Port Hardy, Campbell River and other north Island destinations offer a true chance to get into the heart of the wild, sometimes on land, but more often by sea.

Victoria

Although most written histories of Victoria begin with Captain Cook's arrival on Vancouver Island in 1778, Aboriginal people have been living in the Victoria area for many hundreds of years. There were numerous clans, all speaking variations of the same language, around what are today the Inner Harbour and sur-

The Fairmont Empress Hotel stands over Victoria's Inner Harbour.

rounding bays. They were primarily fisherpeople due to the incredible abundance of the sea, supplementing this rich diet by gathering food from the land, and going on the odd hunting expedition. They had time to develop wonderful art in the form of masks, dance, jewellery and carving. (The totem poles so much in evidence throughout Victoria today are primarily from other parts of B.C., or are replicas.)

For the Native people on

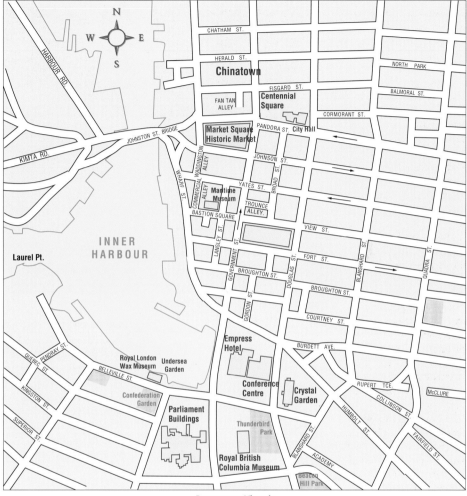

Downtown Victoria

Vancouver Island, contact was as disastrous as elsewhere in North America, due to the introduction of European diseases. On the whole, however, the relations between Native people and newcomers were relatively friendly. Today, the tourism industry in Victoria thrives on the celebration of Native art, as well as the English heritage of the later settlers.

Captain James Cook landed at Nootka Sound, on the west coast of Vancouver Island in March 1778, and found plenty of Nuu-chah-nulth (Nootka) people living there. The first known white person to land near Victoria was Manuel Quimper, a Spanish explorer who landed near modern-day Sooke in 1790 and claimed the area for Spain — in vain, as it turned out, for the HBC was on the move.

By 1842, the Hudson's Bay Company had made it west as far as Vancouver Island, and after some investigation of the eastern side of the island, selected Victoria as the site for a fort and trading post. The fort, originally called Fort Camosack, then Fort Albert, and finally Fort Victoria, was built in 1843 with help from Native people in the area. They were paid in blankets for providing wood to build the fort.

By 1849, the HBC owned Vancouver Island and plans to establish a colony were well underway. In 1862, Victoria became a city, the old fort was

159

British Columbia Parliament buildings at night

demolished not long afterwards, and once the British crown colonies of mainland B.C. and Vancouver Island were united, it was only a few years before Victoria was named the capital of the new colony, in 1868.

In 1871 British Columbia became the seventh province of the recently-formed Dominion of Canada.

Today, Victoria is by far the largest city on Vancouver Island, with a population of just under half a million souls. It's also the capital of British Columbia, rejoicing in the "British" more than any other location in the province. Victoria has the reputation of being more English than the English, and to some degree that's true, with its double-decker buses, its stately homes and gardens, and its tradition of afternoon tea. However, downtown Victoria is also modern and vibrant, a mix of traditions and culture (with a strong Native influence), which makes its true nature Canadian.

Attractions in Victoria

Inner Harbour
The centre of tourist activity in Victoria, the Inner Harbour is constantly abuzz in summer with visitors from all over the world.

Parliament Buildings
www.parl-bldgs.gov.bc.ca
Belleville St., Victoria
250.387.3046
These buildings are a graceful counterpoint to the bustle of the Inner Harbour just across the way. Frequent tours are available for those interested in the history, architecture, and stories behind the scenes of British Columbia's seat of government. Inside are a number of murals depicting episodes in B.C. history, as well as lovely collection of stained glass. The grounds

Ten Things to Do in The Inner Harbour

1) Take a whale-watching tour
2) Jump on the water taxi (Victoria Harbour Ferry) for a 45-minute tour of the Inner Harbour
3) Photograph the beautiful hanging flower baskets (June to mid-Sept.)
4) Admire the crafts for sale, many produced right there by the artists
5) Have a drink or a meal overlooking the water
6) Go deep — into the Pacific Undersea Gardens
7) Toss a loonie or two to a particularly entertaining busker
8) Tour the Parliament Buildings
9) Get dolled up and take afternoon tea at the Fairmont Empress Hotel
10) Sign up for a "Haunted Walk" — and then be brave enough to take it!

The Fairmont Empress Hotel behind the totem poles of Thunderbird Park

Totem Poles

The art of the coastal peoples takes its most unique and recognizable form in the totem pole. Many other Native peoples were not able to achieve this level of artistry due to harsher climates and nomadic lifestyles, but on the west coast an abundance of food allowed people the leisure and means to create these massive works.

The art of creating totem poles appears to have begun in the late 18th century, although carving had already been done for many centuries. It is believed that access to European tools made the carving of these immense trees possible.

Some of the more common figures carved on totem poles include figures representing the beaver, bear, thunderbird (a mythical bird), whale, eagle, raven, owl, frog, salmon, wolf and human. Since the figures are highly stylized, it can be difficult to tell one from another at first, but they do become recognizable with experience. To confound the casual observer further, most totem poles include at least one figure whose meaning is known only to the carver.

There are several styles of totem poles carved by the various tribes of British Columbia, and the art of totem pole carving is alive and well today. For more information, see *Totem Poles: An Altitude SuperGuide*.

Francis Rattenbury

Francis Rattenbury arrived in British Columbia from England in 1892, a brash young architect only 24 years old. One year later he beat out 67 other competitors to win the contract to design the province's Parliament Buildings — at that time, the most important building in the province's history. Construction was completed in 1898. Rattenbury's original bid estimated the cost at about half a million dollars, but once all was said and done the cost was well over $900,000. He later went on to design the Empress Hotel and the Crystal Gardens in Victoria, and many other public and commercial buildings and houses throughout British Columbia.

Despite his considerable talent as an architect, Rattenbury became more famous as a murder victim after his return to England. He had divorced his first wife to marry Alma Pakenham, also a divorcee. They moved back to England, where she began an affair with their chauffeur, who in 1935 beat Rattenbury to death with a mallet. The chauffeur was convicted of murder and sentenced to life in prison, and Alma committed suicide.

Stream in Beacon Hill Park

Craigdarroch Castle

feature many fountains and statues, as well as a majestic sequoia tree.

Royal British Columbia Museum

www.royalbcmuseum.bc.ca
675 Bellevue St., 250.387.3701, toll-free 888.447.7977

With a focus on the natural and human history of British Columbia, the Royal B.C. Museum is one of the most popular attractions in Victoria and certainly a fascinating place to explore. There are three major permanent galleries: the First People's Gallery, the Modern History Gallery, and Natural History Gallery.

The First People's Gallery is enormous, with a huge number of displays. To protect the artifacts, the lighting is extremely dim in this section, and it's very easy to go around in circles. However, this means that all the exhibits can really be taken in. The Jonathan Hunt longhouse

is very impressive, as is the hall with the totem poles.

National Geographic IMAX Theatre

www.imaxvictoria.com
250.953.IMAX
An IMAX theatre is attached to the Royal British Columbia Museum, and the facility often plays host to large-scale visiting exhibits.

Art Gallery of Greater Victoria

www.aggv.bc.ca
1040 Moss St., 250.384.4101
The gallery has a large collection of work, including some paintings by Emily Carr. The exhibits change regularly and run the gamut from contemporary work to historical surveys, with an interesting emphasis on Asian art.

Thunderbird Park

Located beside the Royal British Columbia Museum, Thunderbird Park boasts an impressive collection of totem poles and a big-house

workshop where several Native artisans can be found daily in summer, working on their totem art.

Helmcken House

www.heritage.gov.bc.ca/helm/helm.htm
Nestled somewhat incongruously between the hulking Royal B.C. Museum and the totems of Thunderbird Park, Helmcken House, built in 1852, is the oldest house in B.C. still on its original site. Dr. Helmcken was an important figure in early B.C. politics. The house has been restored and now displays elements of the Helmckens' belongings, offering a glimpse into life in Victoria at the turn of the 20th century.

Beacon Hill Park

www.beaconhillpark.com
Beacon Hill Park was established in 1882 and has been providing beauty and tranquility ever since. Its extensive gardens, ponds, statues, fountains and green spaces are

Emily Carr House

Maritime Museum of British Columbia

www.mmbc.bc.ca
28 Bastion Square,
250.385.4422
The building alone is worth the visit. The restored 1889 Provincial Law Courts of B.C. is a handsome structure with plenty of beautiful wood paneling inside, as well as what is reputed to be the oldest working elevator in the country. The exhibits focus on all things nautical, from dugout canoes to pirates and on to passenger ships and BC Ferries. It's lots of educational fun for children and adults alike.

Craigdarroch Castle

www.craigdarrochcastle.com
1050 Joan Crescent,
250.592.5323

truly outstanding, and this is a great place for a Sunday stroll. There is a large off-leash dog area that flanks Dallas St. and goes along the oceanfront. You can either stay high along here, or cross Dallas to take the Oceanside trails that hug the coast. In late July the wildflowers along the bluffs are astounding.

This "castle" is in fact a lavish 39-room mansion built in the 1890s by Robert Dunsmuir, a self-made coal baron who was for a time the wealthiest man in western Canada. Dunsmuir died in 1889 before the building was completed, but his widow Joan and their children eventually moved in and lived there for many years. Today, the buildings and garden are open to the public and are gradually being restored to period authenticity. The architectural details are beautifully ornate. Be sure to climb the 87 steps to the turret to take in the striking view of the city, the Juan de Fuca Strait, and the Olympic Mountains.

Point Ellice House and Gardens

www.heritage.gov.bc.ca/point/point.htm
2616 Pleasant St., 250.380.6506
This lovingly restored Victorian home can be reached by car, but it's a lot more fun to take a Victoria Harbour Ferry from the Inner Harbour. Arriving from the water, visitors can stroll through the gardens before reaching the house, which was owned by the O'Reilly family for over a hundred years. This is one of the most pleasant places in Victoria to enjoy afternoon tea.

Emily Carr House

www.emilycarr.com
207 Government St.,
250.383.5843
Visit the home of Emily Carr, one of Canada's best-loved painters. She was born in Victoria, and became known for her paintings of the B.C. landscape and of the Native peoples of the province. Tour the house and gardens filled with

Emily Carr

One of Canada's best-loved painters, Emily Carr was born in Victoria in 1871. She spent time studying art in San Francisco, Paris and London before returning to Victoria, where for many years she painted very little due to strained financial circumstances.

When she did return to painting, in her late fifties, she turned to the Native villages north of Victoria and along the coastal mainland, trying to capture as much as possible of a culture that she perceived to be dying out. In 1927 she travelled east for an exhibition of her work and met with members of the Group of Seven. Her paintings of Native villages and of the scenery of the west coast are dynamic and full of life, clearly influenced by the Group's uniquely Canadian approach to painting, but with a perspective all her own.

Carr was also a writer. She wrote five books — her first, *Klee Wyck* (1942), a collection of non-fiction stories, won the Governor General's Literary Award.

Carr died in 1945. She remains a Canadian icon.

reproductions of her work, and visit the People's Gallery, which displays work by Canadian artists.

St. Ann's Academy National Historic Site
www.bcpcc.com/stanns
835 Humboldt St., 250.953.8828
In 1858, four Sisters of St. Ann arrived from Quebec in what would become Victoria, to begin teaching and ministering to the sick. They lived in a humble log cabin at first. In 1871 the first part of the current building was completed. Two other wings and a chapel were added in later years. After operating as a Catholic girls' school, a convent, and an administrative centre until 1973, today the extensively-restored buildings are used for government offices and an interpretive centre. The gardens also offer a wonderful calm place in the heart of the city.

Victoria Bug Zoo
www.bugzoo.bc.ca
631 Courtney St., 250.384.BUGS
This attraction is great for kids and anyone else with an interest in arachnids, scorpions, grasshoppers, beetles, and many other insects. Visitors are permitted to touch certain residents of the zoo — a thought that will dismay some and thrill many others.

Miniature World
www.miniatureworld.com
649 Humboldt St., 250.385.9731
Over 80 "small" displays, including a model of the CPR, Frontier Land, Fantasy Land, the Fields of Glory, the World of Dickens and Olde London Towne of 1670.

Pacific Undersea Gardens
www.pacificunderseagardens.com
490 Belleville St., 250.382.5717
This is a great place to view underwater marine life, through viewing windows. The plants and animals are protected within the Inner Harbour, their natural habitat. Dive shows are part of the theatre experience, and a tidal pond is the place to touch some of the marine life. You may spot seals hanging around the area; many of them were rescued and rehabilitated by the Gardens, and now continue to stay in the harbour.

Royal London Wax Museum
www.waxworld.com
470 Belleville St., 250.388.4461
Life-sized wax figures of famous people are the draw at this museum, which was the first Canadian offshoot of Madame Tussaud's Gallery in London. There are over 300 figures in authentic period costumes.

Crystal Garden Conservation Centre
www.bcpcc.com/crystal
713 Douglas St., 250.381.1213
An indoor tropical environment with a wide range of plants, butterflies, birds, and mammals (including the world's smallest monkeys), the Crystal Garden is also a heritage building with a unique glass roof, modelled on London's Crystal Palace.

Government House
www.ltgov.bc.ca/house/default.htm
1401 Rockland Ave., Victoria
250.356.5139
This is the "ceremonial house of all British Columbians",

Afternoon Tea in Victoria

While afternoon tea at the Empress Hotel is the most well-publicized ritual in Victoria, plenty of other establishments offer the same type of repast. Afternoon tea traditionally consists of scones with Devonshire cream (very heavy and rich) and jam, crumpets and honey, sandwiches, English trifle, pastries, and of course a selection of teas.

Ten Places to Take Tea in Victoria:

1) **Fairmont Empress Hotel**, 721 Government St., 250.384.8111
2) **Museum Tea Room**, Royal B.C. Museum, 675 Belleville St., 250.388.5500
3) **James Bay Tearoom & Restaurant**, 332 Menzies, 250.382.8282
4) **Oak Bay Beach Hotel**, 1175 Beach Dr., 250.598.1134
5) **White Heather Tea Room**, 1885 Oak Bay Ave., 250.595.8020
6) **The Blethering Place**, 2250 Oak Bay Ave., 250.598.1413
7) **Butchart Gardens Dining**, 800 Benvenuto, 250.652.8222 (Note: does not include admission to the gardens)
8) **Point Ellice House & Garden**, 2416 Pleasant St., 250.380.6506
9) **The Gatsby Mansion**, 309 Belleville St., 250.388.9191
10) **Point-no-Point**, 1505 West Coast Rd., Sooke, 250.646.2020

The Gate of Harmonious Interest marks the beginning of Chinatown.

Victoria Festivals and Special Events

Victoria is a festive place — check out one of these festivals to experience some true local colour. Throughout the summer, Bastion Square and Centennial Square are busy with performances and concerts under the banners of Festival of the Arts and Summer in the Square; these are usually free.

January: Polar Bear Swim
February: Flower Count
April: TerrifVic Jazz Party
May: Victoria Harbour Festival; Victoria Day Parade; Literary Arts Festival
June: Jazzfest
July: Shakespeare Festival; Ska Festival, Luminara
August: Symphony Splash; Rootsfest; Shakespeare Festival; Fringe Festival; Latin Caribbean Festival; First People's Festival; Dragon Boat Festival
September: Blues Bash
October: Royal Victoria Marathon

and the 26 acres of gardens are also open to the public daily (whether British Columbian or not). A 15-minute walk from downtown along a street of Victorian houses, Government House's gardens have a wide range of themes and are truly delightful to experience.

Culture

Victoria has many cultural venues. You can take in a play, ballet, opera, concert or symphony almost any night of the week. These two venues are the first places to check out:

Royal Theatre & McPherson Playhouse
www.rmts.bc.ca
805 Broughton St. and #3 Centennial Square respectively
Shared box office 250.386.6121, toll-free 888.717.6121
These two restored venues, both built in the early 20th century, offer a wide range of programmes, from ballet and opera at the Royal (a premier venue for touring attractions) to a more eclectic lineup at the McPherson. Between the

two, there is almost always a show to take in. The Royal is also the home to the esteemed Victoria Symphony (www.victoriasymphony.bc.ca).

Belfry Theatre
www.belfry.bc.ca
1292 Gladstone Ave.,
250.385.6815
Operating out of a restored 1892 church, this local professional company has been offering consistently entertaining quality theatre for over 25 years. Every February and March, they put on a festival of more unusual performances.

Shopping

Government Street
The main shopping street in downtown Victoria, Government St. also connects up many of these other shopping districts. Leading away from the Inner Harbour, this is an excellent place to pick up postcards and souvenirs. Take a look as you stroll along for some stores carrying exquisite Native crafts (including the ubiquitous Cowichan sweaters), and be sure to stop at Munro's Books. There are plenty of unique stores along here, mixing with well-known chains.

Chinatown
The oldest (but no longer the biggest) Chinatown in Canada, the area around Fisgard and Government streets still offers a taste of the East, with an abundance of Chinese restaurants and shops. The Gate of Harmonious Interest marks the beginning of the area, which at the height of the gold rush was the

largest Chinatown north of San Francisco. Be sure to have a look around Fan Tan Alley, the narrowest street in Canada, and imagine it full of opium and gambling dens as it was at its peak.

Market Square

There are lots of one-of-a-kind shops (a dog bakery, a stringed instrument store, and the largest hologram gallery in Canada, for example) and restaurants in this old building, which was once "the bawdy side of the community, where saloons were busy and opium was legal." Today, it's a trendy area only a few blocks from the heart of the Inner Harbour along Wharf Street.

Bastion Square

This is the historic heart of Victoria — the place overlooking the harbour where the original Fort Victoria was established by the Hudson's Bay Company in 1843. Although the fort is long gone, the area is still lively, especially in summer. There is a wide range of arts and crafts vendors and buskers between Government and Wharf streets, as part of the summer-long Bastion Square Festival of the Arts. This is a splendid place to enjoy a meal on a patio, or to discover the range of interesting shops. The Square is also a venue for parts of Jazzfest, the Fringe Festival, and the Folk Festival.

Trounce Alley

Just a block long, Trounce Alley off Government St. features original gaslights over 125 years old. One of the shops here has been operat-

The Maritime Museum of British Columbia on Bastion Square

ing on the same site since 1862, which may explain the historic feel to this little street. This is a great place for unique clothing, with a few excellent restaurants that definitely warrant a visit.

Johnson Street

The site of Market Square, this street has become nicely gentrified and the old warehouses near Wharf Street now hold shops and restaurants.

Flower Count

In late February, when winter still has its icy grip firmly around the rest of Canada, Victorians joyfully count blossoms to celebrate spring (and no doubt to lord it over the rest of the country just a little bit). Citizens are encouraged to call in their personal flower tally, and random prizes are awarded throughout the week. The community within the greater Victoria area that has the most blooms wins the "Banana Belt" designation for that year. (Note to the very literal: counts are estimated; a small flowering tree is worth 250,000 blooms, for example.) The average annual count is well over a billion blossoms.

Hit the Beach Around Victoria

Victoria is blessed with an abundance of scenic lake and ocean beaches, some ideal for swimming and others great for beachcombing and picnicking. Choose from any of these local beaches:

- **Thetis Lake**
  swim in a lake
- **Matheson Lake**
  swim in a lake
- **Willows Beach**
  swim in the ocean
- **Witty's Lagoon**
  have a picnic
- **Coles Bay**
  have a picnic

Take a tour

Horse-drawn tours visit the major sights of downtown Victoria.

Gray Line of Victoria offers a wide range of tours. Check for their picturesque buses outside the Empress Hotel.

By Pedal:
One Day Cycling Adventures with Switch Bridge Tours, 250.383.1466
A fully-escorted tour of some of the astounding scenery that surrounds Victoria. Everything is provided for the visitor to enjoy a full day of cycling.

Paddling a Kayak:
Victoria Kayak Tours, 250.216.5646
Take a kayak tour of the Inner Harbour and get to know Victoria from the water on a guided half-day trip. Or try an extended day of paddling to the Butchart Gardens! You will learn basic safety and handling for the sport, and take in a lot about Victoria as well.

With a horse:
Tally Ho Sightseeing, 250.383-5067, toll-free 866.383.5067
Hop on a horse-drawn tour outside the Parliament Buildings for a one-hour tour of the major sights of downtown Victoria with other visitors, or take a more private "Central Park" style carriage, which offers a little more flexibility and sights to see.

On a bus:
Gray Line, 250.388.6539, toll-free 800.663.8390
How about a double-decker bus tour of Victoria's sights?

Walking Tours of Victoria: Not Your Average Stroll

Victoria has so many stories to tell. On these walking tours you'll learn a thing or two about the city:

Cemetery Walking Tours – These have a different theme every Sunday, but always feature people and events from Victoria's interesting past. Call 250.598.8870 for more info.

Legislature Tours – Take a free tour of the Parliament Buildings and learn about their architecture, the parliamentary system, and information about B.C.'s colourful history. Tours run frequently in summer, less so in winter. Call 250.387.3046.

Lantern tours (every night in summer only) – Stroll around Pioneer Square, the old burying ground, on this captivating tour, and learn about Victoria's history. This is a lively one that will entertain the whole family. Call 250.598.8870.

Harbour Tours – See Victoria from the water on one of these cute little vessels. They roam the harbour daily and make frequent stops at various places of interest. If you want to disembark and spend some time at a particular place, you can hop on a later boat. Call 250.708.0201.

Garden Tours – Visit some of the city's most beautiful public and private gardens with a knowledgeable guide. These small tours of up to six people run year-round, but you must make an advance reservation. Call 250.380.2797.

Architectural Tours (every night in summer only) – Take a free walking tour of Victoria's historic heart, beginning in Bastion Square, presented by the Architectural Institute of British Columbia.

Fort Street

Serious antique lovers and collectors will want to make a visit to upper Fort Street, also known as Antique Row. This is the place to admire — and acquire — fine furniture, paintings, jewellery, housewares, and all sorts of other *objets d'art* and small treasures. A wide selection of shops along this street offer an ever-changing array of wares.

Dining

Victoria — and indeed all of Vancouver Island — is an excellent place for seafood. With its historic Chinatown, Victoria offers plenty of dim sum and other Chinese food.

West Shore

The West Shore is just fifteen minutes west of Victoria, and has several popular attractions. Stop here in the morning and then drive the Coast Road for a complete day trip.

Fisgard Lighthouse and Fort Rodd

http://parkscan.harbour.com/frh
603 Fort Rodd Hill, Colwood,
250.478.5849
Dating from 1860, Fisgard Lighthouse was the first permanent lighthouse on the west coast of Canada. It is now automated, but you can tour the former lightkeeper's abode. Fort Rodd, just next door, was built in the 1890s to defend Victoria (and the Esquimalt naval station). There is plenty to explore in this artillery fort, including the barracks, the guns, and the battery.

Fisgard Lighthouse at Fort Rodd

Most Scenic Dining in the Victoria Area

If you're looking for a restaurant with a breathtaking view, try one of these — and even better, the food is excellent:

- **Laurel Point Inn**, Inner Harbour
- **The Parrot House**, Inner Harbour
- **Boardwalk Restaurant**, Delta Victoria Ocean Point Resort
- **Bentley's Dining Room**, Oak Bay Resort Hotel
- **Marina Restaurant**, Oak Bay Marina
- **Masthead Restaurant**, Cowichan Bay
- **Newport House** restaurant, Sidney
- **The Aerie Resort**, Malahat Highway
- **Sooke Harbour House**, Sooke
- **McMorran's Beach House**, Cordova Bay
- **Blue Poppy Room**, The Butchart Gardens
- **The Victorian Restaurant**, Delta Victoria Ocean Pointe Resort and Spa

Hatley Castle, part of Royal Roads University

Hatley Castle
www.hatleycastle.ca
2005 Sooke Rd., Colwood,
250.391.2600

Another stately old pile to discover, Hatley Castle is now part of Royal Roads University. Completed in 1908 for James Dunsmuir (son of the man who built Craigdarroch Castle), the mansion displays lavish use of fine woods and local stone throughout. Dunsmuir lived there until his death in 1920. The museum here explains both the Native history of the site and the history of the house, which was a naval training establishment during WW II. On the grounds are some beautiful gardens, including an Italian Garden, a Japanese Garden, and a Rose Garden, which are, unsurprisingly, a popular location for weddings. The original estate was almost 650 acres and it is still open as a park, with lots of woods and trails to explore.

Goldstream Provincial Park
204.478.9414

Only a few kilometres from Victoria is Goldstream Provincial Park, renowned for the salmon run that begins in late October and goes into November. This is a wonderful place to watch the fascinating sight of salmon fighting their way up the Goldstream River, as well as females laying eggs and males fertilizing them. After the salmon run is over, hundreds of bald eagles (and the odd bear) come to Goldstream to feed on the carcasses. To prevent their being disturbed, they can be viewed from a specific area through a video camera and spotting scope. A number of hiking trails wind through the lush park forest, and there are abundant colourful wildflowers in the summer months.

Sooke

A short drive from downtown Victoria is Sooke, a charming community with a thriving arts culture. Sooke is surrounded by an abundance of parks and natural areas. This is an excellent place to explore rivers, towering cedar forests, ocean beaches and intertidal zones brimming with life. The Sooke Region Museum (Tel. 250.642.6351) offers insight into the natural and human history of the area, with displays on the subject of Native first contact with the Spanish, and a recreation of a pioneer house that illuminates a day in the life of a Sooke family in 1902.

Visit Sooke Potholes Provincial Park to beat the summer heat. This is a very popular summer getaway only 30 minutes from Victoria. The potholes are a series of clear pools within the Sooke River — incredibly enticing on a hot summer day. Facilities are basic (picnic tables and toilets).

East Sooke Regional Park, over 3,500 acres in size, offers some short walks and picnic sites, as well as a good place to look for intertidal life, on the beach near Aylard Farm. For a more rugged hike, take the Coast Trail — only 10 km in length, but challenging and varied —which follows the

Fore! Golf Around Victoria

Victoria is the only major Canadian city to offer golf year-round, and there are many courses to choose from. Here's a sampling of public courses in the city. Most feature striking views of the surrounding ocean and distant mountains.

- **Olympic View**
  250.474.3673
- **Cordova Bay**
  250.658.4444
- **Gorge Vale**
  250.386l.3401
- **Uplands**
  250.592.1818
- **Royal Colwood**
  250.478.9591

West Coast Road

Waves from the the Juan de Fuca Strait crash into the shore at Point No Point on the West Coast Road.

Highway 14 from Sooke to Port Renfrew leads through Juan de Fuca Provincial Park, where the Pacific comes crashing in with considerable fury and beauty. There are several wonderful beaches along the way, as well as scenic viewpoints. Juan de Fuca is a wild park where cougar and bear still live, and where there is a good chance of viewing marine life offshore as well. Along the way be sure to stop at the following places:

French Beach Provincial Park, 20 km west of Sooke. This is a great place for hiking, whale watching in spring and fall (and other marine life all year round), and an oceanside picnic.

China Beach is another excellent place to spot marine life and to enjoy a short but spectacular walk through an old-growth forest to the beach. There is a waterfall at one end of the beach, and at low tide this is a great place for beachcombing.

Port Renfrew, a tiny community at the end of Hwy. 14, is primarily known as the jumping-off point (or finishing point) for the renowned West Coast Trail, a gruelling but gorgeous multi-day backpacking trip. If you've come out on a day trip from Victoria, this is the end of the line.

Botanical Beach, near Port Renfrew, has incredible tidal pools with an astonishing abundance of marine life. It is best visited at low tide, so be sure to check the tide tables before heading here. There are some short trails to follow, and some picnic areas, but the

Tide pools

main draw are the rock pools. It's never a good idea to get too close to the ocean here — rogue waves may come in, so keep a safe distance.

The Sunken Garden at The Butchart Gardens was once a limestone quarry.

coastline and enters numerous different ecoregions. It's considered one of the premier day hikes in western Canada.

Saanich Peninsula

North of Victoria, the Saanich Peninsula stretches for about 45 km of serene farmland bounded by Haro Strait and Saanich Inlet. Many visitors to Vancouver Island actually see this part of the island first, for the ferry terminal at Swartz Bay and the airport are both located here, as well as several of Victoria's most popular tourist attractions.

Attractions on the Saanich Peninsula

The Butchart Gardens
www.butchartgardens.com
800 Benvenuto Ave., Brentwood Bay, 250.652-5256, toll free 866.652.4422
This is one of the most famous, popular, and busy attractions on Vancouver Island. It really is a must-see for anyone who loves beauty and colour. Every season has its differences — even winter offers colour and texture — but the peak of the gardens is probably in July, when the flower beds are in full bloom. This is a place to blow off a lot of film, so stock up before you head here (though you can buy it at the gardens).

The Butchart Gardens were started in 1904 by Jennie Butchart. In 1909 she decided to reclaim the land that had been excavated for her husband Robert's limestone quarry. She used topsoil from neighbouring farms to cover the rock, and began to plant what is now known as the Sunken Garden. The one remnant of the old quarry can be seen from the Sunken Garden — a chimney from an old kiln, barely visible among the foliage. As the couple's fortunes flourished, they began to travel, and began extending their gardens to reflect their travels. The Butchart Gardens now includes a Japanese Garden, an Italian Garden, and then the English Rose Garden were added to their property. It is still a family-run business that welcomes many hundreds of thousands of visitors every year.

The gardens are a delight day or night — they are lit on summer evenings, providing a fairyland of colour and light. Summer Saturdays see a magnificent fireworks display, and there are special events to celebrate spring and Christmas. Even with the masses of other visitors, this is truly a wonderful place to visit.

Victoria Butterfly Gardens
www.butterflygardens.com
1461 Benvenuto Ave., Brentwood Bay, 250.652.3822
Close to the Butchart Gardens is another lovely attraction — the Butterfly Gardens. Here, visitors can wander among hundreds of brightly coloured butterflies in an indoor rain forest environment. The gardens are also a location for tropical foliage and flowers, exotic birds, and a stream and waterfall. Note that these gardens are closed from November 1 to mid-February, because the insects are sluggish without sunlight, and even Victoria's winters are not bright enough for them.

Centre of the Universe
www.hia.nrc.ca/cu/Who.htm
5071 West Saanich Rd., Victoria, 250.363.8262
This interpretive centre is part of the Dominion Observatory and offers a unique chance to

explore space without leaving earth. Saturday nights during summer, the centre offers "Star Parties", where visitors can watch objects in deep space from the amazing 1.8-m Plaskett Telescope (these are live images; audience members can't operate the telescope). During the day, the centre offers interactive exhibits, a planetarium, and tours of the Plaskett Telescope.

Horticultural Centre of the Pacific
www.hcp.bc.ca
505 Quayle Rd., Victoria, 250.479.6162
While other gardens in the Victoria area aim primarily to dazzle and beautify, these gardens have an educational purpose: to "demonstrate special plants or conditions or landscaping techniques that are suitable for the Pacific West Coast area." Most plants in these gardens are labelled and identified for the visitor's benefit.

Heritage Acres
www.horizon.bc.ca/~shas
7321 Lochside Drive, Saanichton, 250.652.5522
A place to explore the farming history of Vancouver Island, Heritage Acres features a number of historic buildings housing artifacts that bring farming to life. You can explore several acres of grounds, and see the miniature train engines on display.

Sidney
Sidney-by-the-Sea is a charming little community with a likeable claim to fame as a "Booktown", with eight bookstores located near one other.

Even those who don't enjoy reading will have fun browsing the local shops and galleries, or hitting the summer Thursday night open air market on Beacon Avenue.

This is a terrific place to take a whale-watching tour, and several companies offer three-hour tours as well as longer customized ones. Most guarantee sightings of the several pods of orcas that dwell in the waters off Sidney, as well as a chance to spot resident Dall's porpoises, seals and sea lions.

Other places to discover around Sidney are Mill Hill — a lovely spot for a walk, featuring wildflowers, arbutus trees, and views the surrounding area. Lone Pine Park, named for a small, gnarled and very photogenic Douglas fir, is another good spot for a

Whales

Orca breaching off the coast of Vancouver Island

Whales are among the iconic animals of B.C.'s west coast and Vancouver Island in particular, and a whale watching tour is on most visitors' must-do lists. The most commonly seen whales around Vancouver Island are gray whales, killer whales (orcas — technically the largest of the dolphins and not whales at all), minke whales and humpback whales. Lucky ferry passengers may see them in the Strait of Georgia, and they can be seen from land as well, but most people embark on a boat trip in order to get closer. Some outfitters will guarantee sightings of whales, and other marine animals can often be seen from the boats as well.

Whales engage in a number of different behaviours that have been named, but are not all that well understood. Spyhopping, lobtailing, breaching, sounding, flippering, and blowing are some of the whale activities that delight people fortunate enough to observe them. Often, however, just seeing the broad back of an immense whale breaking the surface of the water can be an exciting enough moment.

To learn more about whales, see *Whales: An Altitude SuperGuide*.

Field of daffodils near Sidney

Old farm on Saltspring Island

walk or a picnic. On a clear day, you can get great views of the Malahat area, Victoria, and the Olympic Mountains.

Sidney Spit Marine Park is only a few minutes from Sidney by a seasonal passenger ferry, and is a popular place to hit the beach. The sand is bounded by bluffs, tidal flats and salt marshes, making it an excellent place to bird-watch and look for marine life. There are several hiking trails to explore, as well as campsites for tenters. It's well worth a day trip.

Attractions in Sidney

Marine Mammal Museum
9801 Seaport Place,
250.656.2140
This is a wonderful museum for anyone interested in cetaceans, with exhibits and murals depicting the world of whales. Next door in the Historical Gallery is a section on the pioneer history of the Sidney area, with displays about daily life around the turn of the 20th century.

Marine Ecology Station
www.mareco.org
Port Sidney Marina, 9835 Seaport Place, 250.655.1555
This is an interesting day trip for those interested in life beneath the surface of the ocean. Walk-in visitors can enjoy seeing displays, programs, and research in progress. Excellent summer and school programs are offered here.

B.C. Aviation Museum
www.bcam.net
1910 Norseman Rd., Victoria International Airport,
250.655.3300
Airplane buffs will be interested in this museum, where planes and engines are on display. The emphasis is on B.C.'s aviation history, but there is a good selection of general Canadian aircraft and aviation artifacts, in various states of restoration.

Mineral World
www.islandnet.com/~mineral
9891 Seaport Place,
250.655.GEMS
This is an interesting family attraction, with a free interpretive centre featuring hands-on displays devoted to minerals. The "Scratch Patch", located outdoors, offers the chance to experience panning for treasure — tropical seashells and semi-precious stones. Entrance is free, but to take any treasure home the collector must buy a souvenir bag.

The Gulf Islands
Located between Vancouver Island and the mainland, the Gulf Islands are a delightful destination, whether for a day trip from Vancouver Island or a longer sojourn of island-hopping. Something about disembarking from a ferry makes the sun seem a little brighter and the scenery all the more lovely. Each island — from tiny Saturna with only 326 residents, to Saltspring with 10,000 — has a distinct flavour. Together, they offer excellent activities and a charmingly relaxed pace of life. (For a more complete guide, see the *Southern Gulf Islands SuperGuide*, from

Ruckle Provincial Park on Saltspring Island

Montague Harbour Provincial Marine Park, Galiano Island

Altitude Publishing.)

Sne Nay Muxw (Coast Salish) people were the first to inhabit the Islands, arriving about 5,000 years ago. European explorers arrived in the 18th century, and their names and vessels' names live on in the names of the islands and their communities: Valdes, Galiano, Ganges, Saturna, etc..

Miner's Bay on Mayne Island was the first place colonized by whites, when thousands of men passed through en route to the Fraser River in search of gold in the 1850s. Shortly afterwards, Saltspring Island began to be settled by freed American slaves and other groups. Farming was the basis of the economy, with produce a key export, until the Okanagan began heavily marketing its produce. Today, the major industry in the Gulf Islands is tourism.

Saltspring Island

Saltspring Island is the most popular tourist destination among the islands, and offers the most amenities. It is easily reached from Swartz Bay, further up the Island at Crofton, or from Tsawwassen. Saltspring is renowned for its scenery, its sunny weather, and its artistic residents.

North & South Pender Island

The Penders are two islands joined by a pretty little wooden bridge. Much smaller in population than Saltspring, these two islands have a pastoral appeal and a great range of activities to enjoy. There are ferries daily from Swartz Bay and Tsawwassen, as well as from several neighbouring islands.

Mayne Island

Mayne has some of the best farmland in the islands, but also revels in its heritage as a former rumbustious mining stopover point during the 1858 gold rush. A visit to Mayne Island will reveal both of these aspects of the island's character. There is daily ferry service from Tsawwassen, Swartz Bay and neighbouring islands.

Saturna Island

Saturna has a very small population (326), coupled with amazing scenery and lots of wildlife, which makes it a compelling destination indeed. It was named for explorer José Maria Narvaez's ship, *Saturnina*. It is reachable from Tsawwassen or Swartz Bay via Pender or Mayne Island, which deters

Ten Activities to Do in the Gulf Islands

1) Swimming
2) Kayaking
3) Sailing
4) Diving
5) Cycling
6) Birdwatching
7) Hiking and walking
8) Fishing
9) Gallery exploring
10) Fine dining

SuperGuide Recommendations: The Gulf Islands

Saltspring Island Recommendations

1) Drive the steep dirt road to the top of Mt. Maxwell for a stellar view of the island, the surrounding waters and neighbouring islands.
2) Take the Ganges Gallery Walk and discover the art of the islands at your own pace while exploring the galleries in this charming little town.
3) Take the self-guided driving studio tour to watch artists and craftspeople at work, creating everything from paintings to soap. Ask for a map at the information centre and look for the signs around the island.
4) Shop for treasures at Ganges Saturday market in Centennial Park — organic produce, crafts and art from vendors who have "made it, baked it, or grown it" themselves (April to October).
5) Take in a show at ArtSpring, the island's centre for the arts, featuring theatre and live entertainment year-round.
6) Visit Ruckle Provincial Park to learn the fascinating history of the Ruckle family farm, founded in 1872 and still partly in operation today. Take a walk around the trails that meander along the coast near the campground.
7) Play a round of golf on Canada's only organic golf course, Blackburn Meadows, a 9-hole course that was designed to have minimal impact on the land.

Pender Islands Recommendations

1) Visit the two farmers' markets every summer Saturday at the Driftwood Centre and the Community Hall.
2) Enjoy the peace of the Enchanted Forest Trail on South Pender.
3) Huff and puff up Mt. Norman for a splendid view of neighbouring islands and the distant San Juan Islands.
4) Beachcomb and explore rock pools at one of twenty beaches around the island.
5) Play a round of disc golf in the semi-wilderness area around Magic Lake (and take a dip in the lake afterwards!)
6) Tour "Gallery Row" — Port Washington Rd. between Hope Bay and Port Washington has galleries featuring the work of many local artists and artisans.

Mayne Island Recommendations

1) Pack a picnic and head to Georgina Point Lighthouse — keep an eye out for ferries in Active Pass.
2) Explore the heritage buildings at Miner's Bay, including the tiny jail, which is now a museum.
3) Hike up a pleasant forest trail to the gorgeous viewpoint at Mt. Parke.
4) Birdwatch at Oyster Bay.
5) Enjoy the beautiful Japanese gardens at Dinner Bay. Japanese people originally settled much of Mayne Island, but many were interned during WW II — one of Canada's more shameful historical actions — and few ever returned.

Saturna Island Recommendations

1) Visit Winter Cove Provincial Marine Park to see the tide pouring in, stroll on the beach, or take a walk on the trails.
2) Discover the sculpted rock formations, beachcomb and enjoy the swimming at East Point — keep an eye out for orcas off the point!
3) Drive to the top of Mt. Warburton Pike on a dirt road for a panoramic view. You may also see feral goats, eagles and falcons in this area.
4) On Canada Day, be sure to check out the famous lamb barbecue at Winter Cove Park — an annual tradition for over half a century.
5) Sample an award-winning wine from the Saturna Island Winery.

Galiano Island Recommendations

1) Take in a sunset at Montague Provincial Marine Park (also accessible from land).
2) Rent a mountain bike to explore the trails of Bluffs Park, with its stunning views of Active Pass.
3) Try sea kayaking with a local guiding company.
4) Discover the sculpted rocks and shapely arbutus trees of Dionisio Point Provincial Park (marine access only at time of writing).
5) Walk the 3 km of Bodega Ridge to discover the beautiful views of Trincomali Channel.
6) Hike to the top of Mt. Galiano to get great views of neighbouring islands and the Olympic Mountains.

casual visitors but makes arrival there all the sweeter. There is some accommodation but few services (e.g., no bank machine!).

Galiano Island

Less than an hour from Tsawwassen, Galiano is a favourite place for mainlanders looking for an island break. It can also be reached from Swartz Bay and neighbouring islands. There is a somewhat Spanish feel to the names on the island — and the island's name itself — as Spanish explorers named many of the places in the late 18th century.

The Malahat

(Trans-Canada Highway #1)

Departing from Victoria towards the northwest, the Malahat highway leads into the central part of the Island, offering stunning views, tranquil communities and lots of interesting attractions. There are several scenic viewpoints along the highway, so take your time and enjoy the trip.

Duncan

Duncan is known as "The City of Totems", and there are about 80 totem poles of varying sizes located throughout the town and along the highway commercial strip. It's worth a stop in town to have a look at the more intricate poles. The local tourist information centre has produced a map locating 41 totems, and on this self-guided tour you'll follow yellow footprints through the downtown area. As a major service centre for the surrounding area, the town is a handy place to stock

up on groceries and other items before heading further up the Island.

One of Duncan's more distinctive claims to fame is The World's Largest Hockey Stick, all 63 metres (173 ft.) of it, outside the local community centre.

Attractions in Duncan

Kuw'utsun' Cultural Centre
www.quwutsun.ca
200 Cowichan Way,
250.746.8119,
toll free 877.746.8119
This centre is a must-see for anyone interested in the local Native peoples. The Cowichan (as the name has traditionally been spelled) were the largest Native group in B.C., with a history dating back many thousands of years. This is a place to learn about their history, and to watch demonstrations of totem-pole carving, beadwork, dancing, knitting

and weaving. There is a traditional salmon barbecue on summer Sundays at lunch. A lot of thought has been put into this centre, from the lovely traditional architecture to the special events and activities, such as trying your own hand at crafts.

Cowichan Valley Museum
www.cowichanvalley.
museum.bc.ca
Located in the Duncan train station at Canada Ave. and Station St. (Tel. 250.746.6612), this museum explores the history of white settlers to the Duncan area.

B.C. Forest Discovery Centre
www.bcforestmuseum.com
2892 Drinkwater Rd.,
250.715.1113
This museum features exhibits on the logging industry (one of Vancouver Island's major industries), with restored machines, trucks, and

---

Vineyards of the Central Island

The climate here is ideal for grapes, and there is no shortage of wineries to visit. Award-winning wines are produced in these small and charming estate wineries. There is also a cidery to discover. Oenophiles should try to time a visit in conjunction with the Vancouver Island Wine Festival, which takes place every September (visit www.islandwineries.ca/festival.htm to find out more). Local wineries include:

- **Cherry Point Vineyards**
  www.cherrypoint
  vineyards.com
  840 Cherry Point Rd., Cobble Hill, 250.743.1272

- **Vigneti Zanatta Winery & Vineyards**
  www.zanatta.ca
  5039 Marshall Rd., Duncan, 250.748.2338

- **Godfrey-Brownell Vineyards**
  www.gbvineyards.com
  4911 Marshall Rd., Duncan, 250.748.4889

- **Blue Grouse Estate Winery**
  www.bluegrousevineyards.com
  4365 Blue Grouse Rd., Duncan, 250.743.3834

- **Merridale Estate Cidery**
  www.merridalecider.com
  1230 Merridale Rd., Cobble Hill, 250.743.4293

Chemainus boasts more than 30 murals throughout the town.

trains from the early days of forestry.

Somenos Marsh Wildlife Refuge
Just south of the Forest Discovery Centre is the Somenos Marsh Wildlife Refuge, a major stop for migratory birds and the site of a heron festival every spring. There is a boardwalk and nature viewing platform; bring binoculars to get a glimpse of some of the more than 200 birds that have been identified here.

Freshwater Eco-Centre
www.island
trout.org
1080 Wharncliffe Rd.,
250.746.6722
This is the only trout hatchery on Vancouver Island, and an excellent place to learn about all things fishy. There are permanent exhibits as well as special public programs every Saturday at 1 p.m.

Cowichan Theatre
www.cowichan
theatre.bc.ca
2687 James St., 250.748.7529
A beautiful state-of-the-art theatre featuring a wide range of live entertainment, theatre and opera productions, and so on. Check their performance schedule to see what's on offer.

Chemainus
Chemainus was first settled by whites in the 1850s. These people arrived to farm, oblivious to the gold rush fever that was gripping much of the continent and the city of Victoria at the time. The area quickly grew into a logging centre, with the deepwater port in Chemainus providing a shipping point for the timber. The town evolved around logging, with one of the largest sawmills in the world, and by 1983, when the mill closed, there was very little other economic opportunity for the residents. Some forward-thinking citizens decided to tap into tourism with a downtown revitalization project that included murals. Since then, Chemainus has developed into a thoroughly charming small town, and it's well worth a visit.

Chemainus's main claims to fame are the more than thirty murals dotted throughout the town. Over 400,000 visitors arrive here yearly to look at this outdoor art gallery, which can be experienced in an afternoon of leisurely strolling about town. Each mural has a historic element, be it an old shop or townscape from the early days, or a tableau from the logging industry. The murals were created by a number of different artists, so each has its own flavour. There is an annual Festival of Murals from July through October.

Just a short ferry ride from Chemainus, Thetis Island is ideal for a day trip, though some of the accommodation available should be

Right: Duncan is home to about 80 totem poles of varying sizes.

booked in advance. You can even leave your car in Chemainus and explore the ferry terminal area on foot. If you take a car, head out to Pilkey Point and the Cufra Canal for beachcombing and birdwatching.

Ladysmith

Ladysmith was founded in 1901 by James Dunsmuir (son of Robert Dunsmuir of Craigdarroch Castle fame) as a shipping port for Nanaimo coal. It's a small, pretty town located on the Stuart Channel, with lovely views and no trace of its sooty past visible today. It boasts one of the warmest beaches on Vancouver Island — Transfer Beach.

In summer, visitors to Ladysmith can visit the Black Nugget Museum at 12 Gatacre St. (Tel. 250.245.4846). Located in a former hotel, this museum has a great collection of local mining artifacts and memorabilia, as well as assorted antiques. Be sure to stroll along First Avenue and take in the restored heritage buildings.

If you visit in November, experience the Festival of Lights on the last Thursday of the month. Countless lights and a parade brighten up the town in readiness for the holidays.

Nanaimo

While the Sne Nay Muxw (Coast Salish) were the first inhabitants of the area, the town of Nanaimo was established in the mid-1850s as a coal-mining town. The name is an interpretation of the Salish "Sne Nay Muxw", which means "the great and mighty people". Nanaimo, population

73,000, is now the second-largest city on the Island, with lots of services, a bustling ferry terminal and a busy harbour. The coal industry has faded, leaving logging and tourism as the major economic drivers.

Walkers will enjoy the wide-open views from the 4-km Harbourfront Walkway, and discovering the older buildings on a self-guided heritage walk through the downtown core. If you've got a lot of puff, climb to the top of Mt. Benson for panoramic views of Westwood Lake and the harbour. Once the view has been duly appreciated, take a passenger ferry to Newcastle Island Provincial Marine Park and hike the trails along the cliffs and beaches.

The Bastion in Nanaimo

SuperGuide Recommendations: Chemainus

1) Take a guided heritage tour around the town on a Chemainus Tours trolley.
2) Take in a dinner show (or lunch matinee) at the Chemainus Theatre Company.
3) Browse the intriguing shops and galleries in the downtown area.
4) For a change of pace, tour the sawmill.
5) Hop a ferry to Thetis Island.
6) Spend an afternoon at Waterwheel Park — have a picnic, enjoy the shade of the giant fir trees, or watch a performance at the bandshell.
7) Go for a swim at Kinsmen Beach.

Fore! Golf in Central Vancouver Island

Golfers can rejoice in the gentle climate that makes golf possible year-round. Discover some of the courses in this area:

- **Arbutus Ridge**
  Cobble Hill, 250.743.5100
- **Cowichan Golf & Country Club**
  Duncan, 250.746.5333
- **Duncan Meadows**
  Duncan, 250.746.8993
- **Mount Brenton**
  Chemainus, 250.246.2588
- **Nanaimo Golf & Country Club**
  Nanaimo, 250.728.2451
- **Morningstar**
  Parksville, 250.248.8161
- **Fairwinds**
  Nanoose Bay, 250.468.7666
- **Glengarry Golf Links**
  Qualicum Beach, 250.752.8786
- **Eagle Crest**
  Qualicum Beach, 250.752.9744
- **Arrowsmith** (Executive)
  Qualicum Beach, 250.752.9727

South of Nanaimo, Petroglyph Provincial Park harbours some incredibly intricate rock art that is well worth a detour.

Visit Nanaimo in July and take in the Marine Festival, a four-day family fun event with the highlight being the Nanaimo-to-Nanaimo, 36-mile "Great International World Championship Bathtub Race".

Attractions in Nanaimo

Nanaimo District Museum
www.nanaimo.museum.bc.ca
100 Cameron Rd., 250.753.1821
This museum includes Native, coal mining, and Nanaimo history, and is located on a lovely spot overlooking the harbour.

The Bastion
Front St., 250.753.1821
This wooden tower fort was built by the Hudson's Bay Company in 1853 and is now the last building of its kind left in North America. It was never used for its intended purpose (to protect HBC employees from Native attack), and is now a historic site and museum.

TheatreOne
www.theatreone.org
490 Dunsmuir, 250.754.7587
Take in a live production — often comic, often thought-provoking — at this theatre.

The Bungy Zone
www.bungyzone.com
35 Nanaimo River Rd.
250.753.5867, toll-free
800.668.7771
The only bungee jump on Vancouver Island, this is an adrenaline-filled and picturesque stop. You can go solo or tandem off the 43-metre (140-foot) high bridge, or try the giant swing or zipline for another kind of adventure.

Parksville to the West Coast

From Nanaimo the main Highway 19 splits in two, with 19A skirting the coast more closely. It's a very worthwhile alternative, leading to Parksville and Qualicum Beach, two small towns that have several interesting attractions. If you're heading west to Tofino, take a few extra hours to explore this area first. If you're going north, this part of the island is on your itinerary anyway.

Parksville has one of the loveliest stretches of sandy beach in Canada. The tide goes out a long way to expose countless sand dollars of many different hues. Needless to say, it's a very popular summer destination. Two unusual events bring in visitors over the summer: "Sandfest" in July is a sandcastle-building competition that attracts over 30,000 onlookers, and in August the World Croquet Championships take place.

Sharing the same sheltered east coast shoreline as Parksville, Qualicum Beach offers sandy beaches, towering trees and lovely gardens.

The Nanaimo Bar

One of Nanaimo's tastiest claims to fame is the Nanaimo Bar. Curiously enough, this chocolatey, coconut-y, creamy treat was not invented here. Its name came from the fact that these bars were often sent *to* Nanaimo, to the coal miners in care packages from their families at home in the U.K.

Regardless of origin, the Nanaimo bar is a favourite Canadian treat that will be appreciated by everyone with a sweet tooth. If you take a liking to it, here's the definitive recipe, courtesy of Tourism Nanaimo.

The Original Nanaimo Bar
BOTTOM LAYER:
1/2 cup unsalted butter
1/4 cup sugar
5 tbsp. cocoa
1 egg, beaten
1 3/4 cup graham wafer crumbs
1/2 cup finely chopped almonds
1 cup coconut

Melt first 3 ingredients in top of a double boiler. Add egg and stir to cook and thicken. Remove from heat. Stir in crumbs, coconut and nuts. Press firmly into an ungreased 8-inch-square pan.

SECOND LAYER:
1/2 cup unsalted butter
2 tbsp. and 2 tsp. cream
2 tbsp. vanilla custard powder
2 cup icing sugar

Cream butter, cream, custard powder and icing sugar together well. Beat until light. Spread over bottom layer.

THIRD LAYER:
4 squares semi-sweet chocolate (1 oz. each)
2 tbsp. unsalted butter

Melt chocolate and butter over low heat. When cool but still liquid, pour over second layer and chill in refrigerator.

It's well-known as an arts community.

Stop along highway 4A in Coombs to see the goats on the roof at the Old Country Market. Be warned, though — on bad or hot days they often stay inside their little shelter. The market offers produce and other items to travellers en route to Port Alberni and beyond. There are several other gifty-crafty stores nearby, as well as a mini-golf course.

Gabriola Island

Easily accessible by a short ferry ride from Nanaimo, Gabriola Island offers the same relaxed island atmosphere of the other Gulf Islands, for a day trip or an extended stay. Many residents commute to work in Nanaimo.

Gabriola Island Recommendations

1) Visit the Malaspina Galleries, a series of remarkable sculpted limestone overhangs along the coast near Gabriola Sands Provincial Park.
2) Visit some artists' studios to discover the work of some of the many artists and artisans living and working here. Gabriola is known as the "Isle of the Arts".
3) There is spectacular diving at Drumbeg Park, where you may see giant octopus and many other varied and colourful marine life.
4) Marvel at the petroglyphs around the island. Some of the best are found behind the United Church on South Road.

The Arbutus

Arbutus trees

One of the prettiest trees on Vancouver Island is the arbutus. It is easily recognizable by its gnarled shape and its parchment-like red bark that peels away from the tree. While the arbutus can grow to a height of over 18 metres (60 ft.), most of the trees on Vancouver Island and the Gulf Islands are smaller, clinging to rocky shores near the coast.

A broadleaf evergreen, and the only one native to Canada, the arbutus does not lose its leaves in the fall. In spring, a new set of leaves grows and the old ones fall off. The tree sports small white blooms in spring and has bright clusters of orange berries in the fall.

The arbutus, also known as the madrone, loves sunlight and grows in only a small belt along the Pacific coast.

Natural Attractions in Parksville and Qualicum Beach

1) Rathtrevor Beach Provincial Park has a delightful beach, and a wonderful place to camp amongst old-growth trees.
2) French Creek is a prime fishing spot.
3) In late May and early June, there's an amazing profusion of pink blossoms on the wild rhododendrons growing along the shore of Rhododendron Lake.
4) Englishman River Falls Provincial Park offers hiking trails through the woods. Take a bathing suit for a dip in the crystal-clear pool at the base of the falls.
5) Little Qualicum Falls Provincial Park features a short walk to several cascading waterfalls, as well as several longer day-hikes through the inviting forest. This is also a popular swimming spot.

Immense trees in Cathedral Grove, MacMillan Provincial Park

Attractions in Parksville, Qualicum Beach and Coombs

North Island Wildlife Recovery Association

1240 Leffler Rd., Errington (near Parksville), 250.248.8534
Open to the public from April through October, the NIWRA offers guided and self-guided tours of their wildlife rehabilitation centre. You may see bear, cougar, smaller mammals, and birds, depending on what animals are there at the time.

Old School House Art Centre

122 Fern Rd. West, Qualicum Beach, 250.752.8133
See the current exhibition and watch artists (painters, woodturners, jewellers, and others) at work in the resident studios. You can even have afternoon tea.

The Power House Museum

(mid-June to early October)
587 Beach Rd., Qualicum Beach, 250.752.6441 or 752.6836
This intriguing museum celebrates electricity, and the history of the area, from the daily life of Qualicum pioneers to shipwreck displays. Try keeping the lights on by bicycling. There is also a section on the Esquimalt & Nanaimo Railway. The Vancouver Island Palaeontology Museum (Tel. 250.752.9810) is part of this complex as well, with an extensive collection of fossils and an emphasis on local prehistory.

Butterfly World

Hwy. 4, Coombs, 250.248.7026.
At this colourful indoor tropical garden you can stroll among hundreds of free-flying exotic butterflies and hummingbirds. You can also visit the bird aviary and the outdoor water gardens, which are filled with koi from Japan.

MacMillan Provincial Park

The next stop of interest along Hwy. 4 is known as Cathedral Grove, within MacMillan Provincial Park. Just driving along the highway, one gets a sense of the majesty of these immense Douglas fir, western red cedar, and western hemlock trees, as they form a canopy over the roadway. There is a place to park and get onto the short interpretive trails leading further into the woods on either side of the highway. Some of the trees are 800 years old. This is a refreshing and awe-inspiring stop on a hot summer's day.

Port Alberni

Until recently, Port Alberni was almost exclusively a lumber and commercial fishing town. But with its scenic location at the head of the Alberni Inlet, it is becoming increasingly attuned to tourism. Many visitors come here for the excellent salmon fishing, or to catch a boat to the Broken Group Islands for kayaking trips. Port Alberni, as the self-proclaimed "Salmon Capital of the World", is an excellent place to visit on the Labour Day weekend, when the annual salmon festival takes place.

Summer visitors can browse the shops and take a stroll along the Harbour Quay, or climb the short trail to the Lookout for an excellent view.

Two unusual tours await in Port Alberni. Plane buffs will get a kick out of the massive Martin Mars water bombers, stationed at Sproat Lake (visitors are welcome, though there is no official interpretive centre). Call 250.723.6225. Visitors can also tour a paper mill; call the Alberni Forest Information Centre at 250.724.7890 for details.

Attractions in Port Alberni

Alberni Valley Museum
Echo Centre, 4255 Wallace St., 250.723.2181
This fine community museum has an extensive collection of Native art, as well as permanent displays on the industrial heritage of the area, and temporary exhibits on a variety of local heritage themes.

Maritime Discovery Centre
At the lighthouse on the waterfront, 250.723.6164
Learn about the seafaring history of the area through interactive displays and exhibits.

Alberni Valley Heritage Railway (summer only)
Head down to the 1912 railway station on Kingsway Ave. and hop on a restored steam train to travel around the city and out to the McLean Mill National Historic Site.

McLean Mill National Historic site (year-round).
This 1920s-era mill is the only steam-powered sawmill in Canada, and actually produces lumber for sale. Tour the mill as if you were arriving for your first day of work in this fascinating look at the lumber industry of bygone days.

Tofino and Ucluelet
One of the more publicized destinations in western Canada, Tofino itself is still a very small town, albeit one with a charmingly touristy feel to it. Ucluelet, about 30 km down the road, offers a more genuine feel and a similar range of seafaring activities. The main draw for visitors to the Tofino-Ucluelet area is the Long Beach section

Natural Attractions in Port Alberni

1) The Somass River Estuary has excellent birdwatching and a good chance to glimpse a black bear during the salmon run.
2) Sproat Lake Provincial Park offers impressive petroglyphs.
3) The MV *Lady Rose* is the best way to take in the spectacular scenery and marine wildlife on a cruise to Bamfield or Ucluelet.

SuperGuide Recommendations: Tofino & Ucluelet

1) Visit the Eagle Aerie Gallery and admire the art of Roy Henry Vickers.
2) Look for whales from Radar Hill.
3) Take a whale-watching trip to spot gray whales and other marine mammals.
4) Explore tidal pools to get a good look at smaller, colourful marine critters.
5) Cruise to Meares Island and walk the Big Cedar trail.
6) Learn about the plants of the temperate rain forest (and many more) in the ten gardens at the Botanical Gardens.
7) Experience Hot Springs Cove, located on an island an hour's boat ride from Tofino.
8) Stop in at the Wickaninnish Interpretive Centre to learn more about the open ocean.
9) Try a sea-kayaking lesson in Clayoquot Sound or Barkley Sound.
10) Sign onto a fishing boat in search of huge salmon and halibut.
11) Eat the freshest seafood imaginable — extra points if you catch it yourself!
12) Visit the Amphitrite Point Lighthouse for views of the Broken Group Islands.
13) Take a hike on the scenic Wild Pacific Trail through the rain forest along the coast.
14) Try surfing the waves at Long Beach (lessons available in Tofino)

The Wickaninnish Centre in Pacific Rim National Park

of Pacific Rim National Park. The park is known for its incredible array of marine life, its wild surf, and its temperate rain forests.

Visit in March for the annual Pacific Rim Whale Festival — a celebration of the 20,000 Pacific gray whales that migrate along the coast. This is a great chance to view the whales from shore and to learn more about their amazing journey. There are a plenty of other fun family events as well.

A Short Walk from a Long Beach

The Rainforest Trails wind through ancient and lush vegetation.

Shorepine Bog Trail (1 km). Learn about many of the trees in the park as you hike through a bog on a boardwalk.

Rainforest Trails (about 1km each). One on either side of the highway, these interpretive trails wind through the big trees (some up to 800 years old) and the lush vegetation you only see in a rain forest.

Spruce Fringe Trail (1.5 km). This interpretive boardwalk trail explains the life cycle of the Sitka spruce trees that abound in the area, at the end of Combers Beach.

If the coastal scenery gets drab after a while (unlikely as it sounds), head inland to one of these short hikes:

Willowbrae Trail (2.8 km). This trail follows a series of stairs and ramps to Florencia Bay or Half Moon Bay — great for looking at marine life at low tide.

South Beach Trail (1.5 km). Start at the Wickaninnish Centre for this trail that leads onto South Beach.

Wickaninnish Trail (10 km). This longer trail connects Wickaninnish and Florencia bays — a great rainforest walk along boardwalks, with lovely coastal views.

Schooner Cove Trail (1 km). This trail gives access to the beach past the old decommissioned campground.

Radar Hill Viewpoint (less than 1 km). A short walk uphill leads to a viewpoint with magnificent views on a clear day.

North Vancouver Island

Heading north from Parksville and Qualicum Beach, the landscape becomes less populous and more wild, especially once the Comox Valley has been left behind. This is not an area to rush through, however, as it features some stunning alpine scenery, excellent skiing in winter, and lots of coastal activities.

Most of the communities along the way here offer whale-watching trips and fishing from right in town. They are also meccas for sea kayakers.

The Comox Valley

This valley, located between the Strait of Georgia and the Beaufort Mountains, offers a range of outdoor activities amid splendid scenery. As the southern gateway to Strathcona Provincial Park, this area is ideal for gearing up and heading off into the wild Forbidden Plateau area of the park. Some of the best summer activities centre around Mt. Washington, where a summer chairlift offers incredible views as well as access to mountain biking and hiking trails.

Roy Henry Vickers

One of the loveliest buildings in Tofino is the Eagle Aerie Gallery, which showcases the work of Native artist Roy Henry Vickers. Each work has a story behind it, making the visitor feel a bond with the artist and his experience of the natural world.

Roy Henry Vickers was born in 1946 in Greenville, B.C., to a Native Tsimshian father and a mother of English descent. As a child, he lived in the ancient Native village of Kitkatla, which grounded him in the traditional ways, and he went on to study art at the Kitanmaax School of Northwest Coast Indian Art in Hazelton, B.C.

Vickers' work, with its many layers, bold colours and simple subjects, has been well-received throughout the world and is instantly recognizable. He creates several new limited-edition prints every year. He has also created many totem poles and other carvings. In addition to working on his art, he has established Vision Quest, an organization to help conquer substance addiction.

Storm Watching

Storm waves can reach heights of 9 metres or more

An average of 12-15 ripping good storms per month roll in between October and March. The majority of the substantial annual precipitation (3 metres or 120 inches) falls during this time.

The storms that pound the west coast come in primarily from the southeast, where there is no land for many thousands of kilometres. During this time the winds can hit gale force, and during a severe storm, the waves can reach a height of 9 metres or more. When a storm hits the beaches, the sight is truly awesome.

Instead of allowing the turbulent winter weather to deter visitors, the residents of Tofino and Ucluelet have turned it into a major attraction known as storm watching.

The best thing about storm watching is that no gear or hardship is required. In fact, you can enjoy it best with a glass of wine, a plate of hors d'oeuvres, and a crackling fireplace nearby. The rooms, restaurants and lounges of several upmarket resorts cater to the storm-watching crowd, with excellent views over the ocean. The Wickaninnish Inn was an innovator of the idea and is still a fantastic place to stay, summer or winter.

You can don rain gear to feel the fury of the storm for yourself, and then retreat sensibly into luxury. When the clouds clear, head for the sand to beachcomb and enjoy the rain-washed stillness.

April Farms in the Comox Valley

Thunderbird totem pole in Campbell River

The Comox Valley area is known as the "Valley of Festivals". One of the best-known is the Filberg Festival in early August, a celebration of arts and crafts that is the largest in B.C.

Two parks offer very different activities: Horne Lake Caves Provincial Park features largely undeveloped caves. Visitors here must be well-prepared, with their own lights and warm clothing. Guided tours are also available during the summer months. Seal Bay Regional Nature Park is a great place to see California and Steller sea lions, seals, and migratory birds.

Visit the Courtenay Museum to see the replica of an Elasmosaur and other paleontology exhibits, as well as displays on the heritage (Native and other) of the area, or take an unforgettable scenic flight over the Comox Glacier.

Campbell River

This community, located most beautifully between Discovery Passage and the highest mountains on Vancouver Island, has been known for almost a hundred years as the "Salmon Capital of the World" (yes, another one) and is still a major fishing resort due to the continued abundance of that fish. It's also the major road into Strathcona Provincial Park, and so attracts more than its share of outdoorsy and fishermen types.

One of Campbell River's most unusual activities is snorkelling with salmon. This trip is offered from July through October by Paradise Found Adventure Tours. Don a wetsuit and move up the Campbell River to follow the salmon making their way upstream. You may also find yourself among seals in this truly unique trip.

Take a day to visit Quadra and Cortes islands for fishing, canoeing, mountain biking and exploring. On Quadra, visit the Kwagiulth Museum and Cultural Centre to see an interesting collection of sacred ceremonial potlatch items confiscated in 1922 (and since returned to the museum).

June sees the annual Driftwood Carving competition, but all through the summer Campbell River is a great place to spend a few days taking in the scenery, watching the cruise ships going by from Discovery Pier, and experiencing outdoor activities.

Attractions in Campbell River

Haig-Brown House Heritage Site
2250 Campbell River Rd., 250.286.6646
Roderick Haig-Brown (1908-76) was an influential writer, conservationist and fly fisherman who lived in Campbell River for many years. His home is now an education centre, and the house and grounds are open to the public in summer for tours.

Gildas Box of Treasures Theatre (summer only)
1370 Island Hwy., 250.287.7310
Experience the drumming and dancing of the Laichwiltach people in a colourful performance excerpted from the potlatch ceremony.

The Museum at Campbell River
www.crmuseum.ca
470 Island Hwy., 250.287.3103
With a strong emphasis on Native art, customs and history, coupled with logging and other regionally relevant displays, this museum is well worth a visit.

Tidemark Theatre
1220 Shoppers Row, 250.287-7465
Take in a play, concert or ballet at this landmark theatre, or just admire the art in the lobby.

Campbell River & District Public Art Gallery
1235 Shoppers Row, 250.287.2261
See contemporary works by local and visiting artists.

Quinsam Salmon Hatchery
Quinsam Rd., 250.287.9564
Learn all about the life of the Pacific salmon while strolling through the woods along the Campbell and Quinsam rivers.

Telegraph Cove, Port McNeill and Port Hardy
The tiny town of Telegraph Cove (permanent population under 10 at time of writing) began as the end of the telegraph line in 1912. There is accommodation to house the increasing numbers of visitors who come here for the splendid ocean scenery and wildlife-viewing opportunities.

Telegraph Cove is probably best known for its whale-watching. Take a boat tour with Stubbs Island Whale Watching (250-928-3185, toll-free: 1-800-665-3066;

Harbour at Telegraph Cove

www.stubbs-island.com) for your best chance to see wild orcas, which frequent the area. There is a 90 per cent chance of seeing them in season, plus a very good chance of seeing a variety of other marine mammals.

If staying on land, admire the houses on stilts, stroll along the boardwalk, or engage in a spot of birdwatching

Take a Hike in Strathcona Provincial Park

The Buttle Lake area of Strathcona Provincial Park is accessible from Campbell River by car along Hwy. 28 and is one of the more day-user-friendly areas of the park. There are a number of short hikes that allow glimpses of the glorious wilderness that makes up the bulk of the park. Take a day and do a few of these hikes to get a taste of the area:

Lady Falls (under 2 km return). Start at the Hwy. 28 viewing platform for this short trip to a pretty waterfall.

Elk River Viewpoint (400-m loop). Start at Hwy. 28 for a brief walk to a viewpoint of the Elk River. Learn about and look for the eponymous elk.

Lupin Falls (under 2 km return). A lovely waterfall is the goal of this short forest walk.

Karst Creek (2 km one way). An interpretive trail about limestone, and much more interesting and scenic than it sounds!

Wild Ginger. A short walk through wild ginger plants and large trees. The ginger flowers are dark red, and can be hard to see.

Myra Falls. This short but steep hike leads to cascading falls and broad rocks that people can't resist clambering over. Use caution at the falls.

Alert Bay

Alert Bay totem poles

When in Port McNeill, take a BC Ferry to Cormorant Island and visit Alert Bay. This picturesque village has extensive First Nations art and historic buildings throughout, as well as the Namgis Burial Grounds, with a collection of lovely old totems. Please admire the burial grounds from the road only — the cemetery is closed to visitors. Check out the highest totem pole in the world (53 m or 173 ft. high). Be sure to visit the U'Mista Cultural Centre on Front St. (Tel. 250.974.5403) to view the incredible array of ceremonial potlatch items in this museum, as well as work by contemporary Native carvers and other artists.

What is a Potlatch?

The potlatch was an important ceremony for Native peoples along the west coast. It was held to celebrate a significant event (such as a coming of age, a marriage, or a totem-pole raising), or to underline the power of a chief or tribe. The potlatch recognized the status of both hosts and guests.

A potlatch could involve as many as a thousand people (neighbouring tribes were invited) and could last for several days of feasting, dancing, speeches and celebration. At the end of the event, everyone attending received a gift suitable to his or her status. A typical gift might be a wooden basket, bowl, spoon, pipe, basket, necklace, or a bark container.

Missionaries found the potlatch to be immoral and pagan. The ceremony was banned by the Canadian government from 1884 to 1951, though potlatches continued to be held in secret, especially among the Kwagiulth people. Many of the items traditionally used and given in potlatches were confiscated by the government over this time. A visit to the UBC Museum of Anthropology in Vancouver will demonstrate the immensity of what was taken from the Natives. Literally thousands of artifacts — from mundane everyday objects to magnificent masks, jewellery and other works of art — now sit unlabelled in the visible storage section. Similar items ended up in many other museums around the world.

Today, the potlatch is still celebrated the length of the west coast to mark important rites of passage.

(Telegraph Cove is a major stop for migratory birds). Fishing, kayaking and sailing in Johnstone Strait are also major activities here.

The gateway to the Broughton Archipelago, Port McNeill offers excellent outdoor activities, including whale-watching, sailing, kayaking, hiking, fishing, and diving. Less well-known, but also interesting, are self-guided cave tours at Little Huson Cave Park.

At the very end of Hwy. 19, Port Hardy is the place to go to get on a BC Ferry to explore the world-renowned Inside Passage, for a much more reasonable price than a cruise to Alaska. Needless to say, reservations are essential, both for accommodation in this small town and for ferry sailings.

There are two ferry trips available from Port Hardy to the mainland: the Inside Passage to Prince Rupert, and the Discovery Coast Passage to Bella Coola, with several stops along the way. Both offer stunning coastal and mountain scenery, along with excellent chances of seeing marine wildlife.

Port Hardy is a wonderful place to see bears as well as marine mammals. Take a day-long grizzly-bear tour with Great Bear Nature Tours (August through October, during the salmon run). Call 250.949.9496, or toll-free 888.221.8212.

Port Hardy is also the jumping-off point for trips to Cape Scott Provincial Park, at the very tip of the Island. This is a true ocean wilderness with wild weather and challenging conditions.

Reference

Emergency Contact Numbers

When travelling in most parts of Western Canada, in any emergency, simply call 9-1-1. This free service will connect you to firefighters, police, and ambulance/emergency medical service personnel.

The RCMP is responsible for provincial law enforcement in Manitoba, Saskatchewan, Alberta and British Columbia. If someone at home urgently needs to contact you, they should contact the RCMP to attempt to track you down.

Tourism Bureau references:

Travel Manitoba
www.travelmanitoba.com
1.800.665.0040
Tourism Winnipeg
www.tourismwinnipeg.mb.ca
1.800.665.0204
Tourism Saskatchewan
www.sasktourism.com
1.877.2ESCAPE
Tourism Regina
www.tourismregina.com
1.800.661.5099
Tourism Saskatoon
www.tourismsaskatoon.com
1.800.567.2444
Travel Alberta
www.travelalberta.com
1.800.661.8888
Tourism Calgary
www.tourismcalgary.com
1.800.661.1678
Edmonton Tourism
www.tourism.ede.org
1.800.463.4667
Tourism British Columbia
www.hellobc.com
1.800.HELLO.BC

Tourism Vancouver
www.tourismcvancouver.com
1.604.682.2222
Tourism Victoria
www.tourismvictoria.com
1.250.953.2033

National Parks featured in this book:

www.parkscanada.gc.ca
Parks Canada has launched a new website that provides links to every national park in the country. For information on the national parks as you travel through the western provinces, call the following numbers:

Riding Mountain,
Manitoba: 204.828.7275
Grasslands,
Saskatchewan: 306.298.9257
Prince Albert,
Saskatchewan: 306.663.4522
Banff,
Alberta: 403.762.1550
Elk Island,
Alberta: 780.922.5790
Jasper,
Alberta: 780.852.6176
Waterton Lakes,
Alberta: 403.859.5133
Glacier,
British Columbia: 250.837.7500
Kootenay,
British Columbia: 250.347.9615
Mount Revelstoke,
British Columbia: 250.837.7500
Pacific Rim,
British Columbia: 250.726.7721
Yoho,
British Columbia: 250.343.6783

For further reading:

Altitude Publishing has a complete line of books that can help enhance your journey through western Canada. From guidebooks and maps about specific areas or interests to photographic histories, they are an excellent and widely available resource.
www.altitudepublishing.com

Photographic Credits

J.F. Berger: 45
Big Rock Brewery: 64 bottom
Calgary Stampede: 5 (bull rider), 61 top left and right, 61 bottom, 62, 63 right
David Cooper / Royal Winnipeg Ballet: 23
Craigdarroch Castle: 162 right
Doukhobor Village Museum: 128
Edmonton Tourism: 65, 67 right, 68 top, 69
Frank Slide Interpretive Centre / Alberta Community Development: 81
Forks North Portage Partnership: 5 (Forks), 16, 19
Glenbow Archives: 11 (NA-967-20), 13 (NA-4274-3), 22 (NA-504-3), 32 bottom (NA-4868-211), 42 (NA-3432-2), 52 bottom left (NB-166-56), 52 bottom right (NA-1771-1), 68 bottom (NA-876-1), 72 bottom (ND-8-24), 120 bottom (NA-1194-8), 122 bottom (NA-1444-1)
Jennifer Groundwater: 100 left and right, 148, 192
Harlequin: 22
Jasper Tourism and Commerce: 86 top right, 86 middle, 86 bottom
Donald Lee / Banff Centre: 92, 94
Doug Leighton: 4 (Okanagan), 5 (Mt. Rundle), 6, 7, 54 top, 54 bottom, 55, 67, 71, 72 top, 73, 74 left, 76 left, 77, 82 left and right, 84 top and bottom, 85, 87, 88, 89, 90, 93, 95, 99, 102, 103, 105, 106, 108, 109, 110, 112 top left, middle and right, 113, 114 top, 115, 116 top and bottom, 119, 120 top, 121, 122 top, 125, 127, 129 top, 130,

132, 134, 135, 136 top and bottom, 138, 141 right and left, 142 left, 144 left, 145 top and bottom, 146, 147, 149, 150, 158, 161, 163, 173 left, 181, 183 top and bottom, 185 left, 186
Mission Hill Family Estate: 129 bottom
David Myers: 34
National Archives: 11 (PA 182603), 114 bottom (NA 1949-1), 117
Northlands Park: 70
Parks Canada: 14, 33
Photography by Chris: 133

Dennis and Esther Schmidt: 8, 10, 32 top, 43 top and bottom, 49, 96 left and right, 107, 112 bottom, 124, 156 bottom, 177 right, 185 right, 187
Lee Simmons: 84 middle
Tourism Calgary: 58 right, 63 left, 64 top, 76 right
Tourism Regina: 44 right, 47
Tourism Saskatoon: 36, 38, 40, 41 left and right
Tourism Vancouver: 5 (False Creek) 137, 139, 142 right, 143, 144 right, 154, 155
Tourism Victoria: 4, 156 top mid-

dle, 156 top right and left, 162 left, 167, 169, 172
Travel Alberta: 56, 58 left, 74 right, 79, 86 top left
Travel Manitoba: 15, 25, 27, 28, 29 left and right, 30, 35
Vancouver Sun Run: 153
John Walls: 160, 165, 166, 170 top and bottom, 171, 178
The Wickaninnish Inn: 184
Douglas E. Walker / Tourism Saskatchewan: 5 (Fort Walsh), 37, 44 left, 48, 50, 51, 52
Whyte Museum of the Canadian Rockies: 104 (V439/PS-6)

Index

About the Author

Jennifer Groundwater celebrates her tenth anniversary as a resident of Alberta with the publication of this book. Born in Montreal, she came to Banff in 1993 for one summer. Like so many others before her, she fell in love with the Rockies and just couldn't tear herself away. She now makes her home in Canmore, where she enjoys the mountain lifestyle with husband Scott, a dog, a cat, and a very young son named Finn.

Jennifer has been working in the tourism industry in Banff and Canmore since her arrival here, most recently for Tourism Canmore. She has travelled extensively throughout Canada, as well as other parts of the world. This is her first book.

Acknowledgements

Writing this book has been a wonderful learning experience for me. I would like to thank the many people who have helped along the way, contributing insight, information and encouragement that shaped the book. Any errors in the book, however, are entirely my own responsibility.

I would especially like to thank Doug Leighton and John Walls for sharing their wonderful photographs, which really bring the western provinces to life in the most beautiful way.

Thanks to Stephen Hutchings and everyone at Altitude Publishing, who are a great group of people to work with. My editor, Andrea Murphy, proved a witty source of information and guidance.

Thanks to the following people who helped review the text: Nadine Howard, Cathy Senecal, Colette Fontaine, Mika Ryan, Laura Serena, John Walls and Kara Turner.

Most of all, thanks to my husband, Scott Manktelow, whose belief in me kept me going on this project when I felt I would never complete it. He is a stellar travelling and research companion, and I look forward to many more journeys in his company. This book is dedicated to him.